PEACHTREE

Repeat Until Rich

Repeat Until Rich

*A Professional
Card Counter's Chronicle
of the Blackjack Wars*

♦

JOSH AXELRAD

THE PENGUIN PRESS

New York

2010

THE PENGUIN PRESS
Published by the Penguin Group
Penguin Group (USA) Inc., 375 Hudson Street, New York, New York 10014, U.S.A. • Penguin Group
(Canada), 90 Eglinton Avenue East, Suite 700, Toronto, Ontario, Canada M4P 2Y3 (a division of Pearson
Penguin Canada Inc.) • Penguin Books Ltd, 80 Strand, London WC2R 0RL, England • Penguin Ireland, 25 St.
Stephen's Green, Dublin 2, Ireland (a division of Penguin Books Ltd) • Penguin Books Australia Ltd, 250
Camberwell Road, Camberwell, Victoria 3124, Australia (a division of Pearson Australia Group pty Ltd) •
Penguin Books India Pvt Ltd, 11 Community Centre, Panchsheel Park, New Delhi – 110 017, India •
Penguin Group (NZ), 67 Apollo Drive, Rosedale, North Shore 0632, New Zealand (a division of Pearson
New Zealand Ltd) • Penguin Books (South Africa) (Pty) Ltd, 24 Sturdee Avenue, Rosebank,
Johannesburg 2196, South Africa

Penguin Books Ltd, Registered Offices:
80 Strand, London WC2R 0RL, England.

First published in 2010 by The Penguin Press,
a member of Penguin Group (USA) Inc.

LIBRARY OF CONGRESS CATALOGING IN PUBLICATION DATA
Axelrad, Josh.
Repeat until rich : a professional card counter's chronicle of the blackjack wars / Josh Axelrad.
p.   cm.
ISBN 978-1-59420-247-6
1. Blackjack (Game)   2. Gambling systems.   I. Title.
GV1295.B55A94   2010   2009044751
795.4'23—dc22

Printed in the United States of America
1   3   5   7   9   10   8   6   4   2
Designed by Jessica Heslin

CONTENTS

This is for Paul. It's also for Harriet, Ralph, Ray Kroc, and Jay Sarno. And for the Ballers of Blackjack: you know who you are. And for my mom, dad, and stepmother. And finally (not least!) for the Internal Revenue Service, Wyckoff Heights Medical Center Billing Department, Chase MasterCard, American Express, Discover Financial Services, and everyone else who *believed.*

NOTE ON VERACITY

What's true is I won. Mostly. From 2000 to 2004, I supported myself playing blackjack professionally as a card counter. I won around $700,000 on behalf of myself and my teammates, and I collaborated in sessions that won much more. I was 86'd, 172'd (86'd twice, from the same place), 258'd, or otherwise discouraged from enjoying gambling opportunities at all the finest toilets in Las Vegas—with the exception of the newest Wynn toilet—as well as at casinos nationwide. I was detained in back rooms against my will in a casino in Kansas and another down in Southern California—acts, one could argue, of unlawful detention on the part of these casinos: *criminal* acts, I believe. (Personally, I've never been convicted of a thing. Card counting isn't a crime anywhere in the States. It's *the right thing to do,* in most cases.) Casinos seem to think I'm a threatening guy.

Or was, anyhow. There are some complications to the story. My claims to gambling greatness are offset by the fact that I'm currently broke. I'll say more on that front when it's time. For now I should point out (a) that the story is true, (b) that it's told truthfully, and (c) that I did make some changes.

Identities are veiled—that's the big one. The team activities described here took place in a context of privacy and of intense secrecy while they were going on. In deference to that spirit, and out of respect for the ongoing privacy of my colleagues and of others involved in the story, most but not all names are changed. Where I changed names, I changed other details, too—cities of residence, prior occupations, physical descriptions (sexing everybody up, as a rule, with an eye toward a Hollywood version someday: longer legs, bigger pecs; I went ahead and added a half inch to my own height while I was at it). The exceptions are Robert Jayne, an actor and indomitable card counter who kindly let me use his real name, being perfectly happy to remind the casinos (in particular Mandalay Bay) of the impact he had on their asses, and my roommate, guardian, and best friend, Paul.

I also changed the name of the team. I changed the location of our base in Las Vegas. I changed all the signals we used while we played. Our cornerstone tactic (call-ins) and peripheral tactics (like shuffle tracking) are described as they actually happened. I've omitted occasional secrets at the request of my friends, but it's nothing that goes to the heart of the things we accomplished together.

The incidents are true. The wins and the heartbreak are real. Now and again it gets florid (the prose), and I come off like some kind of pansy. I am, for what it's worth, just your standard Semitic American living on the precipice in Brooklyn these days, drinking bourbon and watching the sky fall, and trying to take care of my plants. My only hope here is to cheer you. If it's florid, then maybe it should be. I did what I could—God knows.

PART I

My Ideas Are Tested
in Nevada

One

They called themselves Mossad after the Israeli intelligence agency. The key honcho was a guy named Jon Roth. I met him just once, and then everything started. I took the subway one evening to Park Slope in Brooklyn, buzzed at the address my contact had given, and was let in by a tiny brunette who introduced herself as Bridget Gould.

She showed me up the stairs. The building was a brownstone, single-residence—all Roth's. He was a retired millionaire from Wall Street. Israeli-born, charismatic, three to six years older than myself. I knew these things from Garry Knowles, my mentor.

At the second floor, I saw a person dealing cards. A dining-room table had been converted into a blackjack table. There was green felt spread over it like a partial tablecloth. Two strangers sat on the player side, chips in the betting squares in front of them. The dealer was Roth, to whom Bridget presented me.

"You're Garry's guy?"

"Right."

He shrugged in response—not without warmth, I thought.

I can't say what I expected, but he was certainly a human being: large head, heavy build. Either he was muscular or he used to be. His hair was a few inches long, and his brow was pronounced. He might in a previous life have been some kind of ape king, a silverback.

The others sat watching me quietly.

Roth said to one of them, "Chuck, you want to check this guy out?"

"For spotter?"

Roth gave the thumbs-up. The person named Chuck was dark-eyed, perhaps Greek or Latino. He was physically attractive, and it bothered me. My habitual nervousness had been about doubled since I got off the subway, but as I shook Chuck's hand, it grew worse. I would *never* fit in with these people.

He led me to a sofa at the end of the room, where he handed me a "shoe" to count down. That's a big deck made of multiple decks mixed together, six in this case. As we sat, he went over the rules. He would remove a dozen cards or so, then time me as I counted the rest. I had to do it ten straight times, pretty fast, with a limited number of errors.

I passed this test. Shortly after that we had a pizza break. Roth ate standing up, as did Chuck and a bearded guy, Aldous. They were discussing an upcoming trip.

No one addressed me again until Roth had finished his pizza and lit a cigarette. "Ready for the table test?" he asked.

"I hope."

This was the final exam. Crusts and paper towels were stuffed into the grease-bruised pizza box. Roth began stacking the deck. The Aldous guy sat on one side of me, Chuck on the other.

I was sitting among strangers in this big brownstone house, playing two hands—perfect basic strategy—and trying to go plus-one, minus-one in my head the way I'd been taught. There's nothing too unusual about that, I guess. Millions of people take blackjack tests every day, or *some* kind of test. But I was less talented, at least than most card counters; this set me apart. Math has never been a strong suit, honestly—I'm more of a speller. Yet I'd *had this dream* ever since I first met Knowles, when he spilled the beans to me about Thorp, MIT, team play, basic strategy, the High-Low count, and all the rest of it, two years before. . . . The dream was to go the full distance, all the way to Moscow, as Napoleon might say: turn pro. Steal money from casinos for a living, and gamble full-time. Scamper around tiny back roads in a forty-eight-valve Italian coupe, looking for games. Up and down the Nevada desert, through the bogs of Mississippi, with so much cash in my Levi's that I couldn't walk. It had stayed a dream, and it might have stayed that way forever if Knowles hadn't met Roth, or if he hadn't played on a trip with Mossad and come back with the stories he did, or if the year 2000 hadn't been bearing down with the slim but notable off chance God might show up—none too amused—bringing apocalypse, or that the "Y2K problem" really would turn the computers either off, or against us, with planes dropping out of the sky and self-realized cruise controls carting pleading families to their doom, exactly at midnight on New Year's . . . or if I had been a little steadier, say. But, sensing opportunity with blackjack— along with the slippage of time and my own steady drift toward dullness— at the end of '99 I quit my job. Mossad, Knowles had told me, eventually might take recruits. It was the only lead I had. I lived off savings, wrote my novella. January passed, and the world carried on. February passed—God was late. Then, last night, with exactly no warning, the call I'd been hoping for *did* come: here I was, in the legendary hombre's dining room, on the fourth and soon the fifth and last shoe of the checkout, the count throbbing in my head like a disorder, each new card a separate problem I had to dispense with instantly, when Roth stopped dealing. He asked for my count, and I told him. He rocked his head back and forth thoughtfully, then looked over at Aldous, who said, "Okay."

The tension rushed out of my body. I'd started to shake. Roth shrugged again. He asked what I was doing next week. I said, "Nothing."

"Better buy yourself a ticket for Vegas, my man."

It started as quickly as that.

Two

The plane seemed to be gliding toward raw desert dust. There was no city. Jesus, we've made a wrong turn. . . . At the last possible instant, a runway appeared just below, and we smacked it, slammed on the brakes, then took a hard right, Strip showing massive on the port side. You could see the black shape of the Luxor. Sunlight reflected off Mandalay Bay like a flock of gold birds taking wing.

I recalled my instructions and pulled my phone out and took one breath. Roth had said to call the *second* I touched down. He answered:

"You're here?"

"Jon?"

"We're just going into the casino," he said. I'll remember those words my whole life. . . . *The* casino, as if it were abstract. A state of being.

"Jon—"

He said, "Listen. Kat Armstrong is coming to get you at Passenger Pickup. She'll know who you are."

"Hey, Jon?"

He made a sound. The call went dead. The plane had halted and was bobbing back and forth. I stood as soon as I could and joined the stream of dazzled gambling aspirants shifting forward slowly toward the Jetway.

When we spilled out into the terminal, the slot machines were waiting. A small oasis of them, clumped like palm trees. I stormed away, moving at peak efficiency toward the baggage claim. My muscles were blazing with purpose.

I leaped for my bag when I saw it and followed a sign for Passenger Pickup. A second sign pointed outside.

Across a pedestrian bridge, a concrete garage structure loomed hallucinatorily, radiant in the daylight. Pickup was inside on the third level. People waited at the curb, their postures suggestive of hookers. Their eyes scanned the windshield of each passing car. Drivers in turn seemed to browse.

Suddenly I wanted sunglasses. And either a tux or a sport coat, but definitely, definitely a shoulder holster. I reflected that I was poorly equipped for secret-agent work. All I was carrying was a duffel bag, the JanSport slung over one shoulder, old pack of Bee 92s in my left ass pocket, and something like twelve dollars cash.

I heard my name, and across the lanes of cars I saw two women. They were standing by a parked Dodge, waving. One was Bridget, and so the other one had to be Kat.

I crept through the tentative traffic.

Bridget greeted me curtly, and Kat held a tanned arm out for a diplomatic handshake, saying, "Mr. Axelrad?"

"Hello."

"Your hair's reputation precedes you."

I thanked her, not quite congruously, running a self-conscious palm over the crop of incipient dreadlocks that dotted my scalp like boils.

Kat opened the trunk, and I dropped my bags in. Bridget took the backseat. Kat secured her Oakleys and adjusted the mirror before pulling back. We crossed the lot and emerged at the top of a ramp so steep it could have been a fucking roller coaster. Down we rushed, Kat asking whether I'd ever been to Vegas before.

"Not in this capacity."

"Good," she said.

"Heh!"

I never know quite what to say to a woman in the absence of sexual tension. *Do you like nasturtiums?* I slumped against the door, feeling drugged. We entered a tunnel, exited, utilized a cloverleaf, banked at impressive velocity onto a broad and Californian ten-laned freeway I recognized as 15 North. The limit was close to three figures here, and Kat took advantage.

Now we were out in the thick of it and holy God—I felt I should cry something out. Sun was falling everywhere with awesome force. Distant streets were gleaming like canals. It was bright and it was bright and it was so strange, so *improbable.* . . . No thinking person would ever have bet on a Vegas sprouting in a wasteland like this.

The towers of the resorts stood separate from each other. Individually their structures were weirder than anything your average gangster or mobster could be expected to dream up without peyote. Green MGM had a pair of big arms stretched out from its body; he actually lay *like a lion.* There was Caesars, which I'll say right now has no apostrophe. Mirage, with gilt stripes, was like a zebra of tomorrow. The perspective shifted oddly as we drove: a result of their size, which was giant.

Hills—some far and others nearer—encircled the entire show.

It was like a vast playpen.

It was like a settlement on Venus.

It was Tatooine. It was Dune.

Kat had begun discussing trip-related business, parts of which I understood. She pointed out the Riviera and said Roth was there. He was "slumming," making his way down a list of neglected casinos; the motive for this tactic had something to do with the direction of the team overall.

"He's able to play?" I asked.

"Sometimes. He can count pretty much anywhere—"

"He *thinks* he can," Bridget said.

"—but betting the money is different. We'll see."

The trip having started last weekend, I was arriving in medias res. There was rather decent news, Kat announced: We were winning forty Gs.

I hummed admiringly but without knowing what the expectations were. Should we be winning $40 million? Was I getting screwed? Bridget, her tone businesslike, said the number was "nice."

"Player-hours are worth two hundred and twenty-five dollars at the moment."

Player-hours had to do with pay. Pay had to do with the bank's structure, which Roth had explained at his house.

There were investing players, there were noninvesting players, there were managers (who also were investing players), and there was no such thing as a nonplaying investor. Anyone other than a first-time participant was invited to invest; nearly everyone did. Four out of five trips won, supposedly. Average return to investors was 4 percent or higher for a several-day bank: pretty sick on an annualized basis.

The group would win or it would lose. In the former case, Sunday evening we would split the cash up approximately sixty-forty, the larger share going to investors and divided pro rata among them based on their commitment to the bank, the lesser share for everyone—investing and noninvesting players both—divided purely by player-hours, the amount of time each spent gambling relative to everyone else.

Red ink, the investors ate alone. They would also reimburse airfare for noninvestors when the win was small or didn't exist.

This meant I couldn't personally lose.

Bridget offered complicated details of where play had gone down already and who was responsible for our win. Chuck Small, the person who'd started my checkout, was a principal BP—a "Big Player"—and he was doing well. Roth of course was here, along with Bridget, Kat, Aldous, myself, a Lawrence, a Neal, a person named Jimmy. She talked about "play groups," and who would play with Roth, and what it meant to play with Roth, and why playing in a group with Jon Roth was "reasonable"—something I had not thought to doubt.

Nearing downtown, we left the freeway. All at once it was suburban. It was the Vegas that Vegas forgot. There were Citgo stations, a Ralphs supermarket. Large housing tracts were defended, as it were, by cinder-block fortifications suggestive of Belfast or Gaza.

The three of us were silent in the car. I thought I saw a mall up ahead, but it turned out to be a casino. As we closed in, the car slowed and my stomach collapsed. I was unready. I needed coffee. I had to warm up. I ought to put a call in to my mom. God—she didn't even know I was out here. . . . If by some fluke I should get thumped by a hypertense security ape gone loopy with his shillelagh, it was better if she had some background at least, some advance warning—before the call came from an ER in Clark County, Nevada.

Kat, nearly at a stop, turned in the wrong direction.

We weren't going to the casino. Ahead, the short road dead-ended at a gate. It was an apartment complex. Kat punched the code at the kiosk. The gate shuddered open, and we parked.

"Here it is."

Bearing luggage, I followed the two women. It was peaceful. There was a pool. Instead of lawns the grounds were covered with small pink stones. Our footsteps crunched, and to me it sounded ominous. There was no one to be seen besides the three of us.

The apartment buildings—numerous and identical—were elongated boxes. Very simplistic. It was architecture out of a first-grade drawing class. They all had Spanish tile roofs. The layout was such that you couldn't guess how many there were, or how far the complex extended. Could be, for example, eight hundred thousand units, and every casino employee in the whole city resided right here—unaware of us lurking so near. . . .

We had mounted a staircase. Bridget, at the top, unlocked a door. She glanced back with a mysterious smile as I entered. "You can drop your bag along the wall."

"Thanks," I said.

I dropped the bags, and I sniffed the air. The A/C was set to a half degree or so above freezing. I was in a living room whose obvious noteworthy feature sat in the corner opposite: a blackjack table. It was full or casino size, with black pressboard struts, ye olde green felt, ye red translucent plastic discard tray upright along the back end. A man leaned behind it where a dealer would be, his butt balanced on a stool.

Our eyes met, and he did the strange thing of just looking. He exhibited, as a psychiatrist observing a patient might note, a lack of affect. Without a word he broke the gaze and resumed shuffling cards.

Kat said, "Mr. Taib. Mr. Axelrad."

She disappeared down a hall. Bridget followed. I had moved about half a yard in, and I was out of ideas.

I stood there.

My heart squeezed blood through my body.

Gradually the other queer aspect of the room became evident. I took in the carpets, which were low-napped, neither gray nor beige. I regarded the sofas, of which there were two. They were arranged in an L shape; they were gray; exactly the color of dolphin hide, not quite as shiny. They had no coffee table before them or side table nearby—no place to set a drink. The entire room, I realized, was wanting. There was no stereo, and there was no television. There wasn't so much as a *postcard*-size Ansel Adams print. The walls were bare, and in general it had the gutted character of a model apartment in a low-rent town. You couldn't envision normal life happening in this space. Thinking of children here, playing, with toys in primary colors helter-skelter on the floor, was impossible. All this hit slowly, as I say; then, with a nonlocalized pang, or perhaps an abstract thud, as of muted thunder that might come either from the sky or from the TV or from one's own empty stomach—all three with equal probability—I was stabbed momentarily by panic, sweat rising over me. A second later it was gone.

Just . . . everything felt so *familiar*.

Three

There had also been déjà vu the night I met Garry. It was at a party, it was on the Upper West Side. Everyone was twenty-six. I was twenty-three, I was old, my best years were behind me. Basic party strategy was consumption of Sam Adams at a ferocious clip for ninety minutes, followed by milling around. This was a time in my life if not of defeat, then of abeyance. I was "napping." I'd been napping for close to a year. I'd found a job because you had to find a job; it was the rage, people worked. In the corporate world, pay is "compensation." That's their bare-bones way of expressing it. Something is being made up for, amends are being made: reparations. If you'd expected of life some vital engagement that shook your soul, broke your mind, drew blood from your eyeballs, breath from your throat, shattered front teeth, minced your fingers and your toes, and left your heart squeezed dry as a juiced lime, you might have been at risk of disappointment, might have turned into one of those effete, wan-faced chumps reading Camus on the subway if you weren't *compensated* sufficiently.

At least that's the way I had come to regard things. Mentally, I was aloof. I wasn't sure what I should want. New York City was like a fire that I had been drawn to, with no thought but to throw myself in.

They gave me a degree—Columbia College did. They gave me a network of contacts. I got a phone, I got a place. I was five foot eleven. Unstoppable. Except I wasn't moving. I had a laptop and a printer—heavyweight cream-colored paper to use for a résumé. I tried to be a temp and bide my time, remain aloof, mull the significant problems. I meant to take nothing for granted. The systems that I was born into I saw as suspicious. I doubted free will, doubted God. I thought of patriots as lunatics. Wealth, I knew firsthand, could breed miserable people. (My grampa was rich and indignant.) Success I couldn't define, happiness I didn't believe was relevant; I had no interest in a career. There wasn't anything that anyone had ever had that I had ever seen that I wanted.

I failed as a temp. I was hired, in a full-time position. A huge Swiss bank corporation that was named Swiss Bank Corporation took me on, on some kind of a whim. My title ("Business Analyst") didn't mean much more to me than the name of our department meant. Somehow I'd had the assumption that jobs were supposed to be like this: nebulous, repetitive—a rehearsal for limbo, or prison.

Still, I had vague expectations; something might change.

The curtain might be yanked away, life revealed glowing underneath.

So I waited.

I drank.

My weapons were beer and insouciance.

♦

Then, in the corner of an overheated room, there was Bill Brace suddenly—a college friend of mine—engaged in conversation with a stranger. I went up near them. I overheard words about gambling. Bill was the listener, the other one spoke. "It's eight decks there, actually."

"People can't count through eight decks," Bill objected.

"As a matter of fact . . ."

Here the stranger launched into an overview of what he called the "High-Low count." Soon he was painting a picture of casinos and gambling as seductive as was possible, claiming that the game blackjack had a loophole built in. A player could win at the game. There were skills you had to learn. By mastering those you could generate a long-term advantage similar to the casinos' edge over most players.

"This is Garry," Bill said to me.

"Hi."

Hence: Garry Knowles. He was lanky, nervous, bright. After each moment of speech, he would cut himself off by applying the top of his beer bottle to his mouth, as if afraid he could bore us.

As if!

I asked how it worked. Garry explained that counting had to do with the role of the deck, how a deck as the source of the randomness in a casino game was different from dice, or from a roulette wheel, or from the microchip inside a slot machine.

"A deck isn't constant. It changes."

Cards get removed with every hand dealt, and they can't appear again until a shuffle. So the deck is in flux—composition shifting all the time. The odds are affected directly. A die will always have six sides; a roulette wheel has thirty-seven or thirty-eight pockets, depending on the version; but a six-deck shoe that starts out with twenty-four aces eventually might have none left. The odds jump around, and it turns out that while the game on average is biased toward the house, as you'd expect, there are moments it's inverted: the house edge disappears, and the player is briefly the favorite.

"Counters just identify those moments," Garry said.

"By what means, exactly?"

"You keep a running tally in your head. This isn't as hard as it sounds. It's just *one number:* this number, the count, represents the relative concentration of a certain group of cards to a certain other group of cards in the remaining deck. It turns out in blackjack that big cards, like the tens and all the face cards and aces, disproportionately favor the player. A deck rich in those cards will become player-favorable. This has to do partly with blackjacks—an ace and a ten make a blackjack, you see, and the more blackjacks the merrier—partly with dealer busts. Dealers play a fixed strategy, and there are certain hands like fifteens and sixteens that they always have to hit, but we don't. So a *high count,* which indicates a deck full of lots of those big cards, means more blackjacks, more dealer busts. The deck favors you, so you bet a lot more. You'll recoup your previous losses that way and come out ahead overall. Fundamentally, it's simple."

Bill laughed. "Doesn't sound very simple. And casinos wouldn't offer the game if it were."

"This 'counting,'" I said, "it's not easy."

"Anyone capable of tipping a waiter eighteen percent with no calculator can count cards," Garry said.

Exactly, I thought. It's impossible.

♦

I might have been wrong, or might not have. I would find in the coming months that the computations you actually had to execute in a casino were tough but substantially learnable. Managing bankroll, analyzing different game conditions (rules at blackjack vary widely from one casino to the next, and sometimes from one table to the next inside the same casino), organizing a play for yourself or for a larger group of counters—these advanced tasks were more challenging. But the immediate trick came down, in Garry's words, to "going plus-one, minus-one inside your head." If you could add and subtract, you could win.

How, I asked, had Garry known all this stuff? He'd learned it in college, he told me. He'd gone to MIT and been recruited sophomore year to join a "team" that played blackjack together. The MIT Blackjack Team—it would later be the subject of multiple bestselling books—had been founded in the late 1970s, shortly after the appearance of an earlier book that unveiled the methods of team play.

"Collaborative play solves multiple problems," Garry said. "It can help with something called 'variance,' and it can help with something called 'heat.'"

Variance means flux, probabilistic ebb and flow: losing when you're supposed to win (or, on the plus side, winning more than you should). From the perspective of a normal, losing gambler, variance is good. When you're playing a losing game (in Garry's more technical language, "placing negative-expectation wagers")—craps, say, or blackjack without counting—if you happen to win, that's variance. Counters play a *winning* game, though. Their expectations are positive, but they'll often lose over the short run. That's variance again, of a less pleasant kind.

Unluckily for counters, the statistical short run can last quite a while. Garry said a single hour's play is just a little better than a coin flip: a competent counter with a healthy 1½ percent edge winds up winning about 56 percent of the time, after one hour. By playing more and accumulating hours, she gets further into the long run; odds of her *actual* result matching her expectation (her *theoretical* result, i.e.—"This we call 'expected value,'" Garry said, "or EV for short") begin to improve. Ten hours in, she's winning 67 percent of the time. It takes about a hundred hours before her odds of being in the black exceed 90 percent. A hundred hours' play could take weeks for a full-time professional to generate, because you can't play as much as you'd like.

The reason you can't? That's heat. Heat—or interference from casino personnel—takes numerous forms, from restricting your bet size to escorting you right off the property. (You can't be arrested for counting. Casinos would love you to believe otherwise, but "thinking while you gamble" isn't technically a crime, even in the state of Nevada.) Heat makes it hard to play a lot of hours.

Garry said, "Heat. That's your problem. Forget counting being hard, because it's not. It's being *allowed* to count that's hard."

It wasn't hard in the beginning, he claimed. When counting was developed—in the early 1960s by a mathematician, Edward O. Thorp, who at the time had just finished his doctorate—casinos dealt from single decks. They don't do that so much anymore; most blackjack is shoe-based today. The added decks boost the house edge, but in Thorp's age the edge was so small that you could crush the game with as little as a three-to-one or four-to-one spread in your bet size. That low-key style of betting would blend in pretty well with the suckers. Counters were hard to identify.

This Golden Age of Counting didn't last, though. Thorp's '62 book *Beat the Dealer: A Winning Strategy for the Game of Twenty-One,* drew enough attention to the loophole he'd found in the game that casinos were forced to react. In 1964 (on April Fool's Day, as it happened), the Vegas casinos did something unprecedented, jointly imposing a set of new rules on an existing game. They altered two aspects of blackjack, disallowing the splitting of aces and restricting players to doubling down only on a total of eleven (instead of on any two cards). In Thorp's own estimate, these changes increased the house edge by about 1 percent. The game remained susceptible to counting, but it was supposed to be harder to beat.

However, as Garry related, the card counters weren't the only ones getting shortchanged. The "desirable" players were, too—and they weren't very happy about it. Revenues collapsed at the tables. Dealers, who depended on tips for their income, began to complain to their bosses. Amid disastrous PR, the casinos quietly rescinded the change. The new rules were gone in one month.

"That might have been the first hint to the casinos that they had common interests with counters," Garry told me. "Although it was anything but the last." The history of card counting is also—and not coincidentally—the history of blackjack's rise from a secondary offering (in the early 1950s it earned less revenue than either craps or roulette) to the number-one table game in terms of house win. Rather than trailing craps (formerly the number one), blackjack today earns about three times what craps earns in Nevada. This, in straight economic terms, is the foremost part of Thorp's legacy. The idea that the game could be beaten made blackjack a phenomenon—even among players who didn't have the chops.

Casinos couldn't afford to get rid of it, but they continued to makes tweaks. Future rule changes would be more subtle and provoke less annoyance. The dominant strategy, though, became the shift into multideck shoes.

Extra decks increase the house edge even when the rules are identical, but they also have other effects. Casinos believed for a while that shoe games were simply uncountable; this was never true. (Thorp's earliest count, the Ten Count, worked in a way that would be very unwieldy with four or six decks; in the second edition of *Beat the Dealer*, he introduced a version of shoe-friendly High-Low, a simplified system as easy to use with four or six decks as with one.) But shoes do offer an advantage casinos might not have expected: with multiple decks, the count tends to fluctuate less. Valuable high counts are rarer. Counters have longer to wait before hiking their bets.

They spend more of their time losing money. And this forces them to take greater advantage when the counts *do* go up. In short, they have to spread a lot more. Three- or four-to-one won't cut it. The minimum bet spread is closer to eight-to-one these days, and professional players push it much further than that.

"This doesn't blend in very well," Garry said.

The counterly pattern is conspicuous in the Shoe Age, and casinos understand what to look for. Upon noticing a bet spread, especially in the case of a large bettor (or, worse, a *periodic* large bettor), the suits on the floor can have surveillance count down the guy's shoes, to see whether his betting is correlated to the count. They'll then take appropriate action. The arrangement works fine for the house, which gets the full benefit of blackjack's popularity while also maintaining a means of identifying so-called advantage players. They still get to offer their lucrative "beatable" game, secure in the knowledge that the few players posing an actual threat will get turned away with relative promptness.

But that's not the end of the story. Shoes have a particular weakness, and the weakness happens to be the very same quality that necessitates big, ugly spreads: slower fluctuations in the count. It was this that would give rise to teams.

A blackjack team is a group of skilled players betting to a joint bankroll and conspiring to fool the casino. Collaboration, Garry explained, helps with variance: by generating hours simultaneously, team counters get into the long run faster than they would on their own; this means they're less likely to lose over any given period of action. They balance one another's fluctuations.

And they can circumvent heat. In a style known as "call-in play," a group of players will enter a casino at the same time, counting down separate shoes in the same area of the gaming floor. The counters will all bet the minimum. When they find a good count, they won't bet it themselves. Instead they'll give a furtive signal to their BP, a roving player who comes in midgame, betting perhaps a hundred times what his counters are betting. The group's overall spread is enormous—*and* hard to discern. The BP, always betting big, doesn't look like a counter at all. And the whole stunt is made possible by the fact that a high count in a shoe game tends to stay high for a while—allowing time for the counter to hand off his count. The multideck innovation, intended to protect the house game, turned out to create further loopholes.

First developed in the early 1970s by a gambler known as Al Francesco, team play was made famous by a teammate of Francesco's, Kenny Uston, who published a book on the concept in '77. The next year, when the Atlantic City casinos opened for business, a new generation of aspiring team players on the East Coast was poised to attack. The MIT group was born at this time—heirs to a recondite tradition that was in its fourth decade some twenty years later when Knowles clued me in. He didn't know it would shatter my life.

Four

It was the next morning, and my stomach burned. Seven stories down, buses were huffing and sighing. My bed was right under the window.

I lived in a room meant originally for a maid, on Broadway, in an apartment I shared with a madman, who was very kind to me. He wore no shirt and had no job. He was fifty-plus and uninsured. He had something wrong with his shoulder that he couldn't afford the operation for. He'd hinted to me that the big, six-room, high-ceilinged, decaying prewar apartment was technically leased to his uncle, who'd died. Rent-control shenanigans were going on. It was low-level fraud, and I'd found it attractive. I'd still been a temp when I moved here.

Left over from the party last night, besides sour guts, I had images burned in my brain.

It was motion-picture bullshit.

Hollywood.

Men wearing suits, with slick hair.

Money, in a person's clutching fist.

Ratty but dangerous figure of a slim kid counting cards in the middle of a circus in Vegas, as the guards start to near from behind him.

Hazy shot of Garry Knowles, grabbing my shoulder on an elevator going down: "We could practice together. I miss it."

I kicked the sheets away. I got out of bed. The floor lurched. The news from the mirror was somber. My cheeks appeared swollen, my throat appeared large. I showered, toweled off with impatience, and slipped my wet thighs into Levi's.

Down on the sidewalk, squinting, I walked into H&H. Behind the counter were the bagels in steel mesh bins, with the kitchen in plain view behind. There were daunting, tall machines like you'd see in the engine room on a cruise ship. That was how the bagels were made.

The clerk nodded impassively. "Yeah?"

"You'll put the cream cheese on *for me*," I ordered.

"We don't do that here."

I said, "Fuck it."

I was out on the street again. Ten months of war against H&H's policy of only selling cream cheese on the side (in those hard silver packets— impossible to spread with a cheap plastic knife!), and I had nothing to show for my protests.

I will wear them down, wear them down, I thought, feeling ill.

I came to the bookstore and veered toward the magazines like a diseased bum near collapse. I drifted through the store. Finally I went to the desk and asked for the gambling books.

"Puzzles and Games," she said, pointing.

The section was up on a balcony. My body felt heavy on the stairs. I looked at the books and thought, Garbage.

There was one entitled *Spin Roulette Gold*.

There were systems for craps.

You could win good money playing the slot machines, evidently.

Nevada was the land of opportunity.

But there he was: Thorp. "The Book That Made Las Vegas Change the Rules," it said on the cover. Kneeling, somewhat doubtful, to peruse, I learned it was the only volume in the whole section published by a company I'd heard of. As I leafed through, I again envisioned Knowles with his arm out, touching me, announcing his idea: "We could practice together. I miss it."

◆

It was basically a lark. Garry was lonely, I think, having just moved to New York to start graduate school. Bill Brace and I wanted to learn. We began meeting each Thursday for practice. Garry, still in touch with MIT (a number of alumni played with the team, in addition to current students), said there was a small chance Bill and I could eventually attend a team trip and try taking a "checkout." That's a rigid qualifying test. If we passed, we might play and get paid for it. But trips were decreasingly frequent, he said. The team was in some kind of slump.

Bill wanted the three of us to try organizing our own trips, totally separate from MIT. We could play smaller stakes on our own money. Garry was skeptical about that. The swings on your bankroll were brutal, he said. It would take over $16,000 in risk capital to play at an expected win rate of $25 per hour.

"Look at you—cautious," Bill said. "Some gambler you are."

"I know."

"Really, you live on the edge."

"Thanks, man."

"You're Zorro. Maybe James Bond."

I didn't like that kind of talk—*I* was Bond. I was also Neal Cassady and Gary Gilmore. . . . All I'd really done was read books, before now. I'd gone to movies. I enjoyed taking in a good film. The sole kind of life I could imagine regarding as real, regarding as true, was the kind that was structured like fiction. The message in stories was always the same:

Life is insufficient.

The world—as they say—is not enough.

Adventure pends, somewhere and somehow.

The Final Reality waits: *Out There.*

Blackjack was perfect for someone like me. It was a hidden universe, different, stranger, richer than daily experience. But it wasn't just a myth. The scientific basis made it credible. Garry's strictness as a teacher helped, too. Before our first practice, he e-mailed Bill and me a chart showing something called "basic strategy." Basic is the collection of mathematically optimal moves for each possible hand. It tells you when to hit, when to stand, when to split or double down, when to make the play called "surrender." (Surrendering is basically quitting a hand without playing it, in exchange for a refund of half your original wager. The surrender option is available only sporadically and seldom found outside Nevada.) We had to memorize the chart, which was color-coded and looked wonderfully complex—this grid with 280 squares on it. Sixteen, when the dealer's showing eight up? You hit. Twelve versus three? Hit again. Pair of sevens? You split against an upcard of seven or lower. It went on and on. You had to have basic down cold so you could play with no effort while separately counting the cards. Anytime you made an error, Garry would get very somber. "No good. A basic strategy error will be an automatic fail on every test you ever take."

The High-Low count itself really was just a matter of plus-one, minus-one—at a superficial level anyhow. The good, player-favorable big cards (ten, jack, queen, king, and ace) all counted as negative one. The bad, house-favorable small cards (deuce, trey, four, five, and six) counted positive, as plus-one. Sevens, eights, and nines you could ignore (they counted as zero). While you played, all you had to do was to tally the numbers—also called "count tags"—assigned to each card you saw dealt. A hand such as twelve (e.g., king-two) would add zero to your tally ($-1 + 1 = 0$), until you hit it with a five, say ($-1 + 1 + 1 = 1$). It was important to scan the table according to a fixed pattern with every new round dealt, so you'd know what you'd already added and wouldn't double-count any cards. Forget where you are and you're screwed.

We practiced each Thursday downtown, borrowing a conference room from the software-development start-up where Bill worked as a programmer. It was the perfect ambience: the building was musty and aged, with high ceilings and old-fashioned, wood-framed windows you could actually open; the conference room's door had a transom. It felt like a scene out of film noir, especially with Garry Knowles presiding from the dealer position across the green baize he brought with him, the chips heaped before him, a six-deck shoe to his left.

He was training us as "spotters" to begin with. The team had four major roles. There were two kinds of counters and two kinds of BPs.

A spotter is an entry-level counter dealing solely with the rough tally: the "running count," it's called. His job in a session is to sit at a table, count down a shoe, move to a different table if the count's going nowhere, and keep moving and keep counting until he finds something nice and hot—a running count, say, around ten. At that point he signals and hands the shoe off to someone else.

The rank above spotter is "controller." A controller is qualified to take the running count and to do additional math in order to calculate bet size. Running count alone's not sufficient for that. You have to adjust your running count to reflect where you are in the shoe. Specifically, you take the running count and you divide by the number of decks left to play—a factor you estimate visually, by eyeballing the discards stacked in a tray at the back of the table. The result, running-count-per-deck-remaining, is called the "true count," and in addition to determining bet size the true count tells a controller when he should deviate from basic strategy.

A controller who also acts as BP, placing large bets in a session, is simply called a "counting BP." The other kind of BP is the "gorilla"—so called because he doesn't count at all. (The term is found in Uston's books.) A gorilla is a dumb ape—or an actor, basically—whose job is to take call-ins from controllers who signal his bets and his playing deviations for him.

Spotting was easy for Bill and less easy for me. You had to add up your hands two separate ways simultaneously: a seven and a six are thirteen, for basic strategy purposes, but they add plus-one to your running count. I was constantly adding the wrong thing to the wrong place and losing my count altogether. Slow at math ever since grade school, I was far from a natural counter.

One day Garry told me his way of holding the count. "I have a separate voice in my head. It's located here, near the back, and it's deep, sort of drones. It says the number over and over again like a mantra. *Nine, nine, ten, ten, twelve, twelve, twelve.* . . . That voice is in charge of the count. With the rest of my brain, I can do anything else, including separate math, and it won't overlap. It's like an autonomous thing, here."

"Wow." I started emulating that, and it worked. But by the time I was getting comfortable with the running count (a few months into our practices), Bill was far along with the true count. This was beyond me completely. You had to get your running count, then do division—sometimes while cards were still coming—and, once you'd computed the true, resurrect the running count you'd started with, then keep counting from there. All at incredible speed.

"I could just be a terminal spotter. Forget about controlling completely," I said. "I'm never going to get this."

Garry shook his head. "You can't do that. The MIT spotter checkout includes a part dealing with the true count. You have to be well on your way to becoming a controller already. Otherwise you're never going to pass."

"That standard's just needlessly high. Spotters only have to use the running count."

"The team has to know you're for real," he said. "They're not just looking for passable, borderline skills. You're gambling, with other people's cash, in a game where the near-term results are dominated by variance. You could vaporize a hundred thousand dollars in a couple bad shoes. They want to know, and you'll want to know, if that happens, it's not because you fucking suck."

"Yes. But I *do*."

Five

Out of the blue, there was a trip. MIT was in Atlantic City. Garry had done some finagling. He got Bill and me invited to go, so we could try taking checkouts down there.

We took Greyhound on Saturday morning, collecting new images throughout the trip: incredible, sullied New Balance sneakers down to the last millimeter of sole and bedraggled as hell, on the feet of the passenger who sat across the aisle talking to himself the whole ride; apocalyptic factories, shipping yards, power plants of northern New Jersey, with sprawling, wild campuses whose buildings interlocked à la Tetris, incongruous colors and metals joined like industrial quiltwork, emitting miasmas of filth; a long peaceful stretch through the woods; the marbled, heavy, oceanic sky as we charged finally toward the coast and could first make out the casinos, organized into a row along the sea, somehow cold-looking and industrial and Jerseyan rather than otherworldly and Disneyfied, as they are in Las Vegas; the trashy, salty reek along the Boardwalk; the area at Caesars where we waited for Boris, our host, the trip's manager, heard the ping and saw elevator doors parting as he strode forth in his neat clothes and fat silver wristwatch and silver bracelet, minutely bowing his head as he said the word "Boys?" for a greeting; Boris holding open the door of the suite they had comped, like some scene out of Ken Uston's books, with a half dozen card counters lounging variously throughout the light-colored living room washed with gray daylight from the floor-to-ceiling windows looking out toward the sea; the now-familiar setup with a portable green felt spread on a tabletop, discard tray, cards, chips; Bill testing first, counting five shoes with no trouble as the woman named Jen dealt severely; yours truly failing repeatedly, hour in and hour out, until no one was willing to deal; the meeting they had pre-session with the counters gathered, ready, on the couch, Bill with his earnest expression looking like he wished he had a notepad; bidding farewell as they went out to play, locking the suite door and throwing myself on the sofa to watch some TV, quite alone; and the weary drive back the next day, seated too close to the john in the aft of the bus, Bill saying what the play had been like and how nervous he'd felt, how surprised he'd been by his nerves, how rare it was in real life for the count to go up high enough to generate a call-in—a stark change from the stacked shoes with their prearranged counts that we were accustomed to from practice every week. Bill voicing various doubts. The play had looked clunky and conspicuous, the signals surprisingly blatant. The pay you could get as a noninvesting player was fine as hourly rates go ($60 or so, by Bill's estimate: "about what a good plumber might bill for his time"), but less fine when you accounted for the scarcity of hours, the relative infrequency of trips, not to mention travel time and the hundreds of hours of practice. "And the ultimate problem," he said, "can't ever be solved." Meaning heat.

"Either you play at low stakes, under the radar, making no money; or you play infrequently like these guys, as a hobby, and make no money; or you play at high stakes, as a full-time professional, and you do fairly well till you're blown," Bill said. "Then you're *hot* and making no money. Any way you look at it, it isn't worth much. I don't see a future in this."

♦

Bill quit practicing. Months and months passed. Garry and I started getting together less often. There *wasn't* a future in blackjack—that much was perfectly clear. I had no aptitude for it, and even if I had, it wouldn't lead anywhere.

I kept dealing cards to myself on my own. I read Thorp's book over and over, in particular chapter 5, "My Ideas Are Tested in Nevada," where the twenty-eight-year-old adjunct mathematics instructor counts cards for real money for the first time. In clear prose, laden with portent, Thorp describes bizarre confrontations with embittered casino employees, like the dealer on grave shift in Reno who spitefully watches him win. "As I picked up my winnings and left," Thorp relates, "I noticed an odd mixture of anger and awe on the dealer's face. It was as though she had peeked for a brief moment through a familiar door into a familiar room and, maybe, she had glimpsed something strange and impossible."

I was hoping for a vision like that, of strange and impossible things where before there had been only tedium. And then one day it appeared.

Garry started telling me about Mossad. A counter friend from MIT had put him in touch with Jon Roth, a full-time professional player whose team had been in action for a couple years. "They're thinking of expanding," Garry said.

I said, "Hm."

Mossad was smaller, leaner, tougher than MIT. They organized banks on a short-term basis, playing really hard for a week or two straight, then splitting up the money and enjoying some time off. MIT's banks, by contrast, dragged on for months; you had to wait a long time before you got your full pay, and this caused motivational problems.

"Also, they're super aggressive," Garry told me over drinks one night after he and Roth had met. "Completely indifferent to heat. Which is good, because they're all really hot. They believe in playing until you're thrown out the door."

I didn't know exactly what this signified, or whether it was possible to play in that way. Bill thought heat meant you were doomed. Mossad seemed to think it didn't matter. In any case, it *sounded* like a sexy approach. Sexy also, to me, was the news that Mossad's spotter checkout didn't involve true count at all. You only had to keep the running count—a thing I could already do. "I'll get you introduced," Garry promised. It was early November.

Later in the month, he said, "Soon. I really think they want to grow the team."

The year was closing down and Y2K coming, heavy with portent and fear. I decided to give notice at my job. For three months I stayed home and I waited. I had beer and insouciance, patience, credulity, cash.

Six

Then I flew to Las Vegas. And suddenly I was in a cold room standing in front of a casino-size blackjack table inside an apartment. Bright sun slashed through the blinds.

The first thing that happened was that Lawrence Taib dealt me a checkout—another. You had to pass a two-shoe, on-site mini-test at the start of every trip. When it was done, he lit a cigarette. "You can count cards."

"Where am I going to play?" I said.

"Nowhere." He smoked. He was smiling. He was right. I was in the apartment all day. He, Bridget, Kat came and went, separately or together, running errands they seldom explained. Roth was "getting down" at Riviera, Bridget said. The bad news was that he was losing.

The afternoon stretched into evening. When night fell, Kat ordered pizza. Roth was losing $20,000. Nobody seemed too concerned.

I must have dealt myself a thousand hands. Now and then one of the others would take the cards, without a word, and start dealing and giving me pointers. I was practicing controlling. Lawrence asked, "How many decks left?"

"Two and a half?"

"Wrong." He turned a card sideways, holding it up to the discards in the tray. "Four decks are the same height as a card turned on its side. These are four decks in here. Two remaining. You see? That's four decks exactly."

"All right."

I was at blackjack sleepaway camp. It was weird. It was cool. I got tired by three in the morning. Roth, at the Riv, had played twelve hours straight. He'd erased the whole win on the bank. People were now sounding stressed. I sprawled on a couch and passed out. Then Lawrence Taib was standing over me. "Hey. It is time. Grab your bag."

I followed him down to a car.

He'd made no offer to open the trunk. I was sitting in the front passenger seat with the backpack at my feet, duffel in my lap, dog tired, thinking maybe he was just going to take me back to the airport and drop me at the terminal, saying, "Sorry. I guess it doesn't work."

"We're putting you up in a fine hotel near here." Those were the last words I caught. We turned left onto Rancho, and then I was out cold.

When I woke, we had pulled into a Budget Suites. It didn't look much different from the apartment complex. Taib went into the lobby and came out several minutes later with a key, then drove me around to the room.

"You're on your own tonight. Enjoy it. Don't let me find any porn on that bill."

"Thank you," I said. "Bye-bye."

Seven

The next morning I woke up alone, disoriented, hungry. My stomach felt inside out, like a Ziploc someone's trying to shake the crumbs from. The suite had no food in it. There was a fridge, which was empty. The cupboards had nothing. No bowl of fruit had been left. I drew back the curtain—oh, God, oh God oh God—I hadn't realized they *had* Budget Suites directly on the surface of the sun. The daylight was blinding. The daylight was more than was needed. The daylight was *all too much*. It was a sunny day, I noticed. Then my eyes recongealed; I could make out the Texas Station, the casino, on the opposite side of the street. I have to be near the apartment. . . . Amazing I passed out last night on what must have been a short drive. I scanned but couldn't see any restaurant. No Arches. Egg McMuffins weren't accessible. The casino would probably have food but it looked like an errand to get there, and I shouldn't just abandon my post. The question was, what do I eat?

I checked my phone. It hadn't rung. I sat down on the couch. I'm a pro, a pro hustler. How great! Hustler on the couch, everybody—clear out. I ended up waiting for the next hour.

I had no other number but Roth's. It was barely noon and I figured he wouldn't be awake yet. I debated calling Garry, but I didn't. Too bad he's not coming this trip—it's lonely, this business, when no one's your friend, when no one tells you what the fuck is going on, when you're stuck in some dump and you're starved and they've lost all the money. At Swiss Bank they had a cafeteria.

My phone rang.

Bridget: "Could you meet me downstairs in eight minutes?"

"Okay!"

I skipped a shower, found my shoes. I ran down with seconds to spare.

I stood in the hot air, waiting.

Half an hour passed. Then she pulled up in a gray car. "Here's the plan," she was saying as I climbed in. "Riviera. They have our money in escrow. Okay? We've got to make a withdrawal."

"All right."

"Do you understand?"

"No."

"Payback," said Bridget.

"All *right*."

♦

We went to the apartment. Jon Roth was coming down the stairs, followed by Kat and a stranger. "We're off," he announced, his voice half chirp, half grunt.

"I have a spotter for you," Bridget said.

"Could you log him in"—he nodded to acknowledge me—"and bring him to the Riv?"

"Does he need the whole speech?"

"Do you?" Roth said.

"Speech?" I said. What I needed was protein and coffee.

"Do a quick version." He kissed Bridget's cheek, winked at me, proceeded down the stairs.

She led me into their bedroom, launching instantly into an overview of the team's accounting procedures. She asked how much cash I was carrying. "About ten dollars," I said.

"Not 'about.' Open your wallet, please."

"Twelve."

Laughing at the small number (but in a friendly way), she wrote it on a special printed form, then handed the form to me. It was a "player sheet." The front was for session results and the back side for expenses.

"Two thousand." She flourished some bills.

Whoa, I thought, taking the money. It was all Ben Franks.

"That's player stake," Bridget was saying. "Only use it for sessions, buying chips. The cash you brought with you is expense money. That's for everything except for chips. If you need to buy coffee or something. Keep the two physically separate."

"Two different parts of my wallet, like this?"

She nodded and then said, "Signals. What do you do for a call-in?"

When a shoe went hot, I was supposed to signal the BP—Roth in this case—by dropping my left hand into my lap. I showed Bridget this. She said, "Good. Pass me a count. Plus-twelve."

I placed my right hand on my left wrist, the right index finger extended.

"Okay. Now plus-twenty-three."

This was right hand on left forearm, two index fingers this time. We signaled the units place of our running count by touching different parts of each arm. The fingers indicated the tens place. For single-digit counts, instead of extending your fingers you made a fist.

"Good," Bridget said. "If there's heat . . ."

She touched her mouth, thinking. She looked delicate—almost like a child—and her voice was amazingly gentle. She certainly didn't resemble any hardened professional gambler I'd ever seen.

". . . rule one is that you ignore it."

I wasn't sure what she meant—ignore heat. How do you ignore armed men cracking your skull with a truncheon? "I do?"

"You shouldn't even look at the pit."

"Oh. Right."

"New players tend to be paranoid."

"Ah . . ."

"Always looking at the bosses, to see if the bosses are looking at them. Which is a good way to cause them to look at you, right?"

"But what if something *definite* happens?"

"Like what?"

"I don't know," I said. "They throw me out?"

"That would be definite. Sure. But casinos aren't actually in the business of randomly throwing out people who come there to gamble, okay? They have to see something concrete. Heat isn't amorphous. It doesn't just come out of nowhere. There's rhyme, and there's reason. The person they go after first, pretty much every time, is . . . ?"

"The BP?"

"Correct. They look at the guy placing bets. Now, if you're controlling—calling bets for a gorilla—eventually they'll check you out also. You spend so much time at the table together. But a spotter just gets no attention. You pass the count and leave."

"Okay."

"But if something *should* happen . . . Oh, well. There's no time. If they tell you to leave, just do what they say. You'll get the full speech later on." Grabbing her purse, she said, "Good?"

Feeling like an actor or an impostor, I stood. "Great," I responded. "Let's roll."

Eight

Bridget drove at moderate speed. But the drive was too short. In minutes we saw the casino. Oh, *no.*

"EOS is McDonald's."

"What's EOS?"

"End-of-session. No one told you that before?"

"Where's the McDonald's?"

"Across the Strip when you get out."

We were coming down Paradise Road. I was suddenly struck with nostalgia. The Papster and I, years ago, when I was in junior high school, used to favor this street. "Paradise east of the Strip and Industrial when you're west." That was my dad's wisdom on avoiding the traffic of the famous main artery. We used to take back roads. We were *insiders,* or he was, and I was a kook, virginal and helpless, thrilled by the proximity to all the strange forces and sex of this town, all the magic. We would come out about once a year and stay free in a model apartment at this complex where my grampa owned a stake; by day we would sightsee, and at night the Paps went to play poker and I was alone. From the time I was maybe fourteen, when he was at Mirage playing stud I was free to go wander, down the Strip and up, along the sidewalk, scintillated by everything. The buzz was in the air. The gas would ignite with a snap in those elaborate glass tubes you could stand really near at Oasis in front of the Dunes. Drunk people came roaring up, arms linked, obstructing the sidewalk, like a wave bounding down on your head in the ocean near where I grew up. I darted, weaved, and got exhausted and was overwhelmed. I kept eyeballing porn. There were brochures full of prostitute ads. Brochure-dispensing racks lined the boulevard, and I would look but never touch: I could imagine the smell of the ink on the newsprint. That's what sex smells like, I thought. Standing at the periphery of a gaming floor, I would gaze out feeling the energy of the slot machines, not wholly believing I would ever be of age. Vegas was a heaven, and not touchable.

Bridget turned right at a small street leading through parking lots to the Riv. We were approaching it the rear way. It looked like a studio lot in Hollywood. The buildings were industrial, pale from the wear of the sunshine.

"Find Kat or Jimmy in there. You should try to sit in view of each other."

"All right," I answered. "Who's Jimmy?"

"You didn't meet Jimmy? Hispanic?"

I shrugged. But then I remembered a Latino man, about my age, coming down the stairs with Roth at the apartment just before.

"Never mind. You'll see Kat. They've started already. Are you nervous, man?"

"What?"

"You'll do fine."

We'd reached the rear entrance. Bridget held her small hand up and slapped mine. Dashing through a swath of hot air, I grabbed the Riv's door and was in.

Suddenly it was cold, and the ambience was even more alien than the Venusian terrain of the valley outside. It had an ill odor, something like an elementary-school cafeteria where the children all smoke.

I was among the outlying slot machines, scattered in small clusters like incipient suburbs far removed from some metropolis. The main action lay ahead, and you could hear it. There was always that illusion as you entered—of widespread, impossible mass jackpots spewing into the drop trays and over the trays to the floor in a flood like a dream: gamblers kicking drunkenly through shin-high mounds of actually silver dollars, cocktail waitresses carrying champagne, wearing snowshoes so they can make their way over all the heaped winnings. It sounds pretty good, every time you're first going into a casino and regardless of how much better you know.

Moving down toward the table games, I felt conspicuous. Knees growing tense: I was limping. I couldn't see Kat anywhere. I gimped among games, scanning the backs of the blackjack players' heads, searching for dirty-blond hair or for a skull that looked Hispanic, while also trying to catch sight of Roth.

Where, damn it, where? I was aware I might be passing right behind them. It was difficult to see any faces. A pit boss was looking my way. I'd come to the end of the pit and was commencing down the other side. Another time around and I'm in orbit, I thought. That Suit over there—is he watching?

I got down to the other end, turned, and had nearly completed a lap without finding anyone when I saw an open stool and took it. The dealer was ending a round, dealing out hit cards. The table had three other players. It was higher than what I was used to, almost at the level of my nipples, so I felt like a young boy. I was fourteen years old again, but now I'd gone rogue and was gambling, at risk of arrest any moment.

"Sir?"

I looked up. The redheaded dealer was waiting. Her hair was a dye job and her elderly person skin wrinkled like elephant hide, ghastly with all the foundation she wore. I waved my hand—"Just a moment"—and she checked the others' bets, proceeding to deal around me. The shoe was half done. You can't start counting in the middle. And still there was no sign of Roth: without a BP it was pointless to play.

But what else could I do? I was holding a $100 bill, still glancing around looking for teammates, when I heard the words, "How would you like that?"

I froze.

She was pointing toward the cash in my grasp.

"Put that down here, on the felt."

"Oh," I said.

"I can't take it out of your hand."

I did as she said. In the course of a second, she'd taken the bill, then called, "Changing one hundred!," dipped into her rack and with a flick of her emaciated fingers shot out in perfect geometric form on the table an arrangement of green and red chips.

"One hundred. Thanks," a boss said. He'd come from nowhere, and I thought he was glowering at me. She thrust the chips across the felt, and I extended a tentative hand.

"Bets?" she said. It felt like a rebuke from a grandma or from a teacher. Everyone else had wagered already. I was still counting chips—in checkouts you had to make sure you were paid exactly right on every transaction, but I'd forgotten to do that just now.

I bet five dollars, the min. I was trying to count the cards on the round just for practice's sake, but everything was going too fast. I hit my hand, busted—I didn't see the bust card. I bet again: I was just gambling. I had no count and no count team. The cards made a whisper as they raced across the baize. I cowered rather low on my stool, feeling smaller than ever, younger and out of control, like a kid who can sense himself getting into trouble but doesn't know how to pull back. My heart was pounding fiercely in my chest. I placed my third bet and saw Roth.

He was crossing the floor, surrounded by Suits. They resembled a pack of Secret Service agents hustling away a bad guy. They brought him up a short flight of stairs, and he was moving for the exit. He was smiling—I caught a glimpse of teeth—and his cheeks shone with color. He was laughing, in fact. He patted one Suit on the shoulder. Then he moved into the daylight and became a silhouette, the Suits standing to watch as he left.

Nine

The team created order out of chaos. First they created the chaos, then they imparted the order. Progress was subtle. You almost couldn't tell there was a method. I thought it was madness at first. I flew into town, money started disappearing, and then they sent me to a doomed session. Then we had lunch. We had a nice, decadent meal. When sessions got going, they might last for whole days straight, but if there was downtime, the downtime could last. We could order up two, three, maybe four Blooming Onions for the table at Outback Steakhouse, plus a couple other appetizers, and entrées the size of a lapdog, and chow until I wanted to barf. Even with nobody drinking, the meals got crazy: voluble gamblers shouting insane yarns; Jon Roth standing up in the booth, producing thirty Gs from his jacket and thrusting it indifferently at Chuck, right out in the open where anybody could see. Chaos. There seemed to be no strategy at all. The check would come, and Roth would say suddenly, "Here's what we're doing. Chuck, you like Mandalay Bay?"

"I'd like to upset them."

"You're the BP."

It was at Mandalay Bay where I first passed a count. It happened on swing shift. (Gamblers think in terms of shifts: day, swing, or grave.) Chuck

Small was betting the money, but Chuck was a gorilla. As a spotter I couldn't call his bets. When I found a count during this session, I was supposed to signal to Bridget, Lawrence, or Kat, who in turn would signal Chuck and control him. It was a relay and not very efficient, but it allowed us to get to more shoes.

Mandalay was different from the Riv. The odor was different. The air had a hint of vanilla and didn't stink of smoke, even though people were smoking. The crowd was younger, too. It hadn't really occurred to me that members of my own demographic would want to hang out in casinos, in a context that didn't involve counting. Who were these people with whom I was meant to blend in? Fraternity and jock types. Lost souls. Investment-banking scum. Money sluts. Atheists, but atheist the *wrong way*. I couldn't understand them or their motives. I didn't look like them. I felt I was standing out horribly in this environment—even before I sat down.

Then, still trying futilely to look normal, I had to watch every card as it fell and, at the same time, maintain an overall awareness of the teammates and where they were and what was going on.

Kat, across the pit, looked completely natural on her game. She was a taciturn woman, in reality a little on the stiff side, but in the casino she wore a sedate smile and a lost gaze that made her look dippy. A few rounds into a shoe, she would stand up—presumably when the count had dropped—and march calmly around to a new game where the shuffle had just then finished.

The team was aggressive. They moved from shoe to shoe rapidly, hungry for counts. I wasn't doing that. It was more comfortable staying locked down on one table, I felt. I was actively hoping the count *wouldn't* rise. The thought of passing it was frightening. I didn't understand yet that my own behavior could have a direct influence on our result. I didn't have the hunger. None of this stuff felt real.

I saw my first call-in, Chuck breaking in to a shoe. Bridget had the count. She was moving her hands on her arms to convey what to bet. Chuck was staring at her doing it, and here came a pit boss, planting himself behind the dealer with his arms crossed, not looking pleased. Chuck was making some silly joke. He put chips down on two spots. The dealer's elbow pumped as she was dealing, and there was Chuck again, staring at Bridget to look for a signal to deviate, all with this Suit just looming.

Nothing was subtle. If you knew who the teammates were, it was easy to see them communicate, easy to see Chuck stall until Bridget shifted her limbs in some way, then immediately continue with his hand. The boss watched for a minute, then wandered away. An hour went by. They were buying it!

Why? The trick was so old and so evident. How could they ever *not* see it? Later I would learn that it came down in large part to allocation of resources. Casinos couldn't simply sweat every guy who showed up from the moment he first started betting. They didn't have the manpower for that. Nor did they have much interest in showing a lot of anxiety whenever someone bet big. The overwhelming majority of blackjack players are losers. And casinos *exist to take bets,* after all. They damn well better take most of them. Before they devote time and energy to scrutinizing a suspected counter, someone up in surveillance or down on the floor has to notice something truly aberrant. Chronically coming in mid-shoe can (and should) be a red flag, but in the first hour of play it's hard for the pit even to be sure that that's what's happening. They have a lot of gamblers to deal with besides your BP. And well-organized count teams with bankrolls large enough to bet like we were betting—up to two hands of $5K apiece on this bank— don't come around very often. The typical guy betting $5K a hand is a fish, even if he plays decent basic.

At a certain point, they will become suspicious. That's when paranoid counters hit the door. But suspicion alone isn't fatal. With very large bettors especially, the pit has to make absolutely certain the guy they're barring is bad; you can't very well run a business where you angrily evict your best customers on the basis of hunches. Making certain takes extra time. That's time a team can spend playing. While they're counting down decks or flipping through pictures upstairs in surveillance, trying to match some guy who's wearing a wig and a big hat and a new beard to a mediocre black-and-white photograph from two years before, we can continue to generate anywhere from $1,000 to $4,000 an hour in EV.

I understood none of this yet. I thought we were just being brazen, and possibly nuts. The heat would come down, it would *crush us*. And then . . . I suppose we'd be crushed. I wasn't really sure what the consequences were. But I was terrified.

My count was going up. It was correlated to my pulse. My breath became shallow, I started to squirm. I was wishing it would go back down again. It got to ten. Ten was when I had to give the signal. Meekly I let my hand fall into my lap, hoping no teammate would see it.

"Excuse me, please." It was Kat, pulling a stool out right next to me. I could no longer inhale.

The count had shot up to fourteen: right hand on left elbow, the right index finger extended. I was trembling as I signaled it. Kat clasped her hands—signaling confirmation, that she'd understood the number I was giving her—then I bumbled up, knock-kneed, seizing my chips in a panic. I hurried off the gaming floor and into a stall in a men's room, where I waited five minutes, not for any very good reason. When I returned, I saw Chuck standing in front of the spot I'd just left, still betting into the shoe. Kat had her narcotized smile and her vacant gaze on, and she looked drunk: totally harmless.

Call-in after call-in went down the same way, Chuck busting in mid-shoe with his big smile, asking to have two spots. He would play until the shuffle. Sometimes he would stand there and wait through the shuffle but leave when the new shoe began. He would constantly look around the pit for other call-ins, and at times he would move really fast, practically making a beeline for the next hot shoe. Other times he'd simply disappear.

Now and then the pit became active. Bosses would get on the phone. A new Suit would appear out of nowhere, strutting around like he owned the place, staring at Chuck with cold eyes. A short while after I'd handed that first count to Kat, one of the younger Suits paused at my table. Do *not* lift your gaze, I instructed myself. Ignore the pit totally—not your concern. I kept counting. He shifted his weight, as if he were making himself comfortable. He hadn't said a word to the dealer. My body was turning to stone. I could barely give hand signals. I couldn't breathe. He couldn't have been four feet away. Finally it seemed so unnatural ignoring him, when the guy was so insistently *present,* I did raise my head. His small brown eyes had been waiting for that. They were utterly motionless, staring, boring in, drilling in. I felt myself start. I tried to keep my neck and head still, but my heart was uncontrollable. My veins were probably throbbing visibly. His lips parted faintly—it was like he was letting a breath out, muttering, "Ah . . ." With a minuscule smile, he turned on his heel and took a step back, then strolled calmly away.

Nothing came of it. We played another hour. Across the pit at last I saw Lawrence Taib touching his neck, pointedly looking my way. It was EOS, out of the blue.

We played at Bellagio, at Rio, both of them nice-ish, upscale, filled with those mysterious people who'd devoted a good part of life to acquiring assets enough that they could piss them away and enjoy it. Chuck continued betting in the fancier joints. He was "clean"—that was why. The better casinos also had better rules and higher posted maximum bets: they were worth more, and reserved for the BP with the best likelihood of getting down. Jon Roth, meanwhile, continued to dabble in "toilets."

On graveyard he bet at the Strat. That's the casino with the tower that looks like the Space Needle. It turns out the place is a dump. Maxes ran mostly to $1K, instead of the $5K found at Mandalay Bay or the $10K they always had at Bellagio. The clientele was shabbier and Riv-like. Action was red, or green in extreme cases (i.e., gamblers were mainly betting $5 red chips, with a few betting in increments of $25), but no one except Jon Roth was throwing purple around.

He should have stood out but didn't. It shouldn't have made any sense for a guy with that kind of scratch to choose Strat over Caesars, Venetian, Mandalay, Bellagio, the MGM Grand. In this dump, if you tried betting $500, they should bar you on general principle. The only plausible reason for a high roller to be here at all is that he's 86'd everywhere else. That's how it seemed to me.

But there was Roth: acting goofy, acting drunk, spilling beer. Wide-eyed, he looked like a child. A couple of Suits were fawning. There was an old fat guy wearing gray and a horrific tie, clutching Jon's shoulder with gusto. When he got to a call-in, Jon had a way of accomplishing exactly what he wanted—dominating the dealer, for example, reading his name tag and saying, "Brian! Hold on. *Do not deal one card,* I'm comin' in!" (once there's a good count, every card left is worth money to us, so a BP wants to prevent any new round from getting dealt before he's had time to place bets)—without breaking character or even in a manner that *augmented* his act. From Garry I knew that Jon Roth had started counting before he was even of age: he used to ditch classes at Princeton and head to Atlantic City. When he got into finance and became a trader, his one goal was to generate a big enough bankroll that he could quit and count cards for a living. He'd been doing it full-time for three years. The experience had made him something awesome. He knew what he wanted in sessions. He could manipulate pit supervisors and shift managers—he did it by acting moronic, but in a frat-boy, Wall Street sort of way that commanded a touch of respect, so the Suits were condescending but cowed, all at once. Roth was creating the big bettor who would most stoke their egos: he came off as richer than they were and more worldly, but also less intelligent. The Suits got to feel superior at the same time they were forced to obey and defer to this person. He calmed them entirely. It was almost a feat of hypnosis.

Brilliant, I thought. I was sitting in a quiet section of the Strat's main floor, innocently counting my shoe, when a big, clear voice from behind said, "Try the other pit, Josh." The dealer looked up, and I turned my head, but Roth had kept going. After a minute I followed him. The rest of the teammates had already moved: Roth had been shepherding people around using a combination of signals and blunt instructions like the one he'd given me, shifting our play to a pit where conditions were better. He could do anything. If he saw a way of boosting EV, he could make it reality. Instead of nervousness and weak hope, he met the casinos with purpose. It seemed like the right way to live.

Ten

I was given an envelope, thirteen hundred bucks in it, then flew home. We had won. It was hard, looking back, to say how. Chuck Small won at Mandalay and at Bellagio. He played Desert Inn, but I think he broke even. Jon Roth won at the Strat. The chaos, heat, and insanity had provided me with two months' rent.

The next trip was in two weeks, and Jon had invited me. In the meantime in New York, I was at liberty, and I was not a crazy dreamer anymore. I had a job. Or I had a *good story,* at the very least. Out with friends at a bar, I got introduced to some friends of those friends, and the conversation took the normal route. They asked what I did for a living.

"Professional gambler," I said.

I loved saying it. But no one knew how to respond. Finally a guy asked, "How long you been doing that?"

"It's been about ten days."

Silence. I might as well have said I was the pope. To an extent, I *felt* papal. Miracles were happening; the curtain had been yanked.

"Tomorrow," I said, "it's eleven."

Eleven

The next week I was back out there, back in the desert, back in that vacuous air that has no trace of wetness—back out again in that sun, in that sun that bears repeating, back in that daylight (that *sun*) that conjures thoughts of Hiroshima, that light that is tactile and into which you are dissolved, in that annhilatory daylight—they tested the bombs out there in Nevada, you began to suspect, because the nuclear explosions *blend in with a typical morning*—back in the apartment (HQ), a burly, happy Jon Roth scratching his face, Bridget drinking coffee with milk, Aldous Kaufman holding a laptop on his lap on the floor, and Don Woolf, whom I'd actually met once before when he was playing with MIT and who now lived in Vegas playing poker full-time, occupying the dealer's seat behind the table.

He was dealing a controller test to me. Five shoes, and I had to calculate and signal bets for an invisible gorilla (we had no one at the table to play the gorilla, so Woolf was just dealing hands to empty spots next to me). I'd gotten in a lot of practice since quitting my job. I was much faster with true count. I'd learned shortcuts, to help me: instead of dividing your running count by two and a half when there are two and a half decks left, you can multiply by point-four, which really just means multiplying by four and then shifting the decimal (this is much easier than the two-and-a-half stuff, which I'd always found mystifying and impossible, and it works out the same); instead of dividing by one and a half, you can multiply by two, then divide by three, which I also found easier.

Not only had my skills improved, but the test was less tough than expected. Mossad's controller test was probably easier than MIT's spotter test. Woolf was just here hanging out, curious about our team, having heard about it from Kat, who herself was an MIT alum, and when I started to make noises about wanting to try a new checkout in hopes of a promotion (controllers got paid twice the spotter rate, and of course I would have to control if I wanted ultimately to turn into a counting BP and become as godlike as Jon Roth), Woolf offered to deal. Jon explained the test requirements to him, and I think he was surprised. Midway through the checkout, I realized Woolf was probably dealing even more easily than Roth had meant; from his perspective the standards must have seemed so low as to verge on nonexistent.

It was in this relaxed context that I passed and became a controller.

The structure of the team was now clearer. Roth, Neal Matcha, and Aldous Kaufman were officially the joint managers, although Roth was pretty obviously the chief. Lawrence Taib and Kat Armstrong were both seasoned players who invested a lot in the banks, and they would help run things as needed. Jimmy Mateo was actually a new counter who had started the trip before I had. Also playing this trip were Chuck Small, another former MIT guy named Clint (he was Kat's friend, too), and a pair of new gorillas named Anthony and Robert. Anthony was here just to train, but Robert Jayne had already checked out and was ready for action.

"Robert can go anywhere. Josh can go anywhere," Roth was saying. He, Neal, and Aldous were standing by the dry-erase board in the kitchen, sketching out possible play groups. Casinos were listed in marker—the highest-value options at the top. It was like a menu at a restaurant in heaven, a restaurant that *paid you to eat.*

We went to the Rio. Robert had a crazy act. He acted like he was coked up, or had maybe snorted angel dust or heroin. BP'ing, "betting the money," demanded an odd set of skills. Technically, you played perfect basic strategy except when signaled to deviate, and you bet as you were told. You also controlled the game's pace. At the end of a round, if your controller needed time to think before signaling your next bet, you would slow down the dealer by asking for change, demanding to talk to a pit boss, or concocting some other ruse. You also had to look natural placing big bets—your character had to make sense to the pit.

The hardest part seemed to be the dead time between shoes. Each of the BP's controllers should have about a call-in an hour. If a BP got lucky, as soon as one shoe ended, he would get called into the next. Often he wasn't so lucky. A call-in would end, and then for ten minutes he would have nothing. He couldn't just run to the bathroom; he had to stay close to the pit—inevitably in view of the pit bosses—so that he could start betting as soon as the next shoe came. What to do? He can't simply sit at a table, refusing to play. And he doesn't want to look like he's waiting for something. Robert would stand blocking traffic, convulsing, eyes rolling back in his head, then maybe stagger around a few steps. He didn't look like he was waiting; he looked like he was struggling to maintain consciousness. When he went to a call-in, he appeared to arrive there at random. He would take wild steps, almost falling, then suddenly get to a table and slap down a bet. He was a hell of an actor. Soon Taib ended the session.

We'd barely played an hour that time, but he won $20K. I wasn't sure why we had ended it. There was an art, evidently, to deciding when to play and when to stop. Each of our sessions had a session leader who would make that decision. Sometimes the leader wouldn't play in a session; instead of counting shoes, he would act as a "heat monitor," our side's version of a pit boss. He would stay removed from the tables—especially in places where he was well known—and study the reactions of the pit from a distance. Roth knew by face many of the shift managers or surveillance guys whose arrival might indicate trouble. Sometimes they kept us playing even when trouble was certain, but at other times they'd want to get us out.

Robert at Venetian was nuts. He had veins standing out on his neck.

His face was bright red. He was losing, and he kept screaming. He looked like he was one lost double-down away from becoming the Incredible Hulk. I had him at my table when the guards appeared. I was signaling a four-unit bet (right hand flat on left elbow: the controlling signals were similar to the count-passing signals for spotters), and there was Robert crying "Noooooooowwwwwwwww!!" at the slow dealer, with two hands of $2K waiting on the felt, when I averted my head from his shouting and saw them: three guards were in position at the end of the pit, watching him.

I shifted my gaze fast, pulse instantly quicker, my body feeling hotter and in a way more alive; down at the pit's other end, there were three more guards in position. They looked ready to close in. The dealer began pulling cards out. I was thinking of looking at Robert and giving him EOS myself, even though I wasn't authorized to do that, when I noticed Taib some distance away, two hands on his neck, nodding.

I clasped my hands before my chest—confirmation—and I relayed the signal to Robert, who had just seen Taib also. Robert abandoned the call-in. I had to stay at the table so we wouldn't be charging out trying to dodge guards in stereo. They probably wouldn't be after me anyhow. Like Bridget had said, the BP gets identified first; a controller is tough to pick out from among all the randoms if his face is completely unknown. I should just wait a few minutes, let the guards dissipate, and then leave.

But it was hard to keep playing and pretend like I was enjoying it. I didn't actually understand why people played blackjack who weren't counting cards. It was hard to get into their mind-set. It seemed both foolish and dull. What could they be thinking about all night long if they weren't doing true-count conversion? To the extent I had an "act" as a controller, I was acting like a guy who would prefer that he wasn't playing blackjack just now. I didn't know how else to behave.

With Robert gone, guards were still looming. A senior-looking Suit was giving instructions to a small group of them. My mouth had gone dry, and my brain had turned heavy. It felt like I had a bowling ball in my skull. It was starting to ache. I lost a hand and stood.

Leaving the pit, I marched right past a guard, lowering my eyes to the carpet. The door was thirty yards straight ahead. The urge was to sprint, but you can't. My strides were as hasty and long as I could make them without looking like a criminal in flight.

Reaching the exit, I stepped out into the night. I was in Piazza San Marco. The Campanile was coated with projected light. Mirage across the street looked palatial. Civilians here and there were taking photographs. It's like they're on a holiday, I thought. Don't you people know there's a war on?

End-of-session was in a parking lot in back of Casino Royale, a tiny dump adjacent to Venetian. I ducked down the dark alley leading that way. Mateo was back there, standing at one of our cars. He said, "Whew. Little hot?"

"Kind of," I said.

"Did they get you?"

"Uh-uh."

"They get Robert?"

"I don't know."

We were in the cloistered lot under the glowing night sky, which was milky gray rather than dark. I felt ravaged and energized—happy. The salmon-colored tower of Venetian's hotel hovered high up, right above us.

Taib appeared, Robert, Bridget, and then Roth, who immediately asked Lawrence why he'd ended the thing. "I sensed a profusion of guards," Taib said.

"You thought that was heat?" Jon's voice became higher. He spoke a little faster when he was upset.

"I interpreted security closing in like that as a negative development, boss."

"There wasn't heat."

Lawrence shrugged, almost mockingly. "Oh?"

"There wasn't heat," Jon said. "They were loving him. They thought he was out of control, that he was dangerous physically. They had security there in case he started throwing punches or something. They *wanted* his action—loved it. Didn't you see the shift manager laughing? Fuck, man."

"It looked really bad to me," Bridget said. Lawrence and she exchanged glances. "I wanted to get out of there, too."

Mateo said, "Yeah."

I nodded agreement.

Jon was looking around at all of us in disgust.

Robert wanted to go back in, but Jon said we couldn't—we'd blown the opportunity for now. He was pissed. Heat could be hard to interpret.

Twelve

R obert won at Rio, lost at Venetian but then went back to Venetian and he ended with a net win at the casino of $30K and then got 86'd. He won another 30 and change at Mirage, and was backed off there, in a session I wasn't a part of. Clint Greene, who was both a seasoned and a clean player, was running around with a crew as a counting BP. He also hit the Rio, hard, for 50. He went into Bellagio—Bridget, Mateo, and I were the counters. It was a day shift midweek, and the casino was empty.

Mateo was heads-up at a shoe, and he got a count instantly. I had just finished buying in when it happened. From nowhere Clint stormed into the shoe, wearing his sport coat and looking dashing, looking calm. He had a mild-mannered sort of act. Generic rich guy, pleasant to be around. He was genuinely a warm person in real life. He was basically just being himself, for his act, except that in real life he was in grad school studying chemistry, instead of being rich. Mateo indicated the count and then was gone, leaving Clint heads-up (a heads-up call-in is a lot more valuable than a call-in at a crowded table, because all the good cards are for you and the dealer and nobody else; you always prefer not to share, even with your own spotter— his minimum bets are a waste of those cards). I was watching my own shoe, but it was hard not to notice Clint applauding or making happy sounds over there. His call-in took a really long time. Security guards came bearing extra chips for his table: a fill, meaning Clint perhaps had won all of a particular denomination of chip in the rack. The shoe took about twenty minutes.

As his dealer was starting to shuffle, Clint looked up and touched his neck. Wow, we've had a one-shoe session. Shortest I'd been in yet. I cashed my chips, left the gaming floor, strolled past the boutiques. I utilized the revolving door, bound north via walkway in the direction of Caesars, wincing automatically in all the sun. I went down a set of stairs, up an escalator, and took the next walkway over the Strip, to the east side of it, where I entered the Barbary Coast at the corner.

Down into the darkness of the musty low-stakes grind joint that happened to be situated optimally at a very busy intersection for card counters (Barbary Coast was the EOS for Bellagio, Caesars, Paris, Bally's, Flamingo— not only was the location convenient, but the small casino had its own garage that almost always had spaces available; it also had miserable blackjack conditions, leaving us free to associate openly here without concern about losing any good playing opportunities), I took a few steps and saw Jimmy. He was drinking a Coke at the bar. Bridget arrived, and in a few minutes we watched Clint Greene appear in the sunstruck entrance as a silhouette, then mosey over to join us. Beaming, he said, "That was a nice shoe."

"Glad you had fun," Jimmy said.

"Result, result, result." Bridget clapped eagerly.

Clint nodded and opened his breast pocket, exposing a manila envelope that was folded in half and weighing his jacket down. He gave it to Bridget, saying, "This is the win. Take a guess."

She felt it from both sides. "Forty."

"Correct within four hundred dollars," he said.

Forty thousand. Oh, we were good.

Not that we were complaining, but the trip was ahead of EV. The number crossed one-fifty, and it kept going. It was an aberrant win: too high. We were all going to take home a bundle.

It began feeling like a normal activity, wandering into some casino in Vegas, buying in for $300 at a $25-min game, playing robotic basic strategy and counting cards, plus-one and minus-one, the running count listing in the back of my head. Six days into the trip, it was like we'd all been doing this forever.

I was sitting at a table—the Paris. I'd never been here before. *Another* new casino I could help pulverize through this amazing little glitch in the game. Neal had just signaled and was giving the first call-in of the session. I was relaxed at my stool, playing through a count heading nowhere, giving no signals, just biding my time till the shuffle.

Oh, we are good. This is *good*. This is how it should work. This is what I wanted from life: magical income in a Wonderland in a hot valley on a foreign planet, with undertones of personal danger.

"Sir," the man said.

Like that. There was no warning. I knew right away what it meant. Raising my head, I saw this strange individual in a costume designed to imitate the flic, or Parisian street cop, complete with a white bandolier. He was standing just behind me.

I should have said, *"Qu'est-ce que vous avez dit?"* But I was too surprised. He had caught me off guard. It was morning, day shift, peaceful. Nothing much was going on. I'd been preparing to sit there for hours. Moreover, *I hadn't done a thing.*

"Mind standing up?" he said. A few feet behind him, a Suit waited, looking rather bored. I got up. The guard asked to see my ID.

Lamely I said, "I forgot it."

He'd been expecting that. "I'm going to have to ask you to leave, then."

"Right. Where's the cage?"

It was like a confession. I'd conceded too fast. I should at least have played dumb—it was very strange for them to get me just now when I hadn't even given a call-in. How could they have known? The Suit remained aloof, just observing. The guard pointed out the cashier.

As I moved in that direction looking straight ahead, I was using peripheral vision, probing for any more bandoliered flics who might be coming to sur-round me, sniffing the air for them, listening, acutely aware of all sound, my body highly sensitive to motion nearby. I was like an animal—a lioness. An attack beaver. Something. I was ferocious, jeopardized and feeling wild, will-ing to defend myself by any means.

In the same hypersensitive state, after cashing my chips I rushed in a near jog down the long sidewalk from the exit to the edge of the property. I glanced back over my shoulder, saw no flic or goon or Suit, but I felt like they were watching me. I tried to disappear among pedestrian traffic. Once I'd crossed the Strip and was riding the people conveyor overlooking the lake at Bellagio, I got Roth on the phone.

"Mr. Axe!" This was a nickname Neal Matcha had given me over the weekend. "How goes it at Paris?"

"I got eighty-sixed."

"Whoa, whoa. What happened?"

I explained the flic coming out of nowhere, asking for ID. When I finished, he said, "That's not an eighty-sixing, that's a backing-off. They didn't trespass you, right?"

"I guess not."

"Do not make that mistake. I know to you it sounds pretty similar, but a backing-off like that and a formal trespass are different. Way different lev-els of heat."

Now I felt more like a lion cub, or a pacifist beaver. For a moment I was almost embarrassed I'd bothered to call. Then Roth said, "Wait a minute. You say you didn't give a call-in?"

"I didn't do anything. I was there five minutes."

"You've never played Paris before, right?"

"Right."

"Axe Man," he said, "you've got bigger problems than you realize."

Thirteen

My cut on the second trip with Mossad was just under $10K. That really got my attention. I flew home across the country in a daze. Again I was paid cash, and I had all of it in my pocket. I was touching it constantly to make sure it was there. The next day I visited the local Chase bank and rented a safe-deposit box. I was handed a metal container and shown into a closet with a door you could lock from inside. I pulled the money out, touching it, feeling the grime on the face of the uppermost bill. It was dirty, sordid, squalid—the kind of money a man could respect. I'd had money already, and for no good reason: when my rich grampa died, it was worth forty Gs to me. I'd had the funds for two years and had spent nothing. It didn't seem respectable getting assets that way. But *this* money here, this was different. It smelled a little like cigarettes or wet newsprint. I planned to leave it all in the box until the next bank, ten days away; I would be investing (my first-ever blackjack investment), and you brought your investment in cash. At the last moment, though, impulsively I held back a handful of bills, thinking I might as well have a grand or so of walking-around money, just in case something came up.

Something did. Things always do in New York. I kept buying dinners for people. I decided I should get some leather pants. I treated myself to a manicure and to a back wax. There were cocktails—several, top shelf. I had a date. Her name was Claire. We'd met via the Internet and gone out the first time the month before. For our second date, we were meeting my friend Paul, who was a puppeteer, with some other puppeteer friends of his in a workshop where puppets got built. We were all drinking beer together, surrounded by half-built puppets, disembodied orb-shaped puppet eyes, reticulated-Styrofoam blocks. Paul looked at his watch. "Shall we head?"

We were going to a party on a boat in the Hudson River. We finished our forty-ounce Coorses and rode the service elevator down from the workshop. As we approached Tenth Avenue, someone said, "Two cabs, I guess? There are five of us."

"Damn," Paul said. Then: "Wait. There's a limousine."

He started rambling drunkenly across the avenue. Claire said, "What is he doing?"

"Hailing a limo, I think." I took her hand, following Paul.

"You can hail limousines?"

"You can hail anything." It felt true. I had $500 left in my pants.

Paul was leaning into the window of a black stretch limo, apparently trying to negotiate. He turned back around, started waving at us. We all scrambled into the car. The guy drove us over to West Street, then started roaring uptown. Paul fell onto the floor and was lying on his back, kicking one leg up, laughing. The sun roof was open. Claire and I stuck out our heads. Through the rough wind and the humidity, headlights were dancing abstractly. We faced each other, kissed. She had a big, sensuous mouth. I held her strong arm as we Frenched. It occurred to me there might be a link between money and the breadth of raw experience a man could get.

Arriving at the boat, we spilled out. I paid admission for Claire. She and I headed belowdecks. The corridors were iron, stippled with rust. Bass was throbbing from the deejay, reverberating everywhere like an earthquake just brewing. I fought to the bar and bought drinks. We wandered down an eerie passageway. We were drunk, and we paused to make out, Claire's shoulder up against the metal wall. Then we found the door to a cabin.

With effort I shut it behind us. The cabin had a mattress on a little frame. I pushed Claire down; she fell back. I got on her and opened her mouth. Her front teeth were crashing against mine. Her thighs were flat against my own. The mattress reeked lightly of mildew. It smelled like a boxful of money. I went for the blouse, pulling two buttons apart, and stared at the size of her boobs. "Ahem!" Claire cried.

I thought, Rats!

She protected her bosom, buttoning up, then bit my neck, and we stopped. We went back to the deck but were kissing again. The wind was very cold. Above and beyond the boat's hulking funnel, the towers of midtown were glowing in some kind of haze; it was the color of the milk from your Froot Loops.

"What if we go get a room?" The words came out of nowhere.

She shook her head. "Where?"

"Someplace good. A hotel."

She said she had to think for a minute. While she was doing that, I got my phone out. I called Sprint information—the 99 cents be damned. "New York," I said, "the Renaissance Hotel." I was connected at no extra charge.

"Do you have vacancy tonight? What's the rate?"

It was $325. A little over half my monthly rent. We were a six-minute drive from my apartment, but that only made it more decadent. Claire threw her arms around my neck: "I won't have sex with you tonight."

I said, "If I had a nickel . . ."

"If you're all right with that, boy, lead the way."

I paid for the cab, too. Fuck it. We got to the front desk, reeking of vodka and pheromones. The desk agent had an expression like a coal miner just come back to the surface after working an overtime shift. Bitterly she keyed in my data. "Address?" she said.

"West Seventy-ninth Street."

"Luggage?" This was sarcastic. Perhaps it's a class thing, I thought. She held out the key, and I took it. I was more excited than I'd ever been.

In the morning I arranged for late checkout. I looked at Claire. "What should we do?"

"Kozmo," she answered.

"Ah. Good."

We called the service up. It was incredible. Kozmo.com was this scam—or, excuse me, "paradigm-transforming business model"—where a man on a bicycle would bring you anything you wanted, anywhere in Manhattan, for about the same price as they charged in a store, and he wouldn't accept tips. You were supposed to use it through the Internet. Or you could call.

"Bagels," Claire said to the phone. "Cream cheese. Oh! The Sunday *New York Times*. Anything else?"

I said, "Toothpaste."

He arrived in twenty minutes. I went down to pick up the stuff. I tried to hand him two bucks but was refused.

"You sure?" I asked the kid.

"Believe me," he said. "They take care of us."

He must have meant stock options, the poor fool. It was May of 2000. NASDAQ had peaked back in March and might never recover, but no one was very concerned yet. The elevator brought me up quickly. I was sure I was on the right path.

Fourteen

A taxonomy of heat: There's session heat, individual-property heat, transproperty heat, local-network heat, and network-network heat. Everything starts with the session.

Heat in the context of one session is more serious the more senior the person giving it. An agitated dealer means nothing. Dealers don't blow you out. If a dealer thinks you're a card counter, nothing will come of it, even if he speaks up, because no one will listen. A dealer cries "Shuffle!" when shuffling, "Change!" when making change, "Checks play!" when large bets are going down. It's up to the Suits in the pit to respond to those calls—in particular that last one—and to interpret what they mean, and to react.

Suits themselves need a taxonomy. The most prevalent Suit is the "floor," short for floorman. The floormen oversee the dealers. Each floor has responsibility for around four tables. In addition to crying out "All right!" in response to a dealer crying "Shuffle," a floor approves transactions above a certain minimum amount, and he keeps track of the buy-in at each table by writing little notes on a pad. Floors, so I've heard, often earn less than the dealers; salaries are low, and they don't get to share in the tip pool. Their job seems miserable. They're on their feet among the slot machines (ka-CHING ka-CHING ka-CHING, BWOOP *BWOOOOP*) all day long getting headaches, breathing smoke. A floor might give some kind of prefatory heat, especially to a lower-stakes counter, but he mostly won't have the authority to blow out a serious bettor. What he can do is alert the guy above him if something looks wrong.

The next guy up is the pit supervisor or pit boss. He also wears a suit. He also wears a few extra pounds. He will have been on his feet eight hours a day, five days a week in that room full of noise for some years. He'll probably have the authority to blow out lower and midstakes counters—to back them off himself, in other words—and he can also put the call in to surveillance, asking them to check you out closely. If surveillance gives the word, he'll probably bar you. But he might defer the final decision to either the table games supervisor or the shift manager. The latter is generally the highest-ranking Suit on duty at any one time.

Casino hosts also wear suits, but they're not "Suits" themselves in the heat-giving sense. A host is a marketing guy. He's basically in charge of free shit. He's the one your BP should milk for the "full RFB"—room, food, and beverage, meaning free suite, free meals, and as many free bottles (of Dom, Cristal, and Johnnie Walker Blue) as he can get. A BP wants to manipulate his host the same way he manipulates the regular Suits, but he needn't fear heat from him. A host, like a dealer, has negligible game-protection responsibility.

In the course of a session, if the only one sweating you is a dealer, you effectively have no heat. A floorman isn't much worse. Once the pit boss gets involved, you may have issues, especially if he tells you you're barred. Still, a backing-off, or any of a variety of what we call "passive countermeasures" (the standard passive countermeasure is the half-shoe, in which the dealer is instructed to deal only half the deck before shuffling; this is the pit boss's way of telling you he doesn't actually know if you're a card counter or not—if he knew, he would just back you off), doesn't necessarily mean you'll have ongoing issues in the property.

To be sure, if you're backed off on a particular shift, you should avoid that shift for some time (*if you can;* if you're without other options, you'll have to suck it up and try again). You don't necessarily need to avoid the casino. Heat only becomes institutionalized if someone bothers taking your picture. If, for whatever reason, the backing-off is dramatic or serious, you can then expect that a picture has been taken; it'll probably be taped to the wall of the surveillance room for a week, perhaps with copies distributed to those podiums they have in the pit, and will be added to their internal mug book. You'll want to wait, then come back looking different.

An 86'ing is graver. This means they're really annoyed. The bosses will have dispatched security. Security will try reading you a statement—an official notification of trespass, complete with the (spurious) threat that you will be subject to arrest if you're encountered on the property again. (Fact: A legal precedent from a 1978 case in Las Vegas suggests that a previously 86'd person must be again asked to leave *and given the opportunity to do so* before becoming guilty of a misdemeanor. In practice this makes a second 86'ing no graver or more significant than a first.) You can be fairly sure in this case that PTZ (point-tilt-zoom) cameras under opaque plastic domes all over the ceiling will be pointing and tilting and zooming at you. Your heat is institutional for sure. You'll have to wait a few months. Disguise will be important upon your return.

Institutional heat can metastasize. Casinos under common ownership (like Mirage and Bellagio) may share information. This is transproperty heat.

Casinos *not* under common ownership may also share information a number of ways. Locally, especially in smaller gambling towns (such as Tunica, Mississippi, or Shreveport, Louisiana), surveillance rooms may simply fax pictures around to their neighbors. They can also communicate electronically through a system known as the SIN, or Surveillance Information Network, sending digital images with the click of a mouse. Or they can communicate through Griffin Investigations, a Vegas-based agency that compiles a notorious book listing highly active counters and that also faxes emergency updates to subscribing casinos when counters are active in their area. These are the varieties of local-network heat.

Most damaging is *network*-network heat: not confined to any particular property, particular chain, or particular region, this kind of heat can be permanent, and it may affect you anywhere at any time. An entry in the Griffin Book is one example. And Griffin also has a competitor: the Biometrica CVI database (originally developed by a former Griffin agent named Andy Anderson), which powers the SIN.

It was one of these last three varieties that probably nailed me that day at the Paris. My dreadlocks were easy to notice. Someone must have recognized me from a flyer. I'd already been hot without knowing it, from some prior session where I must have gotten out before they were able to bar me. I would never learn where it began.

Fifteen

The hot days. Summer. In Las Vegas it was 117 degrees. In Biloxi you had the humidity. Clouds hung low, long, and potent-looking, like warships over the Gulf. In Tunica, forty miles south of Memphis, the heat was smothering the fields. Cotton stretched as far as you could see, modest green clumps specked with white. Some of the casinos were right by the river, where gnarled trees were gathered in the night and the damp, hot air shimmered visibly.

Inside, the casinos were less different. They called female pit bosses "miss" in the South: "Shuffle check, Miss Lydia!" Otherwise you could have been in Vegas. The slot noise got to your head. The backs of your knuckles grew cracked from rubbing on the felt so many hours.

In Vegas we won. In Biloxi we won. In Tunica we lost. I started the trip there humiliated, failing a checkout. They had a different set of rules—the dealer hit on the hand called "soft seventeen" (that's a seventeen made with an ace counting as eleven points: ace-six, or an ace-deuce-four, etc.), instead of standing as normally—and both the bet calculation and strategy deviations were a little different. I hadn't practiced enough with the new math. I failed the mini-checkout twice, and Roth said, "Go to your room." He said it like he was my mom, and quite disgusted with me. "Practice for an hour. Come back, you get one more shot. If you fail, you're a spotter this trip."

I was able to pass. But in other ways I felt that I was failing. I was on the fringes of the team and had no close friends among the players. Jimmy Mateo, only ten months older than I was, seemed more mature and more trusted. He was sometimes a counting BP. I asked Neal at one point if I could do that.

"You're a little young to pull it off," he said, "right? And don't forget, mac—you're hot." He slapped my arm playfully. Hot. I was closer to blazing. By now I'd started getting 86'd. I'd learned how to deal with goons. You move directly for the exit at a calm gait. If they ask you to stop, you say no. If they tell you, "Hold on, we really need to have a word," you reply, without excitement or emotion, that you wish to leave, intend to leave, are in fact leaving, and you simply keep walking toward the door. Your hands should be out of your pockets, arms close to your sides. You should never touch a guard. You must not create a disturbance. Cameras will be watching what you do. They cannot arrest you, detain you, they really can't hinder you in any way *unless* you break actual laws.

At Venetian one night, I was surprised to get 86'd mid-shoe while controlling a gorilla they simply ignored—the heat was on me, not him. He was betting two by $3,000. My wager was twenty-five bucks. I got off the premises and phoned Neal, who was directing the play groups that night. "You won't believe what happened," I began.

"They got you? Hey, look. Aldous is betting at MGM Grand. Get there fast or you'll miss it."

"MGM," I told the driver. "Take Koval." An evocative street, Koval Lane: a single block down from the Strip, it's the inverse of glitz, lightless and not high on charm, crammed with cheap apartment houses advertising vacancies, their front walls cracked or collapsing. It gave me a charge just to witness. Backstage Las Vegas, and I knew my way.

As I marched through the green and gold lobby, passed among the low-profile slots that were only hip-high, and proceeded with purpose down into the broad corridor filled with long pits where I knew the good tables were located, I felt at home, energized, belonging—I wasn't self-conscious at all. Aldous was betting a shoe. I prowled behind the stools like a forager. By the time I was giving a call-in, the pit had grown worried. Telephones rang. It wouldn't be long now. Aldous was quite hot and probably hadn't expected to last here more than an hour. He got to my shoe. I was signaling a four-unit bet. His presence made me suddenly panic. He scratched his chest—angrily, it seemed. This signal meant he wanted the count passed, but I was confused. I had almost lost the count on the round and had to study the cards to regain it.

"Insurance?" the dealer was saying.

Aldous said, "Oh—insurance, huh . . . ," trying to buy time. Eighteen, I was thinking, divided by— *Shit!* I froze up. I couldn't do the math. Taking insurance is a playing deviation—in basic strategy you don't insure. (Insurance is a separate bet placed only when the dealer has an ace up. If you take it, you're betting she has blackjack—a ten-valued card in the hole. It's worth a ton of EV in high counts.) Aldous glanced down at my seat, his brow raised. I shook my head. The dealer said, "Insurance is closed." That's when it struck me: With a four-unit bet, the count's *definitely* high enough to warrant insurance, unless it really plunged on the round. The dealer flipped her hole card: a jack. My mistake cost us $8,000.

"Over here," a man said. A suit. He had a flower in his pocket. The guards waited a few steps behind him. He was talking to me. "Right now."

Standing, I said, "Seventeen," passing the count without hiding it. Aldous clasped his hands in confirmation. He placed a fresh bet. The suit was leading me away. "This man has something to tell you," he said, indicating one of the guards. Then I was between two goons, being escorted to the exit for the second time in forty-five minutes, again blown before the BP got blown—and the BP had seen me screw up. Aldous would not be impressed.

Sixteen

Jimmy might have waved. It doesn't make much of a difference. He was moving through the room and then gone.

In any case I wouldn't have responded.

I had cards on the table in front of me. My left wrist rested on the beige leather cushion. Both feet were flat on the carpet. My neck, shoulders, wrists, knuckles, lumbar area, and butt hurt.

The man I'd nicknamed Bluto was studying me. I'm not going to look, kid, I thought. I'm not in the eye-contact business just now. "Raise," Bluto said.

Oh, God.

Chips clattered. The dealer said, "Raise." Warmth flooded my face and my neck. My cards were no good. I was bad at this game. I shouldn't play. I don't *care* to win, that's the problem. Poker just wasn't important like blackjack could be.

Taking twelve chips from the diminishing hoard, I chucked them at the pot, hoping a fast, manly, taking-no-shit, desperation reraise might provoke a fold. Bluto said, "Raise." No delay. He'd had his chips ready to throw— here they came.

This was so fucking unpleasant. And to think, Jimmy and I on the drive over had laughed half the way, enthusiastic, tired, delirious. The bank had just ended, and the bank break was still under way at the base. The "break" was the eternal accounting procedure done amid reams of player sheets and session-leader sheets and bank logs and receipts in Jon and Bridget's bedroom, sometimes for twenty-four hours. Every misreported transfer gets identified, every wrong balance will have to get fixed before the win can be divided. In the wake of a big and long trip such as this had proved, for those of us not stuck over the laptop entering data it's torturous. *Give us our money!* Pay up, and then let us be. On the brink of complete liberty, usually we were all asked to stay *in* the apartment (and not make much noise), available to answer questions as errors were found in our paperwork. We were allowed to drink. With the trip's gambling finished, the prohibition on alcohol was lifted. We drank, but we seethed. Vegas was out there, man—*right there!* Stratosphere's gaunt red tower was visible from the kitchen. When night fell, light radiated from the Strip; we could see Luxor's beam, linear, dense, and entrancing, like a column supporting the sky. *That* was the place—*out there!* Not here, with this fucking Corona. *Why is it always Corona?* Well, Josh, partly it's Corona in the fridge because those of you interested in other beers don't bother to buy any, do you? Whoever bought the beer bought Corona. I didn't even know who it was. There were never any limes. My cut for the bank I had guesstimated at around $6K. That's a hair more than the worldwide average personal income for an entire year, earned in ten days in Las Vegas, doing very little, as it happened. *Six thousand bucks* I had coming. Oh, but this life was amazing. Then Jimmy secured leave for us from Jon—though the break was ongoing, we had permission to go, romp, play, recreate, procure costly drink, have a leisurely swim, get some exercise, maybe at long last ride one of the roller coasters at the casinos, *do anything at all,* provided our phones were kept on and we could get back to the apartment within an hour or so if we were needed. Anything. We could break loose or explode. Try something wholly unexpected. Stop by an art-supply store and purchase some canvases, portable easels, paint, brushes, sponges, blow a G or two on the equipment and then take a hike, somewhere strange and beautiful like maybe that range of orange hills to the southeast—what are those hills all about?—hike out dodging scorpions and leaping rattlesnakes, and try depicting in thick globs of oil the exquisiteness of this valley. Anything was possible. But: All we wanted really was to gamble some more. And if blackjack was out (personal play being proscribed in Las Vegas as a matter of team policy), fuck it, we'd wager at poker. I would lose, and that was fine.

Fondling my chips, what I wanted was to stand up, mid-hand, neither call nor fold nor raise, abandon the few chips I had left on the felt, and go home. To New York. Where I could lie in bed alone and just sob. Bluto kept his eyes locked on me.

Are you fucking serious, guy? This was the lowest-stakes game in the room: nine-eighteen. (Fixed-limit poker typically has a round or more of smaller bets followed by a round or more of bigger bets, and the stakes are described by the increments of the wagering.) Jimmy meanwhile was playing twenty-forty. I was at the kid's table, basically, and it seemed ridiculous Bluto here was imagining himself as Doyle Brunson.

Reraise? I asked myself.

No. I said, "Call." I hadn't expected to say this. I couldn't possibly win if I called. Bluto shrugged in a way that conveyed some astonishment. "Showdown," the dealer reminded us. I nodded at Bluto, who had to show his hand first. It's last to aggress: that's the rule. He turned up his cards. Pocket nines.

Fucking pair.

I tossed my own cards facedown and hit the muck, the other discards, so the dealer couldn't be sure which cards had been mine if anyone demanded that he show them. "What's that?" someone asked. Somebody else started laughing. On the board there was a king, there was a jack. This would normally mean that a player staying in the hand would at least have two kings or two jacks, but, having lost to those nines, I'd obviously had almost nothing. What could have caused me to reraise back there? What could have caused me to call?

New cards had already come. The time was very late—close to noon. I'd been ingesting, on an hourly basis, a seven- or eight-thousand-calorie drink called a Strawberry Julius, house specialty at the Bellagio, nonalcoholic and loaded with sugar, and my body felt sickly and ravaged, something like an inflatable sex doll whose air has gotten squished out due to violent love. I thought I might easily vomit, pass out, have a heart attack, or shit. Everything was screwy, and my pride was crushed.

Why play poker? It's simple. Poker is a shit game, and the people who play it are shit. Not to say there isn't skill involved, but look: what is the source of the money? The source is the fish. The source is the krill, or the plankton—least protected of the fish. People gone loopy, like arguably I have at present, they form the basis of what Aldous Kaufman terms the "poker economy," and their money gets taken by the bigger fish, who in turn pony up to the sharks. The chain of loss starts with the sickest, really with the degenerates: *los adictos*. That's the foundation here, and it's fucked. That's whose money you're gambling, at bottom. A poker pro is in the moral position of a casino manager, feeding off the weakest of the weak.

But *here*, at the nine-eighteen among the wannabes, hilarity prevailed, in a sense. That was the draw—the hilarity. You could barely buy groceries for the size of these pots. You could barely win a dinner at McDonald's here, yet the so-called serious players on this game dreamed they could be pros. And if they did someday become pros, morally they would be doomed. It was hilarious to me. What a vile fucking aspiration.

Here I was, slumming. A *real* pro hustler, unbeknownst to these clowns, with ball cap low on my face. Surveillance knew us well at the Bellagio. They would tolerate our presence in the poker room, though occasionally the one woman, Jane Durrell, who was kind of high up and had a tendency to get excited, would stop by to watch as we played. We came semi-disguised to deny her the opportunity for good photographs.

Now I was doing this thing. I was mad. The peons weren't acting with deference. I opened my pants under the table. I'd folded a hand, but already in front of me there was another. Reaching under my waistband, I took hold of my overstuffed money belt, unzipped, and was touching a strap.

With my right hand, I lifted my cards. Jack-four. There's potential. No, I thought: no. I tossed them where the dealer could reach. His eyes hitting mine, I took the opportunity to ask, "Cash plays on the table?"

"That's right."

"Thank you." I pulled a $5K strap from the belt. Silently I set it on the table. Bluto saw it instantly, but no one else had. It was an excessive chunk of change for these stakes. You normally buy in for four or five hundred at the nine-eighteen hold 'em. I felt like I'd brought an actual, working light saber to a second-grade show-and-tell.

I came into a pot raising. People were starting to notice the money in front of me. Silence stretched over the table. I lost the hand—had to back out of it. But something had shifted by now. My fellow players weren't sure what to make of me. I had depth, they could see. A normal person, when he's on tilt, and he has five Gs, won't merely stay put at the lowest-stakes game in the room—he'll try something bigger. Not this guy. Another hour came, and then another hour came. I had new poise for some time, and I was deliberative in my decisions. I won a couple hundred, then lost it. The result would form a sine wave if someone were to graph how it flowed. The roster of opponents kept changing. The Juliuses came. I was passing a chip to the waitress. My body felt light, like a sail. Time was the wind; I imagined it blowing forever.

♦

"They give you a key?" Jimmy said.

"Me? Are you kidding?"

"I don't know." He coughed and laid into the doorbell. We were standing outside the apartment. Early evening, and the temperature was infinite.

Jimmy smiled. His eyes were full of gloom. We'd both stayed up through the night. He hadn't gone home after poker; he'd gone to shoot craps for some reason.

Bridget opened the door without speaking. She turned and moved back down the hall. She was wearing short socks made for running.

I followed Jimmy in. Passing the master bedroom, I heard Roth. "Speak of the devil!"

"Morning." I stopped.

"Morning?" he said. "Holy fuck. The sun's setting, Axe. Come in for a sec, grab a seat."

Aldous, with his back against the wall, was perusing a textbook. He gave me a nod as I entered. Roth was standing by the window with a cigarette. The window was open a half foot, A/C notwithstanding. There was no use sweating the small stuff: this we believed. Neal, lying on the bed, was possibly asleep. Bridget had the room's only chair.

Aldous said, "How was Bellagio?"

I was feeling light-headed. "I lost."

"How much?"

"Nine hundred."

"Playing what?"

"Nine-eighteen hold 'em."

He puckered his lips.

Bridget, exhaling. "How long were you in there?" she asked.

"I think twenty hours."

She nodded, glancing at Aldous.

"I guess I could see it," he said. "That's not a great result for that game. Don't tell me you played bad?"

I shrugged.

"Happens," Jon said. His big arms were crossed, and his face, as he drew on the Camel, looked tough suddenly. Then he smiled. "Sit down."

I perched on the mattress's corner, Neal shifting his legs to make room.

"You know what your cut is this bank?" Jon asked.

"I have a guesstimate."

"Yes?"

"Six grand."

Bridget chimed in. "Little more."

"Very, very nice," Aldous said.

Jon nodded severely. "*Nice*. The Axe is a leveraged investor. He barely had to play at all, himself. Why bother? Let everyone else do the work." His tone was playful, but there was an underlying truth here: I *had* barely played on the trip.

"I wanted to."

"Yes. We know," Aldous said.

"I tried to help out around here."

"He muled those funds to Venetian when Greene was getting buried," Neal said. Head on a pillow, his voice was aimed up at the ceiling.

Various eyes were inspecting me. *Muling,* Neal called it: all right. To me it had still felt glorious. Everything we did felt glorious. I'd gotten to the main floor bearing forty Gs emergency funding and happened to find Greene mid-shoe at the very same table where I'd been 86'd on the previous trip. I had my cap's brim in position, practically down to my nose. I was safe—surveillance wouldn't notice some dude who spent less than five minutes on the gaming floor and never sat down at a table. Still, there was a charge just from *being* there. When I followed Greene into the men's room and entered the stall next to his and passed the four straps under the metal divider, everything was buzzing in a gratifying way, and even the sudden harrowing fear that the two of us might get caught, that someone had witnessed the handoff, or that I'd sent the straps the wrong way and given all the money to a stranger by mistake, only augmented the pleasure. It was slightly painful, slightly dizzying, like the fear when a plane's taking off.

Aside from that? Jon was right. My action on the trip had been minimal. I'd played for a while downtown in a micro-limit game worth about $4 an hour. The Mighty Leaders kept me off the Strip. I'd been too recently backed off or 86'd at nearly every good casino, with the exception of Mandalay Bay (everybody *always* gets down at Mandalay; it's like the Giving

Tree). What startled me most was that they kept me out of Aladdin, a brand-new target whose grand opening had been a factor in the timing of our trip. Fucking *Jon* got to play at Aladdin. Everyone else on the team got to go. It was an absolute field day inside, from what they said. There were multiple count teams going at it—I heard stories of multiple BPs from different teams descending on the same table at the same time, because two different spotters had counted the shoe and had signaled their respective guys—and Roth, who knew personally a lot of the high-stakes solo professionals, recognized counters all over the floor. The casino was completely overwhelmed, surveillance not remotely ready. One of our gorillas got down for *four days.* It was a card counter's paradise. There was no sign they used Griffin; if they did, they didn't use it effectively. Why couldn't I play? Why for that matter was I hotter than someone like Jimmy, when he'd played longer than I had? Was it the hair? It was the hair. The hair was ungainly. I was a *funny-looking dude,* let's admit—especially inside a casino, which, frankly, if it hadn't been for blackjack would be the last place on earth I'd want to go. Now it was the last place I *could* go, no matter that I wanted it. Ugh. I had almost no player-hours for the trip. My pay was primarily return on investment, and here was Jon implying I hadn't earned it.

"Axe," he said now, "it's like this." He lit a fresh cigarette. Neal sat up. Aldous continued to read. Roth put his lighter down. "This is a joke. All of us here are aware of it. You don't have a role in this town at this time."

Nobody spoke. Roth took a long, thoughtful pull. "Six thousand for what? Muling funds? I don't mean to say it's your fault."

"Nobody's fault," Aldous said over his book. "Heat is what it is, a force of nature."

"What are you saying?" My voice came out close to a whisper.

Neal said, "Time to hit the hinterlands, mac."

Roth seconded. "There are good games. In some really strange places, you can find EV you wouldn't believe. If you're committed to blackjack, believe me, with all the tribal stuff now—California's just coming online—

there's opportunity. If you want to play on your own, we can talk about that. Axe—don't panic."

Tears were just behind my eyes. I couldn't even tell if they had started to spill out or not. I was *so* fucking tired.

"You're still on the team. Please listen," Roth said.

"I got hot because I played with you guys. All I ever did was what you told me."

"Josh." He was kneeling in front of me. "Listen to what we are doing. We're having two trips every month, minimum. One's here in Vegas. We're going to ask you to lay off those for a couple months. The other will be somewhere else. You're definitely going on those. You're the Axe, and we need you in action."

"Time to be a road warrior, champ." Neal slapped me on the back. "There's games, mac. Don't worry."

"Games?" I said. "Tunica, hit-seventeen? Atlantic City, eight decks, with the one-K max on the floor—no surrender? *Those* games, you mean? Those are shit. The EV is here in Las Vegas. This is where our business *is*."

The only sound was Aldous turning a page. Shaking his head, Roth stood. He flipped through a collection of white envelopes on the desk. When he found what he wanted, he said, "You want to be a gambler? My friend, there are no guarantees. Heat is cyclical. You're hot right now, and you'll be less hot in six months. I've been through this before. Right now some flyer's on the top of every pile in every surveillance room showing Josh Axelrad's picture. New flyers come in with new faces, and you drift down to the bottom. Six months from now, you'll be buried. This is the cycle of heat. Other things are cyclical in blackjack as well. If you really want to keep doing this for a living, Josh, first of all, you can. Secondly, you're going to have to cope, and with worse shit than this." He handed me the envelope, my initials scribbled quasi-legibly on the front side. "Six thousand and change."

I said, "Thanks."

I walked down the hall to the room I was staying in, collapsed on the bed, and when I woke up fifteen hours later I had a voice mail. It was my friend Belle Gadly from college. She lived in Portland, Oregon, now and last I heard she'd been trying to get into medical school. "What's your week like?" Belle said when I called back.

"Pretty free."

"How about next week?"

"Free."

"Are you curious about the desert?"

"I'm in the desert now," I said.

"Nevada?"

"Yes, Vegas."

"You want to come meet me in Portland?"

"Why's that?"

"I have an extra ticket to a special event."

"What event?"

"It's in Nevada. I think you've heard of it before."

"Oh, shit."

"Do you know what I mean?"

"Is it Burning Man?"

"Yes!" Belle cried.

"Holy fuck."

"You haven't been, have you?"

"I've been avoiding it. Hippies," I said.

"There are punks who go, too. There are goths."

"Isn't it just sort of an Ecstasy-driven, second-rate Woodstock rip-off, except in an even worse climate?"

"There's only one way you can know," Belle said.

Seventeen

I made it to Portland. I'd rented a car. The plan was not the best I'd ever had, but I was a free man holding $26,000 in cash, and I had nothing but time. No reason to be in New York, no subsequent blackjack trip scheduled, and El Dorado—Las Vegas—had just been ripped from my arms. I was young and single and alone, and I'd gotten a call from a woman.

That is easy math, right there. The terms might have been ludicrous, but they suited me. First: Hang with Belle a few days at this house where she rented an attic, on a street lined with trees. Of course, I would have to get up there. I opted to drive. I did the road trip by myself, expecting adventure—that shit that goes down on the road, whatever shit it is that people always talk about—but found something else. It was adventure of the psyche at best, worried thoughts teeming in my head as the torpor of the road stretched endlessly.

Vegas! She was gone. I kept flashing back to these amazing moments there. I remembered the Rio, dashing out the door and down the long, curved driveway with security shouting to stop, thinking they were really going to tackle me for once. Or last trip, back at the Riv, when Mateo had been betting on grave shift, and got blown, and we EOS'd at McDonald's on the opposite side of the Strip: the sun was newly up, the sky had a pretty orange tint, and Mateo and Chuck Small and I were lying in a dazzled state on the little wedge of bright lawn under the Arches, waiting for Roth to come get us (no one in the session had a car), and with the beautiful sense of depletion after gambling all night; with the headache from so many shoes; with the dim awareness that the ending count of the last shoe I happened to play was continuing to linger in my brain; with the wig I'd had on for disguise (a woman's wig, long hair over your face being most effective at masking you) wadded like a hankie in my hand, I felt the transformation was complete, that I was a True Rogue inhabiting weird terrain fraught with bizarreness and danger, living very far away from normal things. *This* is the dream, I had thought, and no sooner had the words formed in my mind than I saw the two Suits coming our direction from the Stardust next door. The casino was separated from McDonald's by a parking lot. Were they coming for us? It was possible: by sitting outdoors rather than waiting inside, we'd placed ourselves in view of the casino we'd just been hitting, and in my paranoid state I imagined a phone call going from the pit at the Riv to the Stardust across the street, requesting a favor, a quick look at those guys over there on the lawn at McDonald's—"I think they were just in here counting together, but I can't quite make out the faces. We threw one of them out, the guy betting. Mind stopping by and confirming who his counters were? Get some good descriptions for us. Thanks, Bruce." This was, I quickly realized, a paranoid thought. They were coming for coffee, no doubt. The truly weird terrain is in your brain, Mr. Axe. They neared the McDonald's door but, turning at the last moment, came striding right for us, and in delirium I stood, my arms whirling, almost falling backward, shouting "Guys, guys!" at Jimmy and Chuck. It was too late. The men were staring down at Jimmy, smiling wickedly. I managed to hop behind the gargantuan column supporting the Arches and was crouching there, trying to hide, but they came around in a minute to look at me. They hadn't brought cameras or anything. They were just looking and laughing. One of them, spotting my wig, said, "Look what we've got! A *cross-dresser!*" It didn't strike me as much of a joke, but his colleague was howling as they strolled merrily back to where they'd come from.

The moment meant nothing, except maybe I wasn't so paranoid. People really *were* out to find us, especially in Las Vegas. I feared, driving north through California, that the thrill I increasingly needed—the great Vegas rush of energy and of chaos—was waning, and that without it I'd be lost.

Paranoia on the interstate. I was carrying all this money. I'd gotten used to that lately, or I'd thought I had—trucking it all over Vegas, guarding it during my flights, a money belt worn at all times, ten Gs or fifteen, twenty out to Vegas this last time. It felt safe because it was hidden. No one could rob what they didn't know you had. In a way it was *safer* to tote all this cash: in the event, for example, of a kidnapping, you were able to post your own ransom. You could buy a car in half a minute, in a pinch. You could get a Russian bride if you needed and have her delivered the following day.

There was the possibility if not the likelihood of sudden extreme decisions. Holding bankroll made the world feel different. On the road, all alone, it was worrisome. What if I get pulled over? What if I get pulled over *and* they search the car? Cash in any quantity was legal to possess, but try telling that to a cop. In any number of states, there were asset-forfeiture laws that allowed the police to seize property if they suspected it was related to crime. They didn't have to charge you with a thing; they could just take it, and the problem of retrieving it was yours to sort out.

My mind was throbbing phobically as the miles added up. It pulsed like the stripe between lanes. Nightfall made everything worse. Something about it was bleak. Why has the sun disappeared? I was thinking. The road was a subdued horror show riven with abstract peril. Paired lights in the rearview mirror bobbed in a way that seemed meaningful, like a beckoning or like a warning.

The next day, as I was coming into Portland, thinking ahead to the rest of this intricate plan Belle and I managed to cook up—we hang for a few days, maybe make a little love, stroll romantically through all the greenery the city presumably has, and I return my one-way rental to the National people, then (and this is where it starts getting stupid), because the car Belle happens to be driving down to Burning Man is already booked fully with riders, *I fly to San Francisco* (aha!), where I meet up with Paul's (the puppeteer's) very good friend Bobo Sanders, who happens also to be going, and ride with him over the Sierra, through Reno, to this dubious drug-driven festival I don't quite want to go to but am nonetheless traveling eighteen hundred miles through three states (having started in the same state I'm trying to end up in) over five days just to arrive at, spending non-trivial sums in the process—about the same moment I first glimpsed the miserly Portland skyline with its stump towers wholly outclassed by the green hills higher than they were, I realized, possibly too late, the problem I'd created for myself.

Money.

I'd brought too much cheese.

Eighteen

I tried kissing Belle. This was another mistake. I think I chose a poor moment. It was the end of my second day visiting, and we had just come back from a casino I'd dragged her to, forty minutes north, up in Washington State, so I could show her how card counting works. Of course, nothing happened at all for ninety minutes, as the tables were packed and the dealing quite slow; I was just playing basic strategy, Belle trying not to yawn, no conversation between us, since I would simply stare dumbly at her if she happened to speak (really trying to focus on the count, betting my own money solo for the first real time as I was; the max was just a hundred bucks, but I wanted to squeeze out whatever I could from the game), and then, at last I got a hot shoe and lost eight hundred dollars in six rounds.

Belle maybe was impressed, but in the wrong direction. I don't know what she thought. It was a quiet drive home in the dark. The pass that I made was incongruous, deftly rebuffed. They can sense the fear inside you, like a pit boss.

In the morning she was at work, and I got into my Neon. I started the engine and drove down the street, my backpack lying on the car floor.

What can I do with this money? I wondered.

The problem: Though I hadn't asked Bobo about it, I had good reason to assume there would be drugs in that car we were taking. Cash and narcotics don't mix; it's a rule. The combination of serious money with virtually any quantity of controlled substance in most states elevates the charge, if you happen to be caught with the contraband, to possession with intent to distribute. Moreover, out there in the desert, half the time at least I'd be out of my skull. That *was* the point, wasn't it? There would be mushrooms, there would be acid, and the freaks would probably try getting the dread beast Ecstasy down in my gullet. I couldn't responsibly play the custodian of twenty-six, or rather, twenty-five-point-two Gs in that condition, and there wouldn't be a place I could store it. Tents don't have locks.

What would Warren Buffett do? I asked myself.

There's no way the Buff brings the cheese to the rave in the desert. I had crossed a bridge and was near the center of town, passing a bright green park. I saw men in suits stepping out of a Starbucks, happy as fuck with their lattes. How wholesome, how *stable,* how centered it must be being a man who has a suit on in Portland and goes to a job. Suits in New York are extremists, highly focused and corrupt, who don't give a shit if they're happy. I'd intended to avoid their way of life, but had I overshot the mark? What kind of bind was I in now? I'd been soft-barred out of the whole city of Las Vegas by my own team. For twenty-odd months, I had dreamed of this thing, dreamed of turning pro and going nuts, and now, why, let's see, April to August makes about five months, and Vegas was lost to me, the principal scene in the whole universe of blackjack had gone dark! I had money to show for the loss, but it wasn't enough. I couldn't be described as established, or on firm terrain. In fact the terrain was a quagmire, decreasingly stable. I couldn't survive on my own professionally as a card counter— didn't have the bankroll for a solo career. You needed seventy Gs free and clear, the way I estimated things, and, separate from that, you should probably have a full year's living expenses set aside, so that the near-term results wouldn't shake you and screw up your mind-set and play. On the team my importance was nil. My skills had been shown to be meager. They never were going to trust me in the key role of counting BP, the place where the true glory's found—and it was too late for that anyhow. *Heat.* The only thing less useful than a weak controller is a hot, weak controller, like what I'd become. Mossad didn't need me at all, but I needed them, or I needed something like them, and I knew it. What had happened to my résumé? I'd forgotten it. It had gaps. The gaps that it had were still growing. They were a sign or a symbol of gaps in my mind, or in myself, or at least in the avatar or the impostor I used to send into the workplace. That dipshit could not be restored. He was grated like a cheese at this point, which is what I had wanted. I'd become something different, or I'd tried. The new me was gruesome, disheveled, a bit wilder, with less of a résumé, and he didn't know how to proceed.

In the middle of some street whose traffic was insignificant, to the right, there it was: a banner hung from a building showed a stage coach pulled by horses straining beautifully in the middle of a desert. LOCAL BANKING, NATIONWIDE, it said, and I thought, There we go. If there's a savings bank for nomads, bandits, and cowboys, this has got to be the one.

I parked the car, grabbed my backpack. I dashed up the gray stone stairs.

"Can you open an account here if you live out of state?" I said to the customer-service woman.

"Sure, sweetie. What kind?"

"Um. Checking," I said.

"Just a moment."

She had me wait in the area, on the small upholstered seat, legs stretched in front of me, crossed at the ankles, backpack on top of my crotch.

The room had a quiet and dignity.

The new woman was approaching when it hit me. There might be some flaws in this scheme. My jeans were torn apart at each knee. Strands of ripped white denim spilled out like the guts of some creature. The Negra Modelo T-shirt I wore had not been washed since New York, and it had seen a lot of action in the meantime. My dreadlocks were six inches long, and I looked like a spaz with this beard.

"Sir?" she said.

"Morning."

"You want to open an account?"

She was a grown-up, a Normal, early to mid-forties, with lip gloss, good posture, hair arranged with sculptural precision and Aqua Netted into place, wearing clothes that looked bought in a store rather than found in an alley.

"That's right."

Her smile was doubtful. "This way."

She led me to the cubicle. We sat. I could smell my own foulness. The backpack stayed right on my lap as she asked me the questions. Additional confusion stemmed from the fact that my license was from California, but I told her I lived in New York, and here we were in Portland, with one more surprise on the way.

"How would you like to fund the account?"

"Cash," I said.

"That's fine."

"So," I said, "it's a lot."

She was writing down notes on the form.

My pores had opened, sweat leaching out. I touched the top of the back-pack as she glanced up at me. Neither of us spoke, but her expression was one of concern.

"It's a *lot*," I repeated, more softly.

All she did was nod. I nodded. We were in agreement, strange shit *was* afoot. She swallowed a big, uncomfortable swallow, and I did the same, clearing my throat, unzipping the JanSport, removing the tawdry, flesh-colored, sweat-stained, partly mildewed and rank canvas envelope with the stretched elastic bands dangling from each side, as if it were a nasty kind of lingerie.

I put this down on her desk. She seemed about to shake her head in re-fusal. Unzipping the main pocket, I pulled out a ten-strap, and another, then a five-strap, followed by the change.

She said, "This requires approval."

She left me alone in her cube.

◆

Months later Roth would warn me, "A financial institution is not a toy." This is important advice. The government keeps track of cash. Our BPs had to deal with something called a CTR, or Currency Transaction Report, which casinos had to file whenever a gambler bought in or cashed out for more than $10,000 in a single day. It was due to the CTR that BPs had to give real names: ID was compulsory, and providing false information for the form was itself against the law. (There wasn't otherwise anything wrong with giving fake names in casinos. Controllers did it all the time.) Banks had to file the same thing, and I'd known this already. It wasn't a very big deal. What I hadn't yet heard of was something more serious: the SAR, or Suspicious Activity Report, also filed by banks with the Treasury Department whenever something looked really fucked. I would later see I'd qualified for that at Wells Fargo. I probably had heat with the feds. On the bright side, they took the deposit.

I was aware of no possible trouble as I flew to San Francisco, the new checkbook tucked in my luggage so I could write a check to myself in New York, nor as I met up with Bobo, rode with him and two others through the night, listening to unfamiliar music, hearing the kid named Mark going on about Burning Man and what it meant and how his life had changed because of it. "For a week every year, there's this place in the desert where anything is possible," he said. There's another place, I thought, farther south, fifty-two weeks every year. We came over the mountains, a sign saying DONNER SUMMIT PASS rushing down like a poltergeist, high and benevolent pines in the sky overhead. I felt free. We were passing through Reno at daybreak. Continuing east into sunlight, we ditched the interstate at Fernley, booked north through the small burg of Nixon, saw Pyramid Lake with its giant rock jutting from the middle, shaped just like the Luxor. We were in the wilderness here. The ground lay beaten like sawdust. The sun-weathered road fizzed past like a dead cable channel on someone's TV. After Gerlach the pavement was mingled with dirt, and soon it was only dirt with no asphalt, and we were slowing down. Cars in the distance left dust in their wakes. The desert extended with no end. There wasn't a road, only dust. The road was everywhere and everything. I was cash-free and had nothing to fear. In the daylight it wasn't so scary.

PART II

September, September

Nineteen

Neal Matcha was the closest thing I had to a friend among the team managers. We met the first time in this way:

It was the weekend of my first trip, and I had come out of a session at Mandalay and gone to the EOS at Luxor. Luxor, the pyramid, is black, sleek, otherworldly—a gem—and I remember when it was being built. During trips with the Papster, I saw it develop, the walls creeping upward at an angle I couldn't believe: a real pyramid! Approaching through the parking lot from Mandalay, I kept gazing up at its beam. From the pyramid's apex 42.3 billion candlepower's worth of white light shines, glozes, fulgurates, burns. We don't quite have the verb for it, but they say the beam is visible from space. It was the highest single entity I'd ever seen. The World Trade Towers couldn't compare. The effect as you stared was vertigo-inducing, almost sickening. Not only did it look infinite in extension, but, from this close, the beam appeared to lean in my direction. This might have been due to the light's spreading out from the core the farther it got from its source: light spreads, I suppose, except lasers, and so even when you're not directly underneath the blazing pith, at least a part of that beam really is physically *over* you, creating in people like me sensations of impending doom, of an imminent risk of being crushed, a carnal fear that the biggest single *thing* you've ever witnessed threatens to topple and kill you. Naturally, it symbolized casinos. At the time I still imagined their power as limitless and was doubtful about all this blackjack.

I met the rest of the crew at the Luxor valet. After we'd done the accounting, Lawrence Taib told me to sit tight, that a person named Neal was coming to get me and would bring me to my next session. "How will I know him?" I asked.

"I mentioned your hair. He'll find you."

With that, he and the others took off, and I waited on a bench for ten minutes. It was sometime past three in the morning; the tourists were drunk and in degrees of dishabille as they came shambling out of cabs. Then a pair of headlights was flashing. I walked to the driver's side, and Neal rolled the window down. He had long hair that I soon realized was a wig. He was the first card counter I'd seen in a wig. He had a long face that was somewhat British-looking and masculine, with a knobby chin and a bump in his strong, largish nose. All he said to me was, "Hey, mac. Get in."

We barely talked during the drive. When we entered the Desert Inn and I saw what a handsome casino it was, I couldn't believe that a man in a wig as outlandish as that was planning just to plop down at a blackjack table and start playing, as if it were normal. But that's what he did. If you're hot enough to need a wig, as I would learn, you don't care much about blending in; you're just hoping not to be recognized for who you really are. It *kind* of fit his overall look; he didn't come off so much as a transvestite as he did a heavy metal fan or hippie. The session went down with no trouble. Chuck Small was betting, and they loved him. By 5:00 A.M. all but one or two of the blackjack players still gambling was a team member. It felt like we owned the casino. Most of us had tables to ourselves. It was quiet in there, and I realized why: Desert Inn had the policy of shutting off the prerecorded noises on their slot machines. No alarms were going off—no bleats, no chirps, no jingles, no ka-ching ka-ching could be heard. It was utterly peaceful, and with the count team controlling the pit and the bosses aloof and indifferent, the EV was through the roof. Perfect.

I ended up associating the feeling of that session with Neal. If a known Griffin player in *that wig* could get down, anything was possible. Some of my doubtfulness faded. I had no way of knowing I would never go back, that the Desert Inn would shut its doors August 28 of that year and later they'd implode the fucking thing.

Twenty

September. New York. What to do? I went to an optometrist and got blue color contacts, hoping I could be reborn through the magic of disguise.

I had money. I felt good physically. I had no hair on my back. I was a seasoned pro card counter tracking to make fifty Gs for the year, somewhat less now that Vegas was lost. The loss had begun to obsess me. I thought about it every day, angrily. Mossad's stated policy was that no player who got heat through the team would be kicked off as a result. Such a policy was needed: the team's strategy involved playing into heat, playing until barred; you had to motivate players to do that. Every gorilla who came through the team had the opportunity to learn how to spot after getting blown out. "You'll put on a ball cap and bet the minimum, and no one will see you—even in places you've been eighty-sixed," Roth would always promise them. Former gorillas like Chuck Small and Robert Jayne had both turned into spotters, then controllers. And neither of them had been barred from Las Vegas as I had.

Unfair, wrong, fucked up: I didn't like it at all. I was stuck in New York while the others were hitting the Strip, bringing down the house or whatever. New York! The magic was dead. Each cocktail was like the one before.

The bustle of Broadway couldn't compare at all to the drama of armed goons swarming the pit back at Caesars. The people were too fucking soft in this town.

I tried to go about my life. I needed a different apartment. I would have to get a wife eventually, and you can't raise a family in a maid's room, low rent or not. But vicious emotions kept surfacing. Something had changed in my soul. I couldn't pursue my business in the ordinary way. A broker upset me in Brooklyn one day. "What kind of apartment you looking for?"

I told him what I wanted. He said he had the perfect place. "Hop in the van. I will show you."

Just as we were leaving, a thin-legged girl, maybe nineteen years old, walked through the door of his office. She was looking for something in the same price range that I was—her daddy evidently would cosign a lease. The broker invited her to join us, and she and I sat together in the back of his extremely hot van, suddenly rivals. We were competing for the privilege of paying the man's fee.

Indeed, the apartment was perfect. One bedroom, newly renovated in Greenpoint, complete with garden access and a new fridge, for $1K a month. I wanted it; she wanted it. We went back to his office and sat filling out applications, but I already knew I was doomed. *The woman always gets the apartment:* a fact. Boys smear their feces on the walls, do we not? Plus, she had Daddy, and I had nothing going for me but a cryptic occupation listed as "Private Investment."

I handed the form to the man, shook his hand, went home, couldn't sleep. In the morning I thought, This is war! Ten minutes later I was buzzing outside the glass wall in the basement at the Chase Manhattan Bank, waiting for admission to the vault.

I took out $6,000 in cash from my box. I thanked Bev, the woman who worked down in there. "You enjoy all that sun," she responded, holding the glass door for me and smiling. I rode the L train to Brooklyn, got off at the Graham Avenue stop, and I found myself cursing out loud as I tramped up the street to the broker's.

I stormed through the door, taking the cheese from my pocket and slamming it down on his counter: a five-strap ($5K), with ten bills resting on top. He hadn't yet noticed. He was sitting in the back corner at a separate desk, staring at an ancient PC monitor almost the size of a weather balloon.

He turned, smiled, then frowned, catching sight of the money—he winced as if he'd been stabbed. He assumed a sort of crouch, one forearm in front of his face like a martial-arts posture to defend a blow.

"I want that apartment," I said. "You tell that landlord I'll pay six months up front—*right now!*"

"Put this away!" It was as though I'd pulled a gun instead of cash. He was shrieking: "The apartment is gone—go away! What are you doing?"

Negotiating! What does it look like I'm doing? But the man could not be reasoned with, he was terrified—wanted me gone. I seized the dough and issued a last, disparaging look at his overweight body before backing out, stuffing the cash in my pocket. Marching down Graham, sweat slathering the small of my back, I tried to hum for a minute, but I couldn't. I didn't have that kind of an attention span. Curse words were crowding my brain. The sidewalk was blinding, I noticed. That sun really *was* out in force.

Twenty-one

Next stop: Detroit. Another rental car, another town. Neal gave me the news as soon I'd shut the car door. My multiplier was being raised. "You can invest twenty-six on this bank, mac," he said.

He was driving, Kat Armstrong in the front passenger seat, Jimmy in the backseat with me. "Twenty-six?" I said.

"Yeah. Send it in."

I had to think. It was good about the multiplier—this was a figure assigned each investor, determining how much he could risk, and mine had been stagnant for some time. Controllers' multipliers were higher than spotters', but counting BPs got the highest, and I seemed to be permanently barred from that rank. You could also boost your number through additional effort that helped out the team. At the new apartment where I was living now with three friends in Carroll Gardens, I'd begun hosting practices, helping to train new gorillas, and this was the payoff.

"I guess I should pick up more cash."

"Where?" Neal asked.

"Could we stop at a bank?"

We got off the freeway. Neal started cruising down a boulevard. We were either in Detroit or in the suburbs still. It looked like any other town so far.

"How's that one?"

I said it looked it fine. Neal pulled in to the lot, and I ran in and got on the line. I had my credit card, my license.

You had to bring your investment in cash on these trips, and now I needed five extra Gs. They might well have exempted me from the requirement under these circumstances, but I was reluctant to ask. A real gambler has access to funds; it shouldn't matter where he is or how short the notice. A back-of-the-envelope estimate gave me the impression that a cash advance on my MasterCard, net of the associated fees, would cost less than the expected extra gain from the added investment. Therefore the optimal play was to walk into a strange bank in a Michigan suburb, show an ID from a faraway state, give an address from a third state (on the opposite coast from the second), all the while adorned with thick dreads longer than ever, with a glittery bandanna wrapped so as to keep them off my forehead, wearing new color contacts whose blue looked entirely fake from close range, and ask for five Gs on a credit card.

"Here you are," I told the teller.

She took the slip and looked at what I'd written. "Just a moment," she said.

"Righty-o."

She returned in a minute, asking for a second copy of my signature. I made another loop-the-loop for her. She smiled in a pained way. "Thank you." Then she rushed off once again. I could see her conferring with a Suit in the back of the branch.

More minutes passed. Soon she came out to the lobby, asking me to follow her. I thought she was trying to backroom me. But she handed me a phone, saying, "Please speak with them."

"Mr. Axelrad?" the voice on the phone said.

"Yes?"

"I'm with security here at Chase MasterCard. Would you mind answer-

ing a couple questions for me, so they can go ahead and process your transaction?"

"All right."

He asked where I was born. He asked me for my mother's maiden name.
Meanwhile Neal walked in. He came across the room and grabbed my arm.
I said to the phone, "Hold on."

Neal asked, "Hey—how long is this going to take, mac?"

"They're heating me up. I'm not sure."

"We've got to go fuck up this town, right? Remember. We have to go
incinerate this dump."

"I'll be out in a minute."

"Remember." He raised his finger, nodding solemnly. Then he went out.
I answered more questions, and at last the security guy wanted to talk to the
teller. When she gestured me back to the window, I assumed it had all been
resolved. She dashed off again, though—talked with the Suit a bit more.

When she finally returned to her post, she handed the card and my
license back. "I'm sorry," she said.

"What the hell?"

"We're just not able to help you."

"Look," I said, "this is my card."

She practically gasped. "It's *too much*. You . . . you . . . you . . ." She was
stammering! "Your eyes aren't even the color it says on that license."

"They're contacts. You see, I'm in character. . . ."

She shook her head, blinking—it seemed like she might even cry. "In
character? But . . . *what for?*"

I nodded, altogether serious: intense. "For rock 'n' roll," I said.

We enjoyed a brief moment of wonder in silence. I returned to the car
in defeat.

Twenty-two

"No dice," I said to Neal in the car.

"All that for nothing?" Jimmy said.

"Sorry. But I fucked up that teller at least."

"You fucked up a teller?" Kat asked.

"I gave her a glimpse of the Far Side."

"Holy fucking Christ," Neal said.

"I showed her the Spirit of Rock."

Twenty-three

Then Kat asked, "Spirit of Rock?" and I said, "Yeah," and she said, "You're not fit for society." I thought back to that thing with the broker. "Hm," was all I could answer.

Nor was I fit to play blackjack. Done. I was cooked. I had gotten too hot, and meanwhile my spastic efforts at adopting the wild talk of people like Neal ("We've got to go fuck up this town, right? Remember?") only worsened the freakish effect of my kinky hair, large nose, effete build, and effeminate posture. I didn't fit in with the team *or* without it.

In Detroit we got blown out at once. We were here ostensibly for the grand opening of a casino called Greektown, but that didn't happen till Friday. Thursday night one group tried the MGM Grand and another group tried Motor City. Both of these crews were shut down. There was only one remaining casino where there hadn't been heat, and it wasn't open yet. The nearest backup games were 227 miles away in Indiana. You can see why I missed playing Vegas.

The day of the Greektown opening, Roth sent me along with a counter named Pete Glass and a newly recruited female spotter named Trudy Hayden to try Motor City once more, this time with Chuck as the counting BP. We had to play in a high-limit room on the fourth floor. Another problem with Detroit: The casinos used eight-deck shoes with very low limits on their main floors and were only playable for call-ins in the high-limit areas. Each spotter or controller had to bet $100 a hand. Not only was this expensive, diminishing our spread and hence our edge, but it subjected the counters to extra attention. It was hard to slip under the radar and play anonymously when betting that much. (Casinos like to track players' wagers. They issue cards called "players' cards" or "rating cards"—"rating" is their jargon for evaluating what your play is worth to them—to anyone who wants to earn comp meals or gifts. While they offer these cards to almost everybody playing at a table, they really don't care if a low-stakes bettor declines; it saves them some work. For someone betting black chips to decline is unusual enough to draw heat, though.)

We staggered our arrivals. I was the last. It was a quiet, long room with fifteen tables or so, not overly busy on day shift. I sat at a heads-up game, the dealer announcing her shuffle. "Go ahead," a man said.

I'd dropped seven bills on the felt. I sat there feeling ridiculous, with my eyes badly dried from the lenses. Their color obstructed my sight, leaving me with tunnel vision. The dealer's hands riffled the deck, and the cards made a smooth, purring noise. "Rolling," she said.

"Go ahead."

She took my bills, announced the change, and gave me seven chips. Kindly she patted the table. "Good luck."

"I could use a bit of that."

Two hands in and the count was going nowhere. I felt the man *standing there*, a few steps in back of the dealer. He was watching me play. I slapped my next chip on the square. He disappeared.

A few seconds later, he returned. A new little sign was deposited in the corner of the table, right next to the sign with the limit. The Suit who had dropped it was watching again. I tried not to look at the sign.

I just kept betting. Finally he left. I raised my eyes and saw the words NO MID-SHOE ENTRY in white print, staring me down.

"Bets?" the dealer said.

"Um. Thanks." I grabbed my last three chips and departed the game. The next table down also had no other players. I sat.

The dealer said, "Shuffle."

Only after I'd placed my first bet and lost another hand did he come by again. Again he brought the sign. NO MID-SHOE ENTRY. A problem. I couldn't very well give a call-in if that was the rule. A no-mid-shoe arrangement is sometimes a courtesy offered to high rollers who don't want new players joining their games between shuffles (according to a superstition whose fatuousness is staggering to card counters, some players believe that a new hand coming in mid-shoe messes up "the order of the cards"—said order apparently imparted by a Higher Power during the shuffle somehow), but here it was something else. It felt like a preventive step against team play. The strange thing was that Chuck was taking a call-in right then. None of the others had heat.

I left the room, slipped out to a stairwell, and called Roth to tell him about it.

"Did you try another table?" he said.

"Just did. They followed me with the sign."

"But Chuck's getting down?"

"He's betting right now."

"So nobody else has a problem? It sounds like personal heat, Axe. They get you every time, man. You must be on a flyer or something."

He was flicking a lighter. I was wondering, What happens now? I can't play in Vegas and can't play the hinterlands. These contacts cost $300—I'm doomed.

"Tell you what," Jon said. "What's your balance?"

"I'm carrying Chuck's backup. About twenty-seven."

"They're letting you play, right? It's just this shit with no mid-shoe?"

"I think."

"Fuck it. Go in there and spread." It was a classic Mossadian reaction to heat: try something even more aggressive.

"You're serious?" I said.

"Sure. At the very least, you can be a distraction from Chuck's play. They'll be worried about you, not him. And you might get a count and win money. Who knows?" He gave me some guidelines: Absolutely no cover. He wanted me to spread my bets blatantly. The base would be $100; the unit was $750 on one hand, all the way to table max. What he said made sense intellectually; I had the requisite skills. I understood the *game plan*, I mean. Everything he'd said was familiar, reminiscent of conversations I'd heard between him and other players many times, but I couldn't quite believe he was now putting me in that role. In summary he said again, "Fuck it."

"Okay."

I marched back into the room. The Suit who had given me trouble was having a word with a colleague, and I saw him glance over my way. At the opposite end of the pit, I found a new table, dead again (no players), and as the dealer commenced shuffling, the guy came by with the sign. He set it down, and then he went away.

"How you doing?" the dealer said sweetly. Her name tag said LYNN.

"Really not sure, Lynn," I said. "Let's find out."

"I hope I can bring you some luck."

"Right, right."

She announced that we were rolling, and we rolled. During the first few rounds, I felt relaxed. It was a relief not worrying about call-ins. I wasn't really thinking too much about what it would be like to bet big; that wasn't likely to happen. About one shoe in seven gets a high enough count to be bettable—I thought there was a good chance they'd just go ahead and 86 me before a count came along.

With Lynn smiling pleasantly, I chunked down a chip at a time. Chuck, in the background, was losing. I saw he was pulling out cash. I must have been focused on him—I didn't notice at first that my shoe had gone hot. I had a running twelve, which is bettable, but I'd only bet a single black chip on the round. The cards were out; it was too late.

I hoped the count would just go away. I actively wanted it gone. I couldn't sit here, suspected already, and hike my bet eight fucking times. But the count didn't fall; it went up. I had running fourteen. I bet $400—much less than I should, but it was all I had the stomach for. I happened to win. I stacked the winnings on top of my bet: $800.

Lynn looked at this bet for a moment. Then, patting the table in a friendly way, she drew the next round of cards, and the count rose some more. Again I had won. Suddenly I had a lot of black chips and a true count of four.

My optimal bet, according to the instructions from Roth, was $2,250. But that was egregious. I chunked a few more chips on top. I was now betting over a grand. I wasn't really putting any act on. I didn't *feel* like I was in character, didn't feel like I was some sort of prosperous nut throwing money here and there to get his kicks; it didn't really feel like gambling. I was simply doing what I should. I was part of a system, almost like part of a machine. The count flowed out of the cards, into my noodle, and then from my noodle to the chips on the felt. Lynn was contemplating these. "Checks play," she announced, not loudly.

She pulled the cards out. I got a seven, a four: an eleven, not bad. She was showing a six up—Jesus. The EV on this round was enormous. "Double," I said, putting the chips in position.

She dealt me a nine, then busted herself. Suddenly her fingers were coming at me, stuffed fill of chips: the payout was $2,200. It was stacked, all in black, right next to my bet and my double, so there was this lewd-looking mass of black chips waiting. The true count had climbed up a bit.

I plucked a few off, betting $1,700. That's when I noticed the Suit. He was standing in back of the pit podium just behind the table. Staring. Just staring. I won on the round, and I added a single black chip to my bet. As I did this, another Suit came, and she planted herself by the first. Both of them were watching.

It no longer felt mechanical or machinelike; this was a performance, but a subtle one. Each new chip could put me over the line in the minds of these Suits. Any moment now and they'd spook.

Another winning hand. The count was getting close to true six. I *had* to bet more, it was right, but at the same time it was criminal, it was bald-faced and obscene: I didn't even use a BP. I didn't even have the decency to create some kind of a ruse. My act was that they thought I was a counter.

I did $2,200. This was an obscene stack of chips. It was the Eiffel Tower, it was the Sears Tower. It looked like it could topple from its own weight. I was playing Jenga.

Lynn kept pulling out cards.

Chuck was looking over at me, puzzled.

A fourth Suit had joined the other three.

I won the next hands. Lynn effused, "My *God*."

"I don't know," I said. "I really don't."

"You're on fire."

Right before the end of the shoe, the count fell suddenly. My bet had been $2,400, but now I should return to table min. With the four Suits observing, like a panel of judges or something, on an impulse I knocked down the multiple high stacks I'd been assembling, covering the table with chips.

"Finished?" Lynn asked. I was nodding. She gathered up the chips to make change.

Twenty-four

I t had been only ten minutes. Roth answered his phone.

"They didn't like it?"

"I won eighteen thousand," I said.

"Come again?"

"I found a shoe."

Jon Roth agreed, I *had* found one.

Twenty-five

It took the one shoe. Everything was different after that. I turned from a frog to a prince. Jon embraced me as a counting BP. I had a new role on the team. My face wasn't clean, but my *name* was—I'd never shown ID in a casino. I was less hot than Jon or than Neal, less hot as a counting BP than players like Jimmy and Chuck, who were presumed to be in Griffin already; their names were no good.

In Detroit I was immediately sent in to try my first call-ins (and *run* my first session!) at the MGM Grand, where I lost eleven Gs in twenty minutes and got 86'd. Not all shoes could be like that first. Afterward I went into Greektown and played through the night, and we won. I cashed out at nine in the morning. Having started with forty (a BP carries ample funds, always ready for the worst), I now had fifty-four Gs. Leaving, I couldn't find a cab. I started pacing the deserted streets. Detroit's a lurid city in the middle of the night. Stores were boarded up. Even the graffiti looked hopeless. I was aware of a certain imprudence, stumbling around half lost, at least a quarter mile from EOS, with so much cash in my pants that my gait was impeded.

We went to Chicago; I got to bet there. Then I got to play Atlantic City. I got down some of the time. My act was a crude attempt at leveraging the dreads and my ungainly gestalt. I pretended I was on drugs. I would stagger to call-ins with drool on my face, eyes starting to cross, my head jerking. I claimed to be a music producer.

At Resorts, on the Atlantic City Boardwalk, I got comped some cigars. I was circling the pit with this full box under my arm. Soon there were symptoms of heat. Afraid they would want their cigars back, I dashed into a stall in the men's room, stuffing cigars into the breast and front pockets of my coat; then, as soon as I came out, they backed me off. I went to the cage and cashed out, cramming the straps in my pants. I had forty Gs more than I'd started with, something like eighty grand now padding my midriff and groin, plus cigars, shambling down the Boardwalk in the heavy, wet, gray salt night. I was bound for the EOS at Taj. The stretch of plank I covered wasn't populous. The seagulls had fled or were dreaming. The wind came burly and rich. The moist air felt like a flurry of small rocks pelting one side of your neck. Lonely drifters gimped long of stride, hellish in their silhouettes, plastic bags hung from their fists; they didn't look at me, and I didn't look at them. I was trying not to run. My jacket was bouncing against me. My crotch itched. My antiperspirant had been liquefied. My heart kept beating at its elevated rate. I was entirely tensed up, muscles rigid, each joint pricking or throbbing, exhausted from the session and spooked at the dark of the night. In a state near collapse, I finally caught sight of Jon Roth with his twinkling eyes across the Taj's floor, lowering his chin in approval.

"Plus forty," I said.

I threw my arm around his back and hugged the side of him, I felt so fucking safe, and relieved, in his presence. There was Roth, hugging me back.

Twenty-six

We were walking in the sun. It was two days before Christmas. The palm fronds were making a clacking sound almost like applause overhead. The Papster, my stepmom, her sister Angela the psychoanalyst, and Angela's husband Eric the kazillionaire were strolling along the canal. For a long time, I had admired Eric, whom I'd gotten to know during college when I was new to New York and spending Thanksgivings with them up in Westchester County. He claimed to have spent ten years, until he was thirty, utterly adrift, selling jewelry at fairs as a wandering hippie, but then he went to law school. He told the story in a way that made law school sound as if it took him four weeks. Then suddenly he was rich. He sold insurance to companies who in turn sold insurance to others. I'd had the impression he'd done it all on a laptop in his basement, but there must have been more to it than that. He went from hippie to kazillionaire. He made it seem effortless, random.

One year, after the turkey, when new wine had been opened, we were talking about some minor riot that had broken out at my college, to which the police had responded. Eric listened to the story with a smile. When I'd finished, he gave a speech about cops and his relationship to cops and how he'd used to hate cops and see cops as small-minded, dangerous, testy, malicious armed bastards defending a social structure by which they were in fact oppressed themselves, because that was the one way they could think to get a foothold, and they were all desperate and amoral. Saying this, he lifted his glass, swirling it in a manner that seemed to acknowledge the excellent house where he lived. He brought the glass to his lips, inhaling the wine's bouquet, and, assuming a small but not insignificant smile, said quietly, "I *like* cops." He sipped the wine, put the glass on the table. "When I see a patrol car in the neighborhood now, I think to myself, That's for me. That guy's protecting *my stuff*."

His honesty impressed me, but I'd only ever been a loopy kid and had no way of impressing him back. Now as we walked, I was talking to his wife— yammering, really, hungry for attention, hoping to get to him like that. "Oh, it's hit or miss! Half the time you don't have a chance. In Chicago last month at the Harrah's—actually, it's East Chicago, which is in Indiana—"

"Oh?"

"—and a ghetto like I've never seen, and I mean I've seen some. You have to drive over this quarry. The earth's been hacked apart. The bridge goes right over the pit. It looks like some kind of an autopsy down there. You can feel the *pain* of the *cliffs,* you share in the agony, but that's how you get to Indiana. And then, along the lake, it's industrial wasteland, tow- ers belching smoke, massive cylindrical units holding God knows what noxious shit, and in the middle of this—the casinos!"

"They seem to have touched you."

"*Listen.* We mobilize our crew. We've flown ten thousand miles between all of us, we've paid for our rental cars, our hotels, meals, gas, gone through the process of checking everybody out (that means checking their skills, verifying we're all good to go, all ready to play), and now, at nine in the evening, exhausted from the long day of travel, we roll into action. Two separate cars. We get to the casino parking lot. It's terribly dark all around there. The lake is like the fucking river Styx, if you'll pardon my French. The water pitch black, and the coast crammed with eerie steel *things,* and making it sadder than that is the sight of Chicago—the Sears Tower!—

glowing over there like a fortress, looking beautiful but *so far away*, and here we go into this toilet."

"This . . . ?"

"That means a casino. A riverboat, in this case, though they really should call it a lakeboat. And so the team staggers onto the boat, and I go to the bathroom to kill time because I want all the counters in place before I try to start betting, and I lock myself in a stall. I have fifty Gs on my person. I have to arrange it—you need some of the cash accessible right away, and you want to buy in for a certain amount (say four or five Gs to get started), without showing them more than you have to. I don't want to whip out a ten-strap and buy in with that, because the quantity I'm packing is a secret. Collectively between all of us, we probably have a hundred and fifty Gs, and from the moment we walk on the boat, if things should go south— which they can—we're prepared to buy in for it all. We know we have an edge . . . and so we'll keep going, and keep going all the way to zero if that's how it goes. But the casino doesn't need to be aware of that. Various things can get to their heads and freak them out, and showing a truly bizarre amount of cash right off the bat just gives a heads-up that you're a very serious gambler, you're there with a purpose. It can cause them to think. That's no good. If the session should happen to go that way, where you start losing and keep losing, and you show a ton of money—okay. You deal with that when it happens."

"It's like improv. Which, if I recall, you used to—"

"Yes. Good. Exactly. Right. You're starting to get it. *Improv!* Can't know in advance what you'll get. You could lose, you could win right away. Those require two different acts, though I'd say on the whole as a BP you have less to explain when the variance is in your favor. Then you're just a lucky guy, pushing it. When you're *un*lucky, showing all the money, that's where you have to *perform*. You have to account for the money: how you get it, why it makes sense that you're willing to gamble with those kinds of funds. And if you happen to get blown while you're losing, that's a twofold disaster. The money is gone, and the venue is gone. Your playing life in that particular casino as a BP using your real name is over for good. Your money *and* your life are gone, your money *and* your life. . . ."

On the canal a small man in a long craft that rose only inches from the surface was paddling at speeds that to him must have seemed overwhelming. My father and Eric were talking about the stock market.

Angela said, "So what happened?"

"At Harrah's? I waited, I climbed up to the fourth floor, where the good tables were where we wanted to play, saw my teammates in position, I went to a table, bought in for four K, and while the dealer was counting the cash out, one of the pit guys walks over and says, 'We're going to limit you to table minimum.'"

"Why'd he say that?"

"I didn't know! But one of my teammates—Neal—he told me later he'd glanced into the pit and he'd seen a big flyer on the podium. This pretty face. I was done. But then, later that trip, I won fifteen Gs at the Empress. All the time hit or miss; it's insane."

"It does sound amazing."

"It is."

We'd paused, looking out at the water. The breezes had slowed. Angela said, "As a therapist it makes me wonder."

"What's that?"

"There's such a source of energy there."

"Yes, yes."

"What happens when all this is over? You'll have to get that energy from somewhere, wouldn't you say?"

I said, "That's an interesting question."

The palm trees fell silent above.

Twenty-seven

Every year the climax was supposed to be the Vegas trip during New Year's. I'd been hearing about it since April: New Year's, when counters run rampant. Casinos are drowning in action, high-rolling loons from around the whole world come in. It was the opening night at Aladdin all over again, except this time Aladdin was everywhere. Table-max bets would go down around the clock, and surveillance could never keep up. In the midst of all the natural camouflage, counters could get down readily. Opportunity was staggering, superfluous. I could barely believe, when Jon said I should expect to attend, that my Vegas reinstatement would occur on the trip of all trips. . . .

Then Jon said the word "Stardust," and that put things in perspective. My role was to play in the gutter. I was betting the money, yes, but only at the worst dumps in town. We had clean gorillas as usual, and as usual the high-probability games were reserved for them to try first. My name being (presumably) clean didn't mean I was actually clean, what with all the flyers I'd appeared on. So I got sent to the Dust.

Among other problems the Dust was a notorious Griffin feed (a casino corresponding with Griffin), in part because Griffin Investigations used to keep its offices *inside* the place. Griffin and Dust were synonymous. For a player who's flyered by Griffin to try to go in there was suicide. But suicide was all I was good for.

As it happened, I also had my own private sentiments related to heat at the Dust. In '99, just before Knowles met Roth the first time, I had come into town on a second attempt at passing the MIT checkout. An MIT player named Howie had been trying to organize a trip, but the team was in a fractious, stunted period, and experienced players like Howie, who had a Griffin entry, found the non-Griffin players on the team refusing to go into sessions with them, fearing contamination. He'd sent an e-mail out to the MIT listserv trying to rustle up players for a weekend, but no one would come. Garry had told me about it. And I said to Garry, "Shit, *I'll* go." So Garry made some calls, and it was determined I could go along and try testing once again, provided I pay my own airfare in the likely event that I failed.

I got to the airport, was told to go straight to the Dust. Don Woolf, already living in Vegas at the time, had finagled a comped room there for our use. This was the same Don Woolf who would later check me out for Mossad when he was visiting the apartment at Kat's invitation. As I walked through the lobby searching for elevators, I saw that there was something lackluster and fatigued about the ambience. This caught me off guard. Until that moment I'd continued to think of casinos the way I'd thought of them in childhood: each as a different embodiment of the same sort of magic, and each equally magical, and lovely. I hadn't realized that their character varied so much, that some of them were thriving and others approaching collapse.

Walking down the hall on a high floor in the hotel, I winced at the color scheme: purples and pinks. The word "dump" might have entered my mind in the context of casinos for the first time that day. I knocked on a door and was admitted by Don, whom I had never met before. He wore a pair of eyeglasses with a serious prescription, spoke softly, and sounded depressed. Don mainly played poker, not blackjack, but he was still the first full-time professional gambler I'd seen, and his quietness and somberness surprised me. I'd assumed they would all dress like Elvis, or at least show up in cowboy hats and boots, but not Don.

I failed again and again. Meanwhile the sun had gone down. Las Vegas looked paltry out there, her neon muted by the window's purple tint. Don kept giving me pointers; he was a clear and considerate teacher. All at once there came a sound from the door: Howie had let himself in. He was somewhere between six-four and nine feet tall, and he had a bit of Lincoln in his face. He looked suicidal, quite frankly. His complexion was ashen or whitish. His eyes were sunk low. He had no visible lips, and his jaw was pronounced, his face more a skull than a face. Inaudibly, he said something—his mouth moved at least—then halted in front of the mirror. He was pulling out wadded-up bills. I'd never expected to witness somebody with that kind of cash so *glum*.

"Any luck?" Don asked. Howie said no, there had not been. He'd been out playing by himself. He'd been doing the trick known as Wonging, essentially team play for loners: standing behind tables, counting down shoes, and sitting only if a deck became good. It sounded rather unglamorous and tiresome, and not very subtle to boot. Howie, in fact, had been backed off at two separate places that evening.

"You at least win?"

"No, I did not." He was staring in the mirror despairingly. Then he did something quite odd. Touching his hair in a strange, gentle way, he lifted it right off his head: a toupee. "This thing doesn't work," Howie said. "They know who I am. That's six hundred bucks down the drain." He dropped it on the bureau, sighing heavily.

It was a fine toupee inasmuch as it looked fairly real, but that was the problem as well: the curly black hair of the wig was almost identical to Howie's real hair. His hair was a bit thinner, but black and curly just the same. All the sadness and the great sense of loss in that room—the sense of something invaluable slipping away—was embodied in the useless little wig.

Stardust, house of suffering, the place where counters' dreams go south: I didn't want to play it. But Jon was not a person I could argue with. That night on the swing shift, once the spotters were in position, I departed my stall in the men's room, ambled through the droves of retirees who constituted the main customer base in the dump, came to a table, and bought chips. I felt wholly ridiculous in leather pants, bandanna, thick beard dyed using Just for Men, with the sides of my head shaved clean and the dreads sproinging out from the top like a cluster of feathers. Soon I was rushing to call-ins. You have to stand in the center of the floor in plain sight placing mid-shoe bets, the biggest bets going in the house, and tolerate the gazes so plainly inspecting you: the boss men aren't even subtle. Nor was I, in this getup. I kept wanting to return the look of the shift manager and spread my arms and say, "Yes. Yes I am. You're correct. That guy there is the spotter. Now, could you please bring the guards in and save us all some time?"

I was losing for a while, and they didn't interrupt. Then four hours had passed. The twenty grand I'd bought in for had all been recovered: we were in the black, and it was grave shift. I didn't make the connection till late in the session, but this was the same shift whose bosses had crossed the parking lot to the McDonald's and laughed at me for being a cross-dresser. Looking around, I didn't recognize them. Nor did they recognize me, if they happened to be on duty. You bitches, I want you to see this, I thought: I want you motherfuckers to *know*.

We were winning forty grand around daybreak, six in the morning. No heat whatsoever. I had no intention of stopping. With the hit-or-miss style of play, in a heat-intensive casino such as this, if you manage to get down, you've been lucky. I knew that we had. I knew the second a senior person took a fresh look at my action—perhaps at the start of the subsequent shift—that he would pull the plug without delay. There would be no coming back. When a big score happens like this (forty Gs is big for the Stardust; at Bellagio they might not have flinched, but the average wager in this casino was approximately 25 cents, and a loss of this size would be noted), even if you leave with no heat, you can bet they'll review what's gone down. They'll bar you in absentia. We call this a "retro blow." Next time they see you, they'll go nuts.

Knowing I would never bet money again here, I was prepared to go with no sleep, not stopping to eat, for as long as permitted. But then Jon appeared on the floor. He walked past with a smile, acknowledging the racks full of chips I was lugging, and touched his neck, signaling EOS. I shook my head no. But Jon had already decided. He went around signaling the spotters. Back at the base, he explained he'd been concerned about them, about the quality of their counts after playing for so long. "They're young little guys, they get tired. They can't count for days straight like you and me."

That "you and me" pretty much compensated for the premature ending. But I still had a feeling of loss.

Twenty-eight

Where to?" That was Jimmy's cousin Sammy in the backseat.

I told him what Jon had just said on the phone. "The Aladdin."

"You're kidding."

"Someone's got to do it."

"No they don't."

"What's the worst that could happen?"

"They shoot you," he said.

Fair enough. The kid was even right, in a sense: there was very little point in this exercise. He was one of a couple of new-generation spotters who'd been tearing it up in Las Vegas since I'd been away. Two others were in the car with us: Doug and the quiet one, Philip.

Everybody knew the problem with Aladdin. Things had gone poorly their opening weekend—poorly from their point of view. With the on-slaught of teams that were in there, they might have lost a million bucks for all we could tell. Ever since then they'd been freaked. They shut down the call-in game totally. They made it a house policy that mid-shoe bets would be capped at a hundred a hand. For us, it was a game killer. Some of us had wondered why it took so long for casinos to adopt such a measure. In all the time I'd played, I'd yet to see a legitimate sucker bopping in mid-shoe with a bet above $500. If they eliminated those bets altogether, probably the only customers who would notice it would be us.

A $100 cap was really low. Aladdin didn't want to take bets anymore. We and others like us had broken their spirit. But Mossad being Mossad, once every trip we would send an exploratory crew just to try it and see what they did. This corresponded to Roth's overall philosophy of always taking a shot no matter how poor the odds. "Why *bar yourself*?" he would say. "That's their job! If you refuse to go in, you've effectively backed off yourself."

When we reached the Aladdin, Sammy hopped out. "See you back here in ten minutes?" he joked. Expecting a very short session.

I said, "EOS at Paris valet."

"As you wish."

"Good luck," said Philip, slamming the door. The three spotters had instantly separated; they were entering the casino as strangers. I swung the car around the immense circular valet conduit, entering the confused superstructure of the parking garage, which resembled almost perfectly the interior shots of the (*second*) Death Star when the *Millennium Falcon* flies through in *Return of the Jedi*. I found a space and parked.

The Aladdin casino floor is accessed through a labyrinthine shopping mall simulating a Levantine village: fake blue sky overhead, the storefronts white "stucco" buildings emerging from the sides of an also-fake cliff. I strolled through leisurely.

Listen: We expect nothing. Like Angela said, it's all improv. I had money in place, at the ready. The loose bills were in a breast pocket. I was carrying seventy Gs. Straps were lodged around my body in various places, like pads on a football player. At the table I bought $3K worth of chips. "Purple and black," I requested, meaning $500 and $100 checks. I was coming off the top of a random shoe (no call-in, right after a shuffle) in the hopes of appearing innocuous. They had signs on the table: $100 MAX ON MID-SHOE ENTRY. It was hopeless. The cards began falling.

I played maybe ten minutes, spreading bets moderately and at random between $200 and $800. If the count had really plunged, I would have left, but the cost of a handful of bets correlated loosely to the count isn't high if it buys you some play time. We often started sessions this way.

A host, named Joe, handed a rating card to me. "If there's anything I can do . . ." he said.

"Actually, a room would be great."

"Heh. Yes." His gaze dropped down to my bet: two black chips. "I'm sorry. We've been booked for this weekend for months."

I said I understood. Then I saw Philip with a call-in. I staggered over in his direction, reverting at once to a drugged-looking, wobbly, confused, beaten-down sort of act, inspired by what Robert used to do. Roth had the theory it worked well on me because I naturally looked so bizarre: "No offense, Axe," he'd said, "but it's true. By casino standards you're a freak. It didn't work for controlling, but when you're betting, you just seem to *scare* them somehow."

"Whoa!" I cried out to the dealer. I came in with an undersize bet, $400 on one hand—well below what the count really called for.

Instantly she pointed to the sign. "It's a hundred-dollar-max mid-shoe."

"Look," I said. I lifted the chips, held them in front of her face, then returned all four to the spot. "That's a bet." I was trying to occupy a middle ground between domineering and insane.

"*Sir,*" she said.

"He can go ahead." The pit boss had seen our exchange. He was a stocky and gentle-faced man with a mouth about the size of a Skittle. When I looked at him, he nodded. "Jen—he's all right."

"Jen! What's the matter? You scared?" I left my mouth open, let drool fly over my cheek. Sniffling, she dealt, and I lost. The boss retreated, satisfied. I took the opportunity to add a second spot, "to change up the cards," as I pretended. Jen didn't say another word to me.

I lost. Then Sammy had a count, and I entered with two hands, and the dealer raised his finger to stop me. The boss arrived, repeating the exemption. This dealer shrugged. Soon I was losing $10K. I got to a third shoe and placed my bets, and when the dealer spoke up, I cried, "Boss!" He responded at once. He was issuing a full-fledged sign-off on me. He thought he saw the crazy in my eyes. "Let him bet what he wants."

I said, "Thank you!"

By the end of that shoe, I was stuck twenty Gs. This was always happening to me. I started minus twenty at Greektown, at Resorts in AC, at the Stardust, and all of these sessions had won. It was almost a comfortable spot. Now we battle out of it, I thought. I went from shoe to shoe, lunging, pounding the table, verging on tears several times. Emotions were dense, overwhelming. My heart was going nuts. Slobber was coating my chin. I stayed on my feet while I played, too energized to sit, and also for the purposes of sight lines: I was tracking where my spotters were, always looking for another hot shoe to escape to, in case the present count should go away.

I took a shoe from Doug at the end of the pit. A crowd of civilians was stalking me, ogling the bets. It was Pied Piperish. I came in at two by $2K. The bank for this trip was over a half million, sized to support a $1,000 betting unit: we could bet up to two by ten grand. The max here was only $5,000, but it was still the biggest stakes I'd ever played. I started losing on the shoe, with the count rushing up and a shitload of small cards just bleeding. I had splits and had doubles. I could hear the strangers gasping behind me. I got to running eighteen; there were three decks to play: a true six. This called for two by the max. I placed the bets in orange chips, five on each spot. They didn't *look* like they were worth ten grand, those little disks, but as soon as the dealer reacted—cried out, "Table max!"—and a new Suit entered the pit, and a stranger near my neck whispered, "*Go, man,*" I started understanding that it was big, this was big, this was the true shit, this was the Kenny Uston–level goddamn serious stuff: I might not ever bet this high again, anywhere. So much had to go right before you found yourself in this position. You had to get down; the odds of getting down were growing worse every day. Each session I played, I was closer to an entry in the Griffin Book. I'd been giving my name right and left in these dumps. You had to get lucky, just like at the Stardust, and once you did, part of the joy of the session was feeling it slip through your fingers, knowing that *these* circumstances in *this* particular shithole would never return—by touching the thing, you relinquished it. Those were the terms that we played on.

I heard the reaction from the spectators first. My head was buzzing, I hadn't quite absorbed what I'd been dealt: an eleven. Beside it another eleven. The dealer was showing a jack. Someone said "Shit!" as she slipped the jack under the reader—a device that would show a green light if she didn't have a blackjack or red if the card facing down was an ace. It turned green. People exhaled. But there was no cause to relax.

I had to go into my pocket, having bet my last chips on the round. The dealer was waiting. Four Suits were in back of the table: the boss, who had given the sign-off; some floor kid; the new guy, who looked really senior; and Joe, that host who'd denied me my comp. Part of me was glad to have an audience large enough to fit the occasion. I took out the ten-strap, waved it, and then, tossing it upward, indulging in a cinematic flourish that made it follow an arc to the felt, I said to her, "Double them both."

The strap sat there a moment. Finally she reached, slipped off the rubber band, and started breaking it apart so she could count. The two older Suits crowded round her. Her stubby white fingers were trembling. The gawkers behind me were sticking their arms out to point at the money. Joe was goggle-eyed. I broke the strained silence, saying, "Joe. Do you think you could double-check about that room?"

He had already lunged for the phone, his face covered with sweat. "I am on it."

"Oh. Thanks."

She was spreading the money out carefully, each bill faceup, counting out five at a time, arranging them diagonally in rows. I tried to look around for other call-ins, but I was overwhelmed; I couldn't see straight. Faces were blurring around me. The noise from the slot machines churned. Glancing up, I saw protruding from the wall overhead a discombobulating sculpture of a winged horse, nostrils flaring dreadfully, his huge teeth sinister, seeming to swoop down toward me. Cash was covering the felt. For a fraction of a second, I could see myself standing there, chest heaving, acting out a scene I had daydreamed so often, and that's when it struck me: that this might well be the peak of my life. No experience would ever be as rich, or as intoxicating or gripping. I felt it all slipping away, even as it was ongoing. It might even be terrible, ominous: I'm twenty-six, and now I'm in decline?

She handed the chips across, swallowing apparently in fear. I placed five of these adjacent to each bet. "Could you deal the cards facedown?" I said. They can do this, on request, when you're doubling. She looked to a boss, and he nodded. She pulled the small, fateful card from the dealing device, drawing it carefully over the baize and tucking the edge of it below the original hand. Then she did the same with the following card. She turned to the next player down from me: a middle-aged woman who had a sixteen. Her bet was only $25. Deferentially, the sweet-faced, tourist-type woman looked at me and asked, "How do you want me to play?" She was reluctant to hit and take a card that might have busted the dealer.

"It is your choice."

"No. I can't."

"I think I would stand." I would actually have surrendered, but I stood to gain nothing by flaunting my conversance with basic strategy in front of these Suits, with a hand that wasn't even mine. She did stand. All eyes turned to the dealer.

She took a quick breath and flipped her hole card, exposing a four. I was sure right then we had won, but the full rush of it didn't hit until she pulled the next card, eight of diamonds—busting with a twenty-two. People were screaming. Twenty thousand dollars is a really nice hand. The count remained high, and I continued to bet; we had the session in the black by the end of that shoe. Over the next two hours, the call-ins were steady and the result climbed and climbed, finally soaring. I had a plastic bucket, designed for slot players to keep their quarters in, absolutely filled with a mixture of purple and orange chips. When I came to a call-in from Philip and chunked my orange bets down again, suddenly the same guy who had originally signed off was bellowing at the dealer, "No action!" I was shocked it had taken so long. He looked shaken, badly distressed—probably the same way I would feel if finally, after almost six months, I issued a onetime exemption to a rule intended to thwart team play and the guy I exempted was himself a team player who would stumble into very handsome variance, hitting us for $78,860. It was the most I ever won in a session.

Twenty-nine

N ew Year's was also the trip Elke and I had our first date. I went to McCarran. Three days into 2001. My cut was $10K on the bank. I had won well over $150K betting the money. Much of the team was in town still, relaxing, tanning their skin, and playing hold 'em. Mateo, Jon, Bridget, Aldous, Sammy, and I all lived in the New York area, but none of us had any reason to ever go home, so we lingered in Vegas.

I'd gotten a comped room at the Hard Rock. In the trunk of the compact car that I'd rented myself post-bank, I also had a bottle of Dom, one of Cristal, and a Johnnie Walker Blue. As I took the banked curve at high speed coming into the airport, the bottles in the back rolled noisily.

I parked. I sprang out.

It was a cool, pleasant night in the valley.

I passed by Passenger Pickup. I strolled across the bridge we always used. It gave me a proprietary feeling to know an airport the way I knew this one.

Who the hell would Elke turn out to be? I was curious. We'd spoken only briefly up to now. I'd met her one night in New York, at this event, the Alfred Joyce Kilmer Memorial Bad Poetry Contest, hosted by the Philolexian Society up at Columbia, of which I'd been a member since college. I'd competed in the contest, and I'd lost. Everyone went to Symposium after, the Greek place; they had this sangria. The first thing I learned about Elke was that her head was approaching my lap. She'd stretched herself out on the chairs—crazy chick! Blinking up, she said simply, "Hello."

I was dating someone else at that time. So nothing occurred. We flirted at the restaurant, and then we went out to a bar, and I bought several rounds, but that's all.

Nothing might have come of it. But Jenny and I broke up. Sometime in December, Elke, who had certain strengths, blasted an e-mail out to the whole Philo e-mail list, announcing herself up for auction: she would happily serve as the New Year's companion to whichever man bid the best date.

I came in over the top (so I hoped) with the round-trip airfare and dinner in Vegas. She'd have a room all her own she could sleep in; there were no "expectations," I promised. The catch was that it couldn't be on New Year's itself. It would have to be after the bank.

She wrote back to declare me the victor. Her prose was first rate, and I liked it. She was bright, and she was slightly on the crazy side; we might have potential together. Possibly she was too young. She couldn't drink, but she could board an airplane.

I went through security. You didn't used to have to have a boarding pass to go to the gate. I was riding the conveyor when it hit me. I could barely remember her face. Who is this woman, and what have I gotten myself into?

The passengers started appearing as soon as I came to the gate. Several times I felt a stir of recognition. In a minute I saw her for sure. She wore high heels. Her legs were bare way up her thighs. The minidress was almost unbelievable. Her purse was no larger than a good-size burrito. She saw me, came over. We had a light hug.

"Luggage?" I said.

"Just this."

I took her arm and led her to the car.

Thirty

Elke would become a real girlfriend, but I had no way of knowing this at first. She was seven years younger than I was, and I was pretty young. The whole thing might have been sick. I wasn't sure. How could I know? Unless you're going to break the law and really be a villain and an assailant, it's not actually feasible to date someone substantially younger than yourself until you're at least twenty-six. It was the first shot I had, so I took it.

There were a lot of first shots around then. There were first shots at casinos. There were first shots playing in new states. It would dawn on me in January that if I continued with regular play and my bankroll continued to grow and my investments in the banks could grow with it (this wasn't assured—investment space was allocated through an esoteric combination of formulas and politics), I would have my first shot at a six-figure income: 2001 would be a good year, in fact.

Elke would be there the whole time. I would bring the money and the stories from the road; it was her job to bring the *humanity*. A human body to hold in the form of a cunning young woman would contribute to my grip on reality at a time when the latter was slipping. My life grew episodic through the year—*more* episodic, I mean. I would wake up in an Oregon forest, in a comped double room indistinguishable from the room I'd had the week prior—except that room had been in New Mexico. In each place I would have a new story, new lies for the boys in the pit, explaining my presence in this or that faraway dump with an out-of-state license and buckets of cash. I was a film producer scouting locations. I operated a chain of coffee houses and was thinking of expanding to Albuquerque. I was simply a compulsive lunatic. The lies would work, and eventually they would stop working, at which point it was rough talk and the guards and their guns and the intimidation racket, the cashing of chips, the worried rush out to the car and the mad dash off the reservation. The next day there would be a flight to New York. Elke and I would have dinner. I wouldn't have had time to drop cash at my box—I would tote forty Gs on the subway. Elke, who was only a sophomore, had a way of looking at all this bustle as if it were natural, decent, even heroic in a minor sort of way.

"Come on, *heroic?*" I said to her once. "I lie to get money. Then I spend the money on myself and on you. A preponderance of the money I lie in order to get in order to spend on myself and on you probably was lost to casinos in the first place by people who were mentally ill, addicted, or out of control. That's whose money I'm getting."

"Don't overdramatize, mister." She was holding tea in both hands. "You're the last living cowboy, and you know it."

"Oh, God." I loved that she would say that kind of thing. I understood, too, that the power dynamic was screwy between us and the relationship probably sick. But the way her eyes would glow when I showed her into a restaurant or spun some ridiculous yarn was something I would grow to depend on. The lies would be entirely justified then, or at the very least my doubts would fall silent.

Thirty-one

D aylight! I was alone. I was hungry. I dashed across the parking lot, looking every which way for attackers. I'd cashed out a bunch.

"Mac!" Neal said on the phone. "How'd you do?"

"Good, good." Revving the engine, I lurched and sped out of the lot. Neal, Jimmy, and Philip were in a separate vehicle. We'd just played the Empress in Joliet (different from the Empress in Hammond, where I'd bet once before, although both were in the Chicago area—"Chicago" for card counters comprising a hundred-mile stretch between Elgin, northwest of the Loop, and a place called Michigan City, across Indiana almost all the way to Michigan). These riverboat casinos were frequently in isolated places, without any good spot for an EOS—there was nowhere around you could walk to. We simply EOS'd in our cars, and this usually left the BP driving by himself; in the event he was barred, we didn't want him coming around to pick up the controllers, contaminating everybody else with his heat. "I almost placed a bet at roulette," I said.

"Why?"

"We were thirty-five dollars shy of winning forty grand even."

"Holy shit. That's fantastic."

"I was going to bet my own money on black—thirty-five, push us over the line."

"You should have done it, Axe. You could have used your playing stake for that. An offering to the blackjack gods, right? That's allowed."

This was sort of a joke. I said, "Next time."

"Good fucking job."

"I have you guys to thank for the counts. See you soon."

It was a long ride back to the Holiday Inn where we were staying, across the Indiana line. I was still buzzed from the session. I loved playing with Neal, I loved being a counting BP, I loved getting down in these low-probability dumps where no one else was betting more than green chips. The act this time was a new one, simple in concept, richer than expected in potential: I pretended I was gay. That was pretty much the whole ruse. I was effeminate, and I was gay. I did the leather pants again, leather motor-cycle jacket, leather cap to cover up the dreads, my beard now a heavy goatee, still dyed. I sashayed into the dump, hips rocking, my wrists histri-onically limp. It was absurd. It should not ever have worked. But the small-minded pit crew simply couldn't get over it: Gay! The guy's *gay*. He's a homosexual, apparently. *A gay guy is betting some money.* Look at how gay that guy is! Preoccupied with gayness, they didn't have enough free room in their minds to imagine something else might be happening.

It was a tried-and-true hustle: you created personas that would corre-spond to the pit's preconceptions of harmlessness. The drugged-out, music-producer, Robert Jayne–style ruse was one option and effeminate gayness another. The key was to come off as weak, to come off as helpless. That's what puts them at ease.

So I was gay, and I was drugged, sashaying and blinking and stumbling and drooling and slurring my lisp. An odd moment came when the shift manager, eager to please, offered a comped room, then asked what else he could do for me.

"Recommend a nightclub in the area," I said.

"Uh. I'd have to think. . . . What kind of, you know——"

"I'm looking for a clientele a little more male than female. Do you know what I mean?"

He said, "Right," and ran off. Over the next half hour, as I went about taking my call-ins, I noticed him frantically talking to various guys in the pits. What the hell was he doing? It didn't look like heat. . . . He was preoccupied by something. Then he ran up to me: "Here, here, this way . . ."

"Darling, what is it?"

He brought me over to a craps game, where a young dealer stood waiting and looking distraught. He couldn't have been more than nineteen years old, and as soon as I shook the boy's hand I could see what had happened. The shift manager had just spent thirty minutes (when he should have been protecting his game, looking through flyers upstairs, or just scrutinizing how I was betting) desperately trying to hunt down a gay employee to put me in touch with. The kid explained about a bar that he knew. He was clearly shaken up and unhappy—I don't think he'd planned to find himself outed to his shift boss while working today. Guiltily, I thanked him, and for the rest of the shift I was running amok, heat-free. I regretted the collateral damage; I wished I could have let the kid know there was a higher cause involved.

The next day we drove out to Michigan City. The trip took an hour. As we reached the casino, the Blue Chip, Neal called to ask if I was ready.

"All set."

"If you get close to forty again," Neal said, "you can go ahead and bet on roulette, mac."

"Will do."

"*Muh!*" he said.

I grunted it back in response. *Muh!* had turned into a battle cry. Neal'd started using it recently, and the rest of us soon followed suit. It derived, Neal said, from *"Monkey!"*—a traditional utterance among noncounting blackjack players when they were hoping for a face card to fall. When especially excited, they elided the second syllable, and "muh" approximated how it sounded.

I waited alone in the car a few minutes to give the others time to stagger in. Then I stepped out, sashayed across the parking lot, once more decked out in leather. As I strolled through the lobby and down the ramp, onto the boat, I was examining the locals, not without a touch of compassion. These weren't tourists with money to blow. They were neighborhood people from a blighted part of northern Indiana. I wondered how gambling fit into their lives.

I'd reached the second level, where the table games were. Approaching the blackjack, I heard the word "Sir?" from behind me. Damn, I thought. These guys are quick.

Halting, I turned to face the guard, an elderly man who looked a lot like my grampa on my mother's side. "I'm afraid you're going to have to come with me. . . ."

"Never mind," I told him. I put both my hands in the air. "I'll withdraw."

Before he could speak, I was rushing down the stairs. At the entrance I discovered a welcoming party: a trio of guards and a man in a nice-looking suit. The Suit knew my name. He said, "Joshua!" extending a hand.

As I shook it I said, "Please. Josh."

He smiled. "We're a little busy today. You mind trying again another time?"

"Of course I'll do that."

"It's very kind of you."

"Never bite the hand that gives the doggie treats," I said. With that, I walked out to the car. It was a shame we had wasted time driving here—pity you can't just call, ask for a word with the shift boss, and say something like, "I'm Josh Axelrad. I'd like to play blackjack tonight. Will that be an issue? Would you mind checking in with the surveillance chief? Thanks."—but the cordial exchange with the Suit had almost made the trip worthwhile.

It was heartening to remember we were all human beings in the end: even the scumbags.

The car wasn't far. I crossed a couple lanes, and I was opening the door. In the next lane over from mine, I saw a white van, a funny yellow light on its roof. Could that be security, scrambling? I thought. I laughed. The idea seemed silly. We had ended on such good terms.

Pulling out from my spot, in the rearview I saw the van turning in this direction. There seemed to be an eagerness about the way he came. I felt a hard jolt in my nooksack. That's where it hit—the adrenaline—and I pushed into D, wishing for standard transmission. The lane ended; I turned, radials squealing somewhat. I turned again, zagged, and was cutting through an empty expanse, indifferent to lanes. The van had zagged, too: he was coming.

Sometimes they go for your plates, they want to keep a record of your vehicle. Sometimes they chase for no reason. We have no strong reason to run. Knuckles don't get broken in this business anymore. The cops-and-robbers game is an indulgence, but nevertheless so *intuitive*—when push comes to shove, you just do it.

Leaving the Blue Chip's lot, I spun onto the public road, and I was rolling ahead, ecstatic. So long, I thought. I knew they wouldn't pursue me off the premises. Their authority ends at the boundary. It always felt a little like *The Matrix:* once you hop out of their world, you're safe. Also, the bad guys wear suits.

I glanced at the mirror. The van was at the driveway I'd pulled out of. Then he turned onto the road. He was pursuing me along the public street. No way, I thought. That's impossible.

Ahead, the light was green, and I accelerated to catch it, going straight where I should have turned left. I'd just missed the road to the interstate. But first I had to lose the fucking bogey. We were on a side street, residential; I was tearing up a hill. He was at least fifty yards back. I would not permit him to get near my plates—never mind that it was only a rental, never mind that they *already knew who I was*. Whatever they want, they won't get from me, I resolved.

I made another turn, not sure how I could lose him. Soon I was back at the main artery, Michigan Boulevard. I took the hard right, more squeals out of those tires, money belt squishing my guts as I struggled for breath.

The street had a high speed limit, and I stamped the pedal. I was eight MPH past the limit. I still had the leather cap and jacket, the metallic silver shirt, leather pants. I was holding sixty Gs on my person. Michigan City is not a nice town. Even by the standards of northern Indiana, it's a heart-breaking place, a bit more hellish than otherwise. I was passing shuttered stores, defunct gas stations, weeds growing out of their lots. The dangers here seemed multitudinous. Locals might come after me because of how I looked. I could be wrongfully gay-bashed. Speeding was dangerous as well, tearing down the street with an out-of-state license and a bankroll the size of a cop's annual pay.

He was far back from me now. But I still had several miles to the inter-state. Ahead, in the distance, the traffic was congealing where a light had turned red. Everyone in front of me was stopping. I had no choice but to slow. In a moment I would be at his mercy. Space was about to run out when I saw the right-turn lane—nobody in it. I cut across two lanes to get there, rushed to the light, made the turn. I had no clue where I was heading, but slamming the gas, I continued to speed for a mile. He wasn't coming after me. He must not have seen. *I'd won my first car chase.* I pulled over, called Neal. "Hey, mac. Where are you?" he said.

All I could answer was, *"MUH!"*

Thirty-two

Route 95 ran straight, perfectly linear like something out of a mathematician's utopian scheme for high-speed desert arteries. We'd gone south out of Vegas, taking the Railroad Pass, where we paused to check the truck-stop-style dump at the summit; the maxes were only $300. It was Neal and I exploring, bound for the city of Laughlin, where supposedly there was a shuffle. The rest of the team was in Vegas. The trip was getting buried, down 40 percent.

South of the pass, the road stretched in a line whose regularity, contrasted to the savage terrain all around, caused the jagged hills to look wilder. It was sun-smothered turf, etiolated and haggard, lunar in character, wretched. Vegas must have looked this way before the slot machines.

Into the hills we shot through the village of Searchlight, then proceeded south to the 163. This was almost the tip of Nevada, near the southernmost point of the state. The road rose, and there were cliffs to one side of us, orange, at once pretty and bleak. In a minute we summited, rounding a curve: far down below on the banks of the river, the city of Laughlin appeared. "Well, mac, another gambling town," Neal said.

"*Muh,*" I responded.

He seconded that.

The game was at the Edgewater, and it was good. A trackable shuffle's a valuable thing. Neal was teaching me, live. Not all shuffles are equally random: with multideck shoes, casinos are forced to make trade-offs between the duration of the shuffle and its thoroughness. Whenever they're shuffling the cards, they're taking no bets. The table's effectively closed down. They want to minimize the time they lose from doing this, and sometimes they come up with nice rapid shuffles that guys like us can exploit.

That's what the Edgewater had. Their shuffle broke the deck down into six different chunks: they shuffled each chunk half to death. But that was *all* they did. They didn't mix the chunks with each other. We were using mnemonics to retain the location of certain large packets of good cards that we saw come during a shoe, and then we would follow them through the shuffle, trying to identify chunks where our cards ended up.

There were certain nuances that complicated things; I wouldn't recommend that people try this without careful study. But our game, to me, looked stupendous. Neal, identifying the packet, would wield the cut card carefully after the shuffle. (The cut card is a plastic reusable card, usually bright yellow, serving two purposes. Dealers hand it to players, who slice it into the deck, indicating where they want the cut; dealers then execute the cut and afterward place the card toward the back of the shoe, marking the point where the dealing will stop and that shoe will be shuffled. When the card reappears, yellow and easy to spot in the middle of a round, that round is the last of the shoe.) The cut would go exactly to our packet. The tens and the aces would gush out. I would bet two by the max, which was $1K here. From the casino's perspective, we didn't look like card counters at all, betting off the top and then *continuing* to bet as the count itself actually plunged. We lost money somehow—bought in for forty-five Gs.

It was unlucky. Technically, I think we were rocking, the EV very good. (A good tracking game even in a low max like here can have extremely high value, in part because you're betting every shoe instead of one shoe in seven.) We'd blasted through so much cash we had to call Vegas for backup.

Jimmy drove all the way down—ninety-eight miles—at four in the morning, then turned right around and went back.

We'd expected to stay for one night, hadn't known that the game was as good as it was, nor that we'd lose so much money. We ended up there for five days. We became committed. Of course we wanted to dig out, then to realize some winnings, since the game was really fine; there was also emotion involved. On the swing shift, the first night, Neal got to talking with the shift boss while I was away in the bathroom. "My friend won't quit gambling," he told him. "We're supposed to be driving to Vegas." (This was our act, that we were en route to Las Vegas.) The shift boss just shrugged. "He'll quit when he's busted," he said.

It was the pleasure, combined with the brutish confidence in the boss's voice, that got Neal pissed. "Axe Man, we'll teach him a lesson." From then on we couldn't back away. We secured our adjoining comped rooms, and we dug in, restricting our play to the day shift, which had the best dealers. It was important to take breaks with this game: you couldn't play around the clock as you could when you were merely counting cards. We played eight hours each day. Then we enjoyed a free steak downstairs in the Hickory Pit and went up to our rooms for our baths.

Our second day we got into the black. The conditions were perfect. They gave us a heads-up game. Neal was in charge of the tracking; I more or less followed along. We would communicate by grunting *"muh!"* during the shuffle when the dealer grabbed the packet we preferred. Whenever our *"muh"*s coincided, I was filled with pride. I was starting to handle this game. I had never done advanced games before. (In addition to tracking, there were a number of other high-level tricks that pretty much no one but Jon, Neal, or Aldous was authorized to tangle with. They were judgment-intensive, considerably more technical than counting.) I hoped, dreamed, prayed, thought possibly I might be earning Neal's respect.

Then there was another day, and then another. We'd established a routine. We came down ten minutes into day shift, and we played with no break until swing. The shift manager was named Rick Buford. He was a really great guy. "Morning, you guys!" he would say with a wave. He'd get our special game going. Then we would blast for eight hours. If heat is conspicuous (and once it's serious enough, it always is), the absolute absence of heat is equally conspicuous to counters. No one was worried at all. They weren't even bothered a bit. Their decision was already made; I would play until "busted," they thought. By the fourth day, our clothes stank—we'd each brought just one extra shirt. I'd given up recycling my boxer shorts. You'd think after that many days the spectacle of two guys sitting at a blackjack table with that kind of endless avidity would start to look a little weird. It was actually exceptionally weird: Neal mostly didn't even play. He'd put an occasional bet down, but mainly he just watched, constantly fixed on those cards, never missing a round, for *four days*. We got ahead sixty Gs. What kind of person would just continue sitting there, forgetting the trip he'd had planned to Las Vegas, forgetting all else in the world? They must have believed we were maniacs, and they *liked it*—it sheds a degree of light into the mind-sets of these motherfuckers.

In Vegas the bank was stalled out, still very much in the red. We could almost forget we were part of that nightmare. We were in a different world here. The casino was smallish and grubby. On day shift most of the customers were senior citizens, and they roved around in packs, having come in together on junkets. It was just them and us and Rick Buford, who was starting to behave rather strangely.

He'd begun dogging our game, watching us for hours straight. It didn't feel like heat. He looked more hopeless than skeptical. He chewed on his thumbnail, leaning over the back of a stool, observing but not interfering. His only definitive action came after a particular run of bad shoes where we'd given back about ten Gs. A new dealer entered the pit—this would happen every twenty minutes. They dealt twenty minutes, then swapped. But as soon as the new guy appeared, Buford jumped up, ran in there and grabbed the guy's elbow. He whispered in his ear for a second. The new dealer listened, then turned right around and departed. Our current dealer looked a bit confused. Neal glanced over at me with a smile, as if to ask whether I'd noticed what had happened. Oh, yes: Buford, it seemed, was keeping the dealer on the game because *we happened to be losing.* In other words, he thought she was "lucky." We'd reduced the poor guy to the kind of inane superstition he usually preyed on in others.

Oh, it was good. Oh, it was dreamy, was *good:* it was like we'd found a home. It was far and away the longest relationship I'd had with a casino as a BP. We recovered the ten, and by the end of that day we were up over $70,000. In my suite that night, I was taking my bath as I did every night. There were jets built into the sides, like a mini-Jacuzzi. My skin had turned instantly pink. It was near-scalding water—just right. I imagined my flesh boiling up, curdles of skin flaking off and disappearing in the bubbles. My muscles began to relax. The ache of the long day spent squatting on the stool slipped out of my body completely. *This* was the right way to live.

I'd just put on my fetid jeans again when Neal called. "How 'bout we talk, mac?"

"Sure. Come on over."

A minute later he was standing at my window. "I think we should call it."

"Call what?"

"It's time to get out of this dump."

I was stunned. "Leave voluntarily?"

"I think so."

I had never heard of such a thing. Neal pressed his hands against the window. The building was washed from below with these floodlights; they made the night simply look blank. It didn't appear dark so much as *voided* out there. "Look where we are," he said.

"So?"

"You bought in for forty-five Gs, right? We're winning, what, seventy?"

"About."

"This is a really small town, Axe. You realize basically everyone in this casino knows how much money you have. I keep overhearing things."

"Really?"

He nodded. "They're talking about you, for sure. They're probably going home and saying things to their wives. You think which room you're in is a secret? I don't mean to get you freaked out, man. I'm sure we'll be safe."

"Now you've got me wondering."

"Don't worry. I just think in a case like this where we've pushed things as far as we have, we don't have to go all the way. I don't especially want to get barred here just now. We're not in Las Vegas. We don't know a lawyer in this little town. We don't know what cops are like here. Metro sucks ass in Las Vegas, but at least they're professional. Here? We don't know. I don't want to have to explain how shuffle tracking's different from felony cheating to some guy on a horse with a shotgun over his back. . . ."

"You think it's that bad?"

"Look, I'm kidding. But there's no giant upside to us finding out." He grabbed my shoulder. "Hey, mac. Relax. It's a suggestion."

An hour later we were downstairs, Neal acting as sort of a bodyguard while I cashed the chips. We had security escort us to our car. Soon, on the 163, we were back at the summit, and Laughlin had vanished behind us.

Thirty-three

Look, mac."

"What?"

"Do you see?"

"What? The road?"

"Something spectacular, mac."

"I'm witnessing my youth fade away. Does that count?"

"There in the sky."

"Oh. Oh."

"The beacon. Like a homing beacon, mac. They say you can see that from space."

"It's bizarre. Astronauts, as target markets go, you would think would have limited value."

"Maybe they like to play big."

"Maybe so."

"You get kind of restless on the shuttle."

"I'll bet."

"Come back with some steam to blow off, you head straight for the Luxor."

"Heh."

"Still," Neal said, "it's amazing."

"It is."

"You think of all the energy it burns. You think of what pays for that baby, you know?"

"You refer to other gamblers than ourselves."

"It's like a measurement of irrationality."

"You refer to the sickos. The rubes."

"It's basically a giant physical beam composed of poor decisions people made."

"Ideas. Transformed into substance."

"Really just fucking amazing."

Thirty-four

Other lights waited around the United States. Some were only stars, blazing over New Mexico, where Jimmy, Sammy, Chuck Small, and I stood in the parking lot of our hotel, a single day into a baby-size, four-person bank already ahead forty Gs—and no one else but us had a piece of it. Known as a "cell play," these smaller banks afforded a chance to play in remote locations where the limits were low but opportunities could be unusual. At Isleta Gaming Palace near Albuquerque, they allowed us to spread with impunity. We didn't even have to run call-ins. They acted like counting didn't exist. One hand of $25 up to three by $500 drew no consternation from them. With the help of that game and another nearby, we'd instantly started to win. The next morning someone pounded on my door.

I sat up, bewildered. Desert sun was flooding through the gaps around the curtains. Chuck Small, my roommate, was snoring. Through the peephole I saw Jimmy's ball cap. He entered, shaking his head, dashed across the room, collapsed in the chair, and hunched forward, arms crossed over his stomach. "I lost half the win."

I sat on the mattress across from him. "Where?"

"Isleta. I couldn't sleep. I figured I ought to be in there; it's the reason we're here." He snorted as if he despised himself.

The sun was burning on the wall behind his head. Jimmy was almost in silhouette. He'd taken some cash from his pocket and started to count. The bills whispered in a stifled, angry way. I said, "Jimmy, you had some good counts?"

"They were high."

"You ship the fucking money in?"

"That was the problem."

"Don't let the variance get to your head. You have heat?"

"None at all."

"We'll be fine. They're holding that money in escrow for us."

Sighing, he said, "Yeah . . ." He straightened his back, stuck his legs out. Calmer, he went back to counting bills. The moment felt hazy and half real, as happened so often in blackjack.

A few weeks later, I was driving through woods, alone in Wisconsin, forty-two Gs in my pants. A duck rushed heedlessly into my lane, her ducklings in a neat line behind her. I eased off the speed for one sec, with no luck—I would roll the fucking car and still plow them before I could brake. There was no way I could stop. It was certain; the family was doomed. I sped up: veered, *fast,* into the opposite lane, hoping I could somehow make it past (the ducks were also heading right to left) but just then, the mama having noticed me, *she* sped up, too, and was heading straight into my path, running at top duck speed across the right lane for the left, with her imps sprinting after her. I hit the horn—BWWAAAAAANNNNK!!!—and she banked violently in a U and began dashing back where she'd come from. Each of the ducklings proceeded to make the same U, in the very same spot. They didn't break formation, I mean, in order to hurry to safety: kept going, danger be damned, turning only where their mommy had turned. The last of them nearly got hit, but, checking the rearview, I saw the lane clear, no lump of roadkill behind me—I could see them disappearing into the trees.

Variance was everywhere, wasn't it? The fuck am I doing, I thought, all by myself (this was my first solo trip) bearing my four-G win farther into crazy wooded areas? Jon had told me not even to go on this trip. Solo, without a lot of bankroll, your EV is small, and the variance completely overwhelms it. It was better, he said, to save my gambling for the bigger team banks. "You could easily lose. It's a coin flip. If you do, it cuts into your investment on the next trip with us, which by the way is better than a coin flip, by a lot. Basically, that's a disaster."

He was right. I was wrong. I was an idiot and a dreamer. But my goal wasn't purely EV—never had been. Otherwise I would have kept my job at the bank. I was in it for *moments like this:* ducks out of nowhere, variance, wins as well as losses that got to your heart, beams of light blasting into space. Beyond money, they paid us in spectacle.

From Wisconsin I crossed into Michigan, and I drove to the village of Watersmeet, having no clue what I would find in the tribal casino out there. I walked through the door and bought in. "Shuffle!" the dealer announced. As soon as I saw what she did, I was certain I would be there for a long, long time.

The max was only $200, but the shuffle—my God! It was *lewd.* The game was just sitting there, naked. The cards were barely randomized at all. It was the quintessential trackable game.

Gorgeous, gorgeous, gorgeous: you bet, track, cut, and repeat. I started losing money right away. Just like with regular counting, with tracking there's plenty of variance. You know when the tens and the aces will come, but that doesn't mean you'll win hands. An exemplary round would come out with four "good" points (four player-favorable big cards) but result in a loss: for me a twenty (king-queen) and a nineteen (ace-eight), but the dealer would show an ace up and have nine in the hole. I would take insurance and lose, then lose with my nineteen and push with the twenty. The effective true count on the round would be plus-thirty-five—the EV enormous but useless. And this kept happening.

I got in for $5,000. The win on the trip was erased. The torment was steady. The tens and the aces kept making bad hands. The consistency was astonishing: the dealer always sitting there with twenty. It was enough to drive you nuts. It could make you doubt the underlying concepts. Maybe that Thorp was a fraud. Maybe Jon Roth had gotten *lucky* for years but counting had nothing to do with it.

It felt different from losing on team trips. With the bankroll entirely mine, my share of the loss was transparent. One dollar equaled one dollar. It hurt, too, that no one else cared, that no one was in this thing with me. The losing was physical, palpable—in my chest, where the stress was growing constantly, but also in my groin area and lower belly, where the money belt had notably shrunk.

The dealers were chatty—they tried to be nice, but they kept saying confounding things, mentioning (first occasionally and in passing, in such a way I barely even noticed, but then repeatedly and at length, insistently even) this . . . *light*, or apparition, spectacle, thing, this enigma. "It's just down the road," one said.

"Right in those woods, down yonder," said another.

"You really ought to see it while you're here," they all said.

"It starts as a pulse," I was told.

"Starts tiny, then it *blows up*."

"It's just a little *point* at first, and then—"

Are you people crazy? Or is it me, here, lost, alone, adrift, hallucinations setting in—is that it? Is this even happening? Really? A *light*?

"If you're familiar with the television program *Unsolved Mysteries*, well . . ."

"It's been on *Unsolved Mysteries* twice."

"*Two* times."

"They keep showing the thing on TV!"

Three days into my stay, stuck now only two Gs but for some reason feeling no better, I fled from the table, chips crammed into my jeans and creating a bruise in my thigh, I went for my standard comped dinner, munched the tasteless pasta semiconsciously, took advantage of the self-serve frozen yogurt (really going nuts with the sprinkles), then went and got into the car. The woods were all around, and it was dark. The road appeared haunted already. I drove as directed, three miles, encountering no other cars, and I found the sign to Robbins Pond Road. This was a bumpy dirt lane disappearing into thick trees. I proceeded at a nervous little crawl. The darkness was troubling. I had all forty Gs on my person. Possible headlines kept flying through my mind: MYSTERY DEEPENS: HALF-EATEN BODY ON ROBBINS POND ROAD CARRIED MONEY BELT WITH $40,000 CASH.

Suddenly there was a barrier, a low piece of bent metal marking the end of the road. The dealers had mentioned this spot. I stopped the car, killing the engine. I sat in the dark in the woods. Beyond the barrier, over a long meadow there, was the place it supposedly dwelled. I'd been told that I might have to wait. Most nights, they said, it appeared, but of course—the typical bullshit with stories like this—sometimes it didn't show up. ("It's *there*, though. This is *real*. You know it's been on *Unsolved Mysteries*—twice?")

A light rain began. I could hear it against every window, like a special effect of the stereo. The darkness turned slightly kinetic, the rain close to visible but not quite. Through the blur of the shower, something almost seemed to appear, far ahead. As soon as I noticed it, it vanished.

The light reappeared; it was pulsing. Get the fuck out of here, I thought. It was faint, faint gray, like a flaw in a black-and-white photograph, but as the tempo increased, it grew redder. By this point I no longer doubted. There was a red flashing light in these woods. Then the light started to move. It *darted*, or seemed to dart, forward, but quickly withdrew. It darted again and retreated again. The next thing I knew, it was swelling.

It might have been a hundred yards back. I felt for the keys, to make sure they were in the ignition. My thigh ached throbbingly from the chips. The light had blown up quite a lot, shifting from red to a mild white color. Was it globe size? The size of a beach ball? The size of the ball in Times Square? Hard to know. Enlarged, it began to dart forward again. Its brightness was reflected on the trees.

Holy fuck, it's really getting close. The apparition, mac, she's coming near. She stopped again, forty feet off, lighting up the meadow beneath her. It was easy to think she was checking me out, that the intrigue flowed both directions. Are you scared, Ball of Light, the way I am? Do you fear that my intentions are bad? Do you want these woods to yourself?

She rushed toward me anew and was instantly so close that the car's interior was brightened. My cheeks were touched by it, my nose was lit up. She pulled back suddenly and, having retreated, welled up even bigger, and now she was twitching, alternating between a softer yellow hue and a blazing bright white. She seemed to be approaching some climax. Something fantastic was coming. I would *really* have a story for my dealers tomorrow. Then she was flashing, looked like she might have been spinning, parading dazzlingly through every different color she had shown up to now. It occurred to me she might impose harm—I had a hollow awareness somewhere near the middle of my throat that the light could *attack*, electrocute, scintillate, burn, snuff out; I felt physically heavy, resigned, and in a way almost eager: Come for me, you ghost bitch, *do it*. Reaching her largest size yet, she flew rapidly backward, began to deflate, color growing soft, and then she was pulsing in red, and then gray, a dot barely visible among the raindrops, until she petered out totally. I continued to shout (in my mind), Bitch, *come*.

Thirty-five

I got into the black at Watersmeet and left of my own accord, with no heat. I'd seen enough variance for now. I'd won $7K on my first solo trip and was happy with the result. With two days till my flight, I went for a drive, drove along Chequamegon Bay in Wisconsin, got a little room at an inn with a view of Lake Superior.

I'd brought a laptop along, since I thought of myself as a writer. I'd barely ever written, but I might. One never knew. The spell could hit at any time. I booted it up, and I sat there. I was thinking of the woods, the apparition: the Paulding Light, it was called. I didn't know what it was—nobody knew; theories included swamp gas (doubtful, I felt), headlights from a road in the distance (didn't comport at all with what I'd seen), or the ghost of a railway brakeman (most apt)—but I wanted to record the moment, how it felt, what it meant or might mean.

I sat there.

In a while I had written, *The light.* I stared at that, deleted it, and made it, *The Light.*

The Light, the Light, the Light, the Light, the Light . . .

Hot damn, I thought, it's blank verse. Wait a minute—surely I can nail this. If I am on a hunt, as I appear to be, for spectacle and weirdness, for the dangers peculiar to blackjack—dangers, that is, within limits, a rogue-like lifestyle that nonetheless involves no actual crime, that ultimately keeps us safe, sane, not really at odds with society, and whose safeness we're rather punctilious about—isn't this thing, this enigma, terrifying but ultimately harmless, mysterious but surely explicable—isn't it the absolute nuts, symbol-wise? Isn't it the object of the hunt?

I thought about that, couldn't decide, remembered a casino down the road, drove to it and parked. It sat on a hill overlooking gorgeous islands in the lake, but the casino itself was a toilet. It had one open table and a $50 max. Only a $2 min, though. It was probably worth six bucks an hour to play, but table min to two hands of $50 didn't bother anybody. I played. Fuck it, I thought: it's EV.

Thirty-six

J eff Toffler didn't look to be having much fun. We were shooting down
I-15 under so much sun it could cook us, Springsteen on the stereo as
usual. What's not to like?

"This was my first live concert!" I shouted.

Jeff turned his big, sullen head. His response was to wrinkle his nose.

I made the thumbs-up, smiling hugely. "L.A. Coliseum, '84. I was ten."

"I don't like arena performances."

"Awesome," I said. "Good to know."

The Boss was lamenting a woman he'd lost. Jeff, clutching his carry-on
on his lap, gazed ahead miserably. I had an urge to seize his elbow, say,
"*Awesome fucking valley*—look!" and then slap his face really hard. But you
can't go slapping gorillas.

He'd had a rough trip. The reason was this: He was bad. Not a natural
by any means. He was terrified betting the money. He looked like he wanted
to cry anytime he bought in. Then he played hands like a robot—he would
pause the same amount of time on every hand, giving his controller a window to signal, in case a deviation was in order. Not all hands have deviations, though; I'd struggled to get him to realize this. There was no point
pausing on a hard fifteen versus six—just wave the shit off! But the Toff

required fixed procedures. He was a stubborn neurotic. Pit bosses hated him everywhere. He appeared to have been flyered on his first night in town; eight days later he was probably in Griffin already. He was done betting money in Vegas for good.

"Is the heat like this every time?" He was shouting. The roof of the convertible was down.

"Pretty much. You expected something different?"

"I knew it could happen. It's just that it happened so quick. Did I do something wrong?"

"It's not you." There was no point hurting his feelings. "Just the nature of the game."

"You guys must be really hot."

"Some of us, in some casinos . . ."

"I put a lot of work into learning that stuff."

"You did good. You're going to make some money. Looks like the trip's going to win."

"I don't see why I can't do it again."

"Bet the money, Jeff? Oh. Probably not."

"But you guys keep going back."

"Sure, to *count* . . ." We were just pulling in to the airport.

"Why can't I change my appearance and use a fake name?" His tone had grown sharper. I could see he was exhausted—not thinking straight. He knew about CTRs, knew you couldn't bet under a fake name.

"Southwest?" I asked. Jeff nodded. As I pulled the car aside, I took my sunglasses off. "You can learn how to count. You know that. Learn to spot, then you can play. You can go right back into those places. There's no betting under a fake name. It's a beautiful thing, all this stuff, but the limits are real. You have to respect them. That's the only way it can work."

He mustered a fractional smile.

"You had a good trip, Jeff." I held up my hand. He considered a moment, then slapped it. *"Muh!"* I said.

"Yeah. Yeah, muh." Sighing, he stepped out of the car.

♦

I feel for him, though. Really do. The Toff has seen into the heart of it.

I drove into the tunnel, picking up speed, the cylinders working, the engine showing off its easy strength, and the Boss Man wailing. The tunnel! She was a constant in life now. The whole route back from the airport was, too. Here came the high-speed bank onto 215, and that *sun.*

I see how this looks, Jeff. I do. Neal has a new car, so does the Axe—and the latter of us doesn't even live in this town! Good God, the kid lives in Brooklyn. *You can't have a Mustang in Brooklyn,* you know; he garages it here in Las Vegas. Potentially comes off as decadent.

All of this—us, the cash, Roth giving orders, Aldous inscrutable over his laptop, answering questions from Neal about variance or this or that technical nugget in a language that sounds like code—decadent, the whole little show. Running crazy in the valley like we own the place, and someone always bossing you around.

Look, Toff. Listen: *I know.*

I know what you saw on the white board, under "Investments": there were my initials, JBA in for fifty dimes on this bank. I know how those numbers come off, like we must be made of money. Rich—not a care in the world. I used to stare at that board on my first trips. It seemed to me, then, so insane—fifty or seventy grand shipped into a gambling venture run from a Vegas apartment. The figures were unthinkable. I thought anyone gambling that high on one bank would have to be a millionaire already.

Not all of us are. You'll notice it's a 'Stang, not a 'Vette. It's the blue-collar muscle car, really. Her name, by the way, Toff: *Surrender.* I took a lot of shit for that from Roth, let me tell you. "Surrender, Axe?" he says.

I say, "Yeah."

"What kind of name is 'Surrender' for a card counter's vehicle, man? You should have called it something aggressive. 'Table Max,' 'Double Down' . . ."

"Surrender's a pretty good rule."

"So is double after split—call it that."

The car was accidental, understand. Bank before this one, our gorilla actually got down pretty well in a couple of dumps, with the result that good money was won. I dropped some off in my box—I have a box in Vegas, too, now, incidentally—but I kept a few Gs in my wallet, just 'cause. Almost like I had a presentiment.

Lo and behold, I'm on Lake Mead Boulevard. Suddenly here comes a Ford place. I walk around, see the white Mustang. Figure I should take it for a test drive. You know the rest of the story: leather interior, stick shift, Dolby stereo, has only seven thousand miles, and the price isn't bad. Not that I've shopped around or anything like that, but the guy brings me in, we sit down, he asks what do I want to put down (I didn't know how all this stuff worked), so I open my wallet. "How's this?" Next thing I know, I'm a vehicle owner.

Then, though, Toff, see, because, because there are *wrinkles* (even when you have a bit of cash), I get to New York, I call the toll-free number for the car-insurance firm represented by the humorous gecko in ads—the firm of which my idol Warren Buffett is the boss—and I ask to insure my new Mustang. Well! The quote comes back eleven Gs for one year. The car only cost twenty-one. GEICO is of the opinion that a car of this type will be totally lost once every twenty-four months. I call somewhere else, get a similar quote. Now I'm beginning to worry. I'm going have to register it soon, do you see? I find a Ford dealer guy in Manhattan, call him. "Where can I insure this new Mustang?"

"What borough you in?"

I say, "Brooklyn."

"You can't have a Mustang in Brooklyn," he says. "The theft rate. Car is uninsurable."

Eh? That, Mr. Toff, is a wrinkle, especially nettlesome, too, as I surrendered my California license only this spring—finally got legal in New York, after almost nine years in the state. (I'd been betting the money a lot,

CTR'ing all over the place, and I'd begun to grow concerned about claiming my mom's house as a residence on all these government forms.) But at least the solution was easy. Had to move back to Orange County.

I know how this sounds. I'm aware. I am hypercognizant. Sounds like I'm drowning in assets. Life is a walk in the park. I book the flight with two days' notice, at plenty high cost, also buying Elke a ticket. And we get to Vegas, and don't you know I manage to cadge comped digs from some douchebag host at the Aladdin—despite being already backed off? Sometimes you really get lucky.

We go into VIP check-in. I want to show my woman the ropes: viz., how to check in to a four-figure-a-night-type suite in a casino you're already blown in, leaving only $40 for deposit.

The room, by the way, Mr. Toff—holy shit. Aladdin's a toilet, but toilets can surprise you now and then. It's down on one end of the building. It's as big as the whole team apartment. These windows cover one of the walls, and the wall projects out, so you get like a 180 view. I need not mention the hot tub. We really go nuts with the comps. This is why you never leave a credit card. We order up dinner, dessert, a Cristal, a Johnnie Walker Blue, *and* a Patron. I'm planning to get a nice breakfast, including a couple more bottles, but no sooner have I called in the order next morning than the phone rings again. That's a *bad* sign. "Yes?"

"This is Bob Buttlick, your host," guy says.

"Hi, Bob. What can I do ya for?"

"I see that you've just ordered breakfast."

"We have."

"For three hundred ninety-six dollars."

"I think the menu's slightly overpriced, to be honest."

"Your dinner was almost eight hundred," he says, "and you haven't placed *one bet.*"

"As a matter of fact, I was just—"

"You can either put a deposit down or show us some action."

"Ah . . . yes . . ."

I hang up the phone. Elke's all, like, What happened? "I'm starting to crave a McMuffin," I say.

"*Me, too!*" Elke cries.

So we get the fuck out of that dump. Grab the car and tear cross-desert. At the DMV near my mom's, I surrender the license I just got four months earlier and say to the woman, "I'm back." I'm still in their database—easy. I get a California license, insurance, smog-checked, registration. I'm saving $8,000 a year. Elke and I hit the road a day later, again with no roof, hot, nearly blind for the sun, stinking of sweat, the Boss Man crooning some song about driving on highways. Elke starts laughing. I say to her, "What?" She's laughing. "What? What?" Howling. "What gives?" She's got her legs going over the door in this dubious skirt, she's wearing glasses and I'm wearing glasses, and we're both *too cool to smoke.* She's chewing gum, though. Moving that jaw. Finally she says to me, "Look at you."

"Eh?"

"I can see my legs reflected in your shades. It *might* be over the top."

"What? Me?"

"The girl, the money, the car . . ."

"Right, right. The girl, the money, the car, the spiritual emptiness, the sense of intellectual withering, squandered potential . . . All in the name"— Elke frowns as I move toward the finale—"of this evanescent dream you can feel dissolve in your grasp from the moment you touch it."

"Bah," she says. "Life is a dream."

You see, Toff? It isn't so easy.

♦

Roth was in the kitchen. "Get rid of the Toff?"

I said, "Yeah."

"Thank God. Now we can go have some fun. I've drawn you up a list, Mr. Axe. Kamikaze time, baby. The hot crew. You down to try betting some cash?"

"I'm always down for blowing up toilets."

"Good man. I've drawn up a list of every big place on the Strip where you haven't been trespassed by name."

I looked at the list. "Hm, Paris. That'll last five or six minutes. Oh, and then Caesars? You kidding?"

"You only have to do it if you want to."

Caesars was sort of a problem child among the Vegas dumps. They were big Griffin users, for one thing, but beyond that, they'd started giving attitude. Counters were getting backroomed. It had happened to people Roth knew, including to seasoned solo pros who knew their rights full well and could assert themselves. It was a recent development, too; in the old days, Caesars was famous for being laid back as far as counting was concerned. "They never liked team play," Roth said once. "That, they shut down right away. But if you were a solo guy, they kind of respected you. It was almost like they thought of us as equals. Guys in the pit would just shrug, you know, until your win became something significant." Everything changed when Caesars got bought, late in 1999, by Park Place Entertainment, same joint that owns Paris and Bally's. Suddenly they started freaking out. Mossad had had a number of near brushes and attempted backroomings since then. A particular douchebaggy character who actually, in real life, called himself "Inspector White"—*Inspector*, like he's Scotland fucking Yard—and expected us to call him that, too, kept blowing out sessions with vehemence. We didn't like to admit it, but the heat they were giving annoyed us. It did impede our willingness to play there.

"I'll try it," I said. "They use Griffin. It's a low-probability shot."

"Tell them your name is Joe Schmo. So long as you don't buy in for more than ten grand, it's no problem. Let them CTR you on the way out, when you're cashing the chips. That's all right. You're already blown at that point. Just win, Axe—it's easy."

I said I would try. This business of giving fake names in the hope you don't have to buy in very much was reserved for senior players on the team. You had to get lucky to pull it off—it was hard to play big without buying more than $10K in chips. We didn't even discuss it around junior players, because the overall policy (do *not* fuck around with CTR laws) we wanted to keep super clear.

After Paris and Caesars, Jon's list *really* went south. He had MGM Grand on that puppy. I'd been 86'd three separate times—admittedly, never by name. But such was my duty. I'd try it.

"Take Philip, Virginia, and Buck," Jon said. "See if you can make something happen."

Thirty-seven

EOS at Barbary?" Buck Zinn said. He was an old counter friend of
Roth's who had lately been joining our trips.

"That'll work."

"You really going in in that helmet?"

"We're grasping at straws. This is the best I came up with."

"What's your story going to be?"

"I'm a Viking."

"He won't be there long enough to tell a story," said Virginia. A new
player who'd been in action all summer, Virginia was a dishy blonde from
Northern California, a cooking-school dropout, and *hot*.

"Come on. Just find us some counts." I reached out my arm. They each
put a hand over mine. On three we all shouted "*Muh!*" The counters sprang
out of the car.

Alone, I pulled down the driveway, made the turn onto the Strip, then
the quick right onto Flamingo, left into Barbary, corkscrewing up the narrow ramp. Parking was easy. Only problem with the Barb was the elevators
being damn slow. Once I was outside, I used the pedestrian bridge to get
over to Bally's. Tourists were dense on the sidewalk. In the plastic Viking
helmet (comped, I believe, from Excalibur), I felt every bit as irregular as

I used to when I was fourteen, struggling through the drunkards on this very same street. Bellagio across the Strip occupied the lot where the Dunes used to be. At times I would have the illusion I'd been walking up and down Las Vegas Boulevard every waking minute of my life.

Over the driveway the sign in the shape of a hot-air balloon announced your arrival at Paris. I entered through the same set of doors the spotters had used just before. The gaming floor was mobbed. People were weaving dangerously, some of them flourishing souvenir plastic cups in the shape of the Eiffel Tower, fat straws protruding from the tip. The hubbub of voices joined with the blaring of slots, producing a Dantesque sound. As I got to the pit, I saw Buck with his hand in his lap.

"Pardon, monsieur!" I cried, dropping three Gs on the felt. The dealer was startled. Buck signaled running fifteen. Before I had the chips a Suit had arrived at the table. "Care for a rating?" he asked.

"Not so much." The words came out the wrong way. He glanced at my mid-shoe bet and was clearly displeased. "What's your name?" he demanded.

"Bob Carter."

He nodded, then left. It was bad. It felt intuitively off, like a first date that's not going to gel. Bob Carter? I thought. You dolt. What kind of Jew Viking shows up with a name that goyish?

It only took five rounds before security showed. "Mr. Carter?" asked a flic.

"Please. Bob."

"Step away from the table," he said.

"Qu'est-ce que vous dites?"

It was futile.

We met at the Barbary, went through the session accounting. I pointed toward Caesars, just across the Strip. "Next stop," I said. "You guys down?"

"It doesn't bother me," said Virginia. "You're the one they're gonna backroom."

We put our hands in again, shouting *"Muh!"* I let the spotters lead the way, entering a few minutes after. On an impulse I stopped at a craps game to buy two yellow chips, acting like I might want to bet them. Then I pretended I had chickened out. I fled the game, chips in hand, abandoned that part of the casino, came to the high-limit pit. Philip, Virginia, and Buck were all there. I decided to wait for a call-in rather than incur the variance of a set-up shoe in a casino where it probably wouldn't help: when you expect only a few minutes' play, every bet should have a real edge.

When Philip gave the signal, I descended the stairs and glided to his table. I might have been gay or might not have been. The act was little more than being a guy in a helmet. I was a crazy dude, hopped up or hepped out or strung in some fashion—that was all I really had in mind. Reading the count from Phil's hand on his arm, I slapped the $1,000 chips on two spots. The dealer called out, "Yellow action!"

A floorman rushed over. The round had been dealt. "You have a rating card?" he said.

"*I'm Josh Berg!*" Berg is my middle name. I had shouted at the guy in a deranged way, and now I was leering. I winked.

"Your card . . . ?"

"I was playing here last night for three hours." I insisted I was in the system from the night before but hadn't brought my card. He said he would check the computer. He was blinking a lot, looking flummoxed, a little stressed out. In a minute he was back, asking exactly when I had played. I said I'd been awake for days straight and the nights were all blending together. I had no idea when, but I had *played*—that's how I'd gotten the chips. "Didn't they give me credit for my action?"

"No, no, Mr. Berg. Don't worry. Your comps are all there."

"They'd best be." Virginia had a count, and I rushed to her table. I was already losing eight Gs. The CTR threshold impended: minus $10,000 and out is a rough way to go. Once I was in for $12K, the floorman returned and I coughed up my license. He had already printed a rating card for me; what would he do upon realizing that "Josh Berg" was actually Josh Berg Axelrad?

Soon he was back with the license. "There you are, Mr. Berg. Better luck."

"Thanks, boss." Was I really in the clear now? Doubtful. Probably they'd copied the license. Somebody somewhere down the line would notice the error, and that would be end of it. I proceeded to run from Buck's game to Philip's to Virginia's, seemingly heat-free. I got in for $30K. Then things *really* turned south. By the time grave started, we were stuck fifty Gs. Roth said to play through the grave shift.

Somehow they let it go down. The middle-name gambit had worked. Or it might have been the helmet and the vinyl pants. The loss couldn't have hurt the act either. By 11:00 A.M., down sixty Gs—the largest buy-in I'd had to do yet—I hardly had to feign being on drugs anymore. The weakness in my knees, the confusion, the spasms, and the drool were all genuine. When day began, Roth said to call it. Day was a tough shift to play on, and fatigue had become a concern. "We'll try again tomorrow," he said on the phone.

Yeah, right, I thought. Surely they would blow it out retro. We went home; I slept a few hours. Caesars had comped me a room, but I was too weary to bother with check-in, I had to take the spotters back in any case, and I was concerned about waking to security pounding on the door. Late in the afternoon, I drove down by myself to attempt checking in—the purpose was to see if they had barred me yet. Apparently I was still good. At the apartment I got gussied up in shiny clothes made out of synthetic polymers, gathered a rotated crew (Virginia again, along with Jimmy and Robert this time), and we rolled into action, Jimmy saying, "Thousand-dollar unit?"

"That's right."

"Have you got up to two by ten K yet?"

"Not yet."

"I'll see if I can make that happen for you."

"Muh!" I dropped them at Caesars, parked across the street at Barbary Coast (leaving your vehicle off premises facilitates the exit if there's heat), walked back over, then went up to my comped room. Inside, I sat on the

floor for a minute. I crossed my legs and tried to breathe deeply. The room was incredibly still. The hum of the HVAC was soothing. The sheets reeked sweetly of detergent. Some part of me was resisting getting started, but I took a last breath and jumped up.

Approaching the pit, I paused, leaning on a column with a view of the high-limit area. I recognized Suits from last night. There was still a good chance that I was barred but they hadn't thought to take away the comps yet. I saw the three counters in action—it was always a strange feeling, this moment before your first bet, when the pit doesn't know you're there and everything looks so calm. When I saw Jimmy signal, resistance flared up in my chest, but I forced myself out. Again a dealer hollered, "Yellow!" A floorman responded, approaching. "Mr. Berg, good to see you back."

I said it was good to be seen. He smiled and was gone in a second. Oh, oh, oh, this is good. The call-ins began to fly by, amid stunning variance. This $1,000 unit just isn't a joke. The result was swinging $10K every few minutes. Jimmy was active, rushing from one shoe to the next, delivering a flurry of counts. At one point we'd nearly gotten even—the session was up sixty Gs. It fell back again after that. Again we continued to grave shift. Roth, Neal, Buck Zinn, Lawrence Taib, and Bridget Gould had been over at Mandalay Bay, trying to get down with Zinn betting. Around five in the morning, they joined us. We had the pit completely covered. The session was truly a massive one, and improbable: nearly everyone had had major heat in this dump. I thought of Toff just begging to be allowed to come back, give a fake name, and try betting again—the truth was that it *could* be done. *If* you're a believer, Mr. Toff, the most dubious thing becomes possible. Your faith and your aggression should be limitless. Think like you're on a crusade.

It was very late when the phone calls began. The phone in the pit kept ringing. This must mean the endgame was starting. Roth had a call-in just then. As soon as I got to his table, he pulled his own bet back so I could play it heads-up. But he didn't step away from the game, as you normally would when delivering a heads-up shoe. It can look strange to just sit there, but

Roth was smiling hugely—he wanted to watch. He hadn't even handed me the count; he was just signaling bets to control me. I was betting on one spot instead of two—it's mathematically preferable playing one spot with the shoe to yourself. He had me at six Gs the first round, then seven the round after that. A senior-looking guy had stepped into the pit and was talking on the phone in a not-happy way. They seemed to have reached the state in the blow-you-out process where they're not even watching your action—the guy wasn't looking my way. Now they're just making the arrangements, I thought.

I'd won another hand and saw Roth signaling nine units. His face looked a lot like a child's. His cheeks were lit up, his eyes shone. I was standing very close to him, feeling the shared energy between the two of us, touching my chips. He said, "Wait."

"Ten?" I said, communicating openly.

He sucked air through his teeth, staring at the discards in the tray. I knew, if it was in any way mathematically defensible, that Roth would round up, not down. We are so fucking close, Jon—please let me get to ten Gs, at least once.

In the end he said, "Leave it." The bet was $9K. As it happened, I got two aces. With the split we were up to $18K. Another ace fell, so I resplit. Twenty-seven thousand on the felt. The hand ended up as a wash. It was also the last of the shoe. The cut card appeared. A moment later so did security. I saw Jimmy with a call-in and ran, but a guard reached his table before me. Jimmy was blown. Suddenly the senior-looking dude with short gray hair was beside me, saying, "If you come back again, we'll arrest you." Then he was gone. He was taking off after Jon. The session seemed pretty much over.

I had to wait on line at the cage. I was cashing something north of $70K. We'd recovered the loss from last night—actually won ten Gs overall. Depleted, and confounded by the sunlight leaking through the main door, I stared at the straps she was counting, amazed. Awful lot of cheese; it's really just pretty to watch.

I was being watched as well: the shift-manager dude and a short, fair-haired douche in a trench coat of all fucking things—he corresponded exactly to descriptions I'd heard of the infamous Inspector White—were standing a few yards away. They were observing me, discussing things between themselves. I almost felt I ought to go and thank them. "We never imagined we'd get down for more than twelve minutes, you guys. Consecutive shifts, on *two nights*? You're the best!"

"That's everything," the cashier announced. On the counter it looked like a mess: seven ten-straps, a five-strap, and change. I asked if she might have a bag. She was able to procure a paper sack. With the cash in, it looked a doggie bag.

As I turned to leave, the boss dude stepped forward. "Hope you had fun," he said darkly. "Your face is going to be all over this town by the end of the day. You can't play with those guys with impunity, pal."

Huh? I couldn't understand what he meant. My face was *already* all over this town, and it had been for almost a year. Then White joined the show, saying dramatically, "Welcome to Vegas."

Astonished, I strolled outdoors, toting my doggie bag cheerfully, drowning in the brightness of morning. They *still* thought my last name was Berg. "Welcome to Vegas"—what else could it mean? The sons of bitches thought I was a greenhorn, here on his very first trip. Oh, Mr. Toff: maybe we can be immortal after all! Faith, Mr. Toff. Life's a dream!

♦

A couple days later, with cash in my pants, the top down, no shades because it was night, the big beam of light in the rearview mirror looking more than ever like a symbol of hope, I was hauling ass out of the valley. I went into Utah and over the Rockies to Denver. More of everything was waiting, I believed. The country was small when you drove from one coast to the other, but the thing was that you could keep circling, east to west and west to east eternally, at least until the Saudis stopped shipping us oil.

As I rolled through Nebraska plains, my thoughts kept turning to Elke.

I was on my way to meet her mom and dad in Chicago—we'd come to that point; I was glad. Her arms would be around me that night. Maybe I should ask her to marry me, out of the blue—shock Mom, shock Dad, shock her, shock me. "Well, son, she isn't done with college yet."

"A certain kind of truth is eternal. Nothing will change. I could marry her now or I could marry her twenty years hence, but we belong to-gether, sir. . . ."

I was moving through Iowa, looking at hills, smelling the grasses and the corn, smelling the sweet, rich shit from the dairy farms, liking it all. . . . It was nature and something beyond, this incredible fusion, the fruit of human history and human thought, mixed with the raw stuff from God: wilderness and interstates; the power of chance and the power of money; a whole nation left half bare and riddled with parks and with madness but still veined with roads, all of it accessible to anyone with credit cards to pay for his gas; across the rural part of Illinois, beyond the Mississippi and Daven-port, I was loving the earth and its scent, feeling pangs over our history and loss on behalf of the Natives, almost wished that we could give it back, until in the twilight, gray, magisterial and domineering, of almost impossible scale, jutting out like some kind of eruption, the Sears Tower came into view. If you're an American, without Native blood, the sight of that beast forgives everything. All of what we'd had to do was justified. No harm had ever been done that could not be let go and forgotten. Oh, but we are bad, and we are strong motherfuckers; our credit-card limits are high. The gas belongs to us, as well it should, for we *build shit like that*—claim the sky, claim the moon, and we're gunning for Mars next, folks. The spirit that built us that tower could easily keep going, and a part of it's even in me.

Approaching the Loop, downtown, I got out my phone to call Elke. Nine P.M. meant I was late. The date was the tenth of September, I'll note. It didn't mean a thing at the time.

PART III

Over the Top

Thirty-eight

Zinn was at the wheel, and Trudy in front. I was in the backseat be-hind Zinn. I must have ended up back there as a result of the way we had exited due to the heat at Lake Charles.

It could have been three in the morning. We were upbeat, thanks partly to the variance, which had been generous, partly to the fact of where we were, with two days left on our trip, riding I-10 in the direction of Baton Rouge. After Baton Rouge is New Orleans, after New Orleans is Bay St. Louis; Gulfport is next, then Biloxi. You understand there's a plea-sure, almost a decadence, having all those towns with all those games lined up along one highway, waiting for you in the night? And you have the crew, and the money? No shortage of gas?

We'd been on the bridge a few minutes. Technically the name for that part of the road is the Atchafalaya Swamp Freeway. It goes on for eighteen miles. This is an elevated stretch where I-10 flies through a swamp. It's the biggest swamp in the nation. A lot of Louisiana, from the vantages you get on the interstate, looks like anyplace else, but not here. Murk extends as far as you can see. You coast above the ominous waters.

The speed limit's lower on the bridge, but ol' Zinn hadn't made the ad-justment. From where I was sitting, with my head leaned left I could just see the gauge. I considered speaking up once again, but this is delicate. Formally, I was the boss man running the trip, but we were all friends, to an extent, and Buck Zinn was older than I was—he had a law degree, for God's sake, and more years playing blackjack than I did.

Earlier in the day, when we were coming out of Marksville going south on obscure county roads, I *had* spoken up. "Remember, Buck, that story Jon has about his counter friends who got pulled over?"

"I do."

"What state was that in?"

"Louisiana."

"Cops find the money?"

"They did."

"Did problems ensue?"

"I'll slow down."

Trudy was talking, rambling on to Buck about her graduate work in artificial intelligence and linguistics. Buck was pretending to listen. Crammed in the back were Virginia, myself, and a counter named Perry Clutch, recruited by Buck in '01. Way back.

The flash came like an idea—a sparkle of blue light so evanescent I wasn't even sure I'd seen it. Then it resurged. It reflected off windows and ceiling. It throbbed with an urgency, ghostlike.

Thoughtfully Zinn said, "Hmm."

Cops, but . . . for us? Not for us?

I squirmed, looking out the rear window. It was as bright and uncanny back there as the landing scene at the end of *Close Encounters of the Third Kind*. Headlights like two little stars, blazing close behind, crowned with that spangle of blue.

"Here we go," Buck said.

It was us. He slowed and began pulling over. The voice came over the bullhorn once we had stopped. *"Driver! Step out of the car."*

"What the fuck?" Trudy said.

Buck eased the door open, peeking back to make sure there was no car coming. When he got out, the cop appeared near Trudy's door, on the passenger side, beckoning. Zinn stepped around cautiously, not quite holding his hands up.

The cop gave an order. We couldn't make it out in the car.

Zinn shifted around, and he planted his hands on the hood.

All I could see of the cop was that he was white, cop-shaped, uniformed, possibly young. Patting under Zinn's arms, along his sides, he eventually came to his pockets. That's where he stopped. He was touching the right pants pocket, looking at Zinn very strangely. Zinn had a troubled expression. I saw he was speaking.

Their low voices warbled unintelligibly. Occasional cars whooshed past. None of us inside was saying a word. Perry had his forehead to the window. Virginia's mouth was open in an O. The blue lights continued to pulse.

Zinn and the cop were talking, Zinn still with those hands to the hood. The cop wasn't writing a ticket or anything reassuring like that.

After a long round of questioning, Zinn stood erect. The cop walked back toward his own car. Zinn returned, carefully treading. He opened the door and got in.

"How did that go?" Trudy said.

"Not great. I have thirty grand in my pants."

He was staring ahead with his hands on the wheel, the engine still off.

"He felt it. He asked what it was. I thought about what I could say. I don't *have* to answer, but fuck it—he's going to find out anyway at that point. I told him, 'It's money,' and he asked me how much. So I told him. He says, 'Why do you have that much money?' I was trying to explain about card counting. . . ."

It wasn't clear how much of this the cop had understood. But he did ask Zinn whether others in the car were carrying cash like that, too, and Buck told him yes, that we were. At the cop's request, he estimated the total among all of us. "I told him one-twenty."

I said, "That's actually low."

"What happens now?" Trudy said.

Buck shrugged.

We waited in silence.

The flashers shone over the swamp.

Thirty-nine

Perry Clutch was staring at his lap. His face looked gray tinged with green. He had an amalgamated appearance, seeming maybe fifteen years old due to a softness in his facial structure, a gawky gentleness about his hazel eyes, but, simultaneously, with his louche mustache and the dense, very large-bore and dark, manly black stubble standing out on his blood-drained cheeks, also looking old and destroyed.

Perry's your problem, I thought. He doesn't have any confidence. My leadership is suspect to him. Maybe to Buck, too, and certainly—most dangerously—to *me*. I have about the self-confidence here of a twit like G. W. Bush if he hadn't been born into wealth and found God.

We continued to wait in the car.

A second police cruiser had arrived on the scene, and the lights on the swamp had redoubled. The leafless bald cypresses lurking out there—each standing aloof from the rest—seemed nearly to move, looking like gaunt skeletons in a stop-motion trick. Coming toward us stealthily, mischievous.

White Cop had been joined by a Black Cop. They strode up together, the latter in charge. He signaled Perry Clutch to roll his window down.

"You-all are doing *what* in Louisiana?"

"We're gamblers," I offered. "Play blackjack. We use a method known as counting cards. It's a legal, legitimate system for winning money at the game."

"Counting cards?" he said.

"Yes." Offering to explain, I told him that all we did was some math in our heads while we played.

"Where you coming from tonight?"

"Lake Charles."

"Where are you going?"

"Baton Rouge, at the moment."

"At the moment?" he said.

"Yes, sir."

"You're going to count cards in Baton Rouge?"

"We're going to try."

"What does that mean—you're going to try?"

"Casinos don't always . . . allow it."

"Why don't they allow it? It's legal."

"Oh, yes." It seemed worthwhile repeating that point. "But casinos don't like you to do it. It genuinely works, and so they end up losing money, and they don't approve of that. If they realize you're doing it, sometimes they ask you to leave."

"They ask you to leave at Lake Charles?"

"They did."

"Where else you been playing?"

"Cypress Bayou. Marksville before that."

"They ask you to leave?"

"Yes, sir."

"Anyplace else?"

"Up in Shreveport."

"They ask you to leave?"

"Yes, they did."

"Which casinos up there?"

"Um—"

"All of them?"

"We never went into the Hollywood, so . . ." My voice trailed off. The cop's eyes had started to bulge. He looked like a temperamental drill sergeant in a war movie.

"You, you, you, you—licenses."

Trudy, Perry, Virginia, and I passed our IDs to him. He and White returned to their cruisers. Perry was moving his lips, but he wasn't saying anything. Zinn hummed morosely. Trudy turned to face the backseat.

"Is this bad?" she said. "Empirically it *looks* bad."

Her blue eyes were resting on me. Answer the woman, I thought. Take charge. Manage the emotions of the crew. Speak with the authority Jon Roth would have in a moment like this. I was frozen.

In over my head, that's a fact. I wasn't Jon Roth. I wasn't going to be Jon Roth. I should never have tried to be. Bin Laden, you've fucked me again. The process of team breakdown and dissolution had begun with the terror attacks, though it's possible the fissures had already started by then. But things were sped up.

There was just the phone ringing at first. I woke, not knowing where I was. The room was a decent-type room. The ceiling was high, and the paint on the walls had a sheen. The TV was newfangled. I remember sun was glowing in the curtains. I could have been comped in anywhere from Vegas to Atlantic City, for all I knew at that moment. It was the room line ringing; my cell phone was off. You don't answer the room phone in this situation. An unexpected call when you're comped is bad news. Security saying to get out. Then I remembered: Chicago—this isn't a comp, but who's calling?

Elke. She gave me the news. I explained why that news was impossible. This caused Elke to yell. In an effort to get the TV going, I knocked the remote to the floor and then under the bed. There was a moment of slapstick, yelling back and forth on the phone while I got down on all fours. By the time the news was on, both towers were already toast. Twenty planes, they said, were unaccounted for still. The hotel I was in was a W, directly kitty-corner to the Sears Tower. "I've got to get the fuck out of here."

"*Yes.*"

Assuming escape mode, I fled the premises—pausing downstairs to get into my box for the bankroll, lest it be buried and lost when the tower came down—hopped into Surrender, went north via Lake Shore Drive to the tony little hood where Elke's folks lived. Her father just stared when he answered the door. (Our meeting last night had been awkward. Elke hadn't told them what I did for a living. They weren't exactly thrilled to find out.) Then he extended a hand and said somberly, "Welcome to history."

"Right!" What does one say? I didn't know. *No one knows.* I wasn't enough of a man for this shit. We spent the day watching the footage.

That night I got Roth on the phone. "We still doing this play in Seattle?" I asked.

"I don't see any reason why not."

"I'm going to start driving in that direction."

"Have fun. Let me know if you find any gems in those tiny North Dakota games, Axe. We'll see you in Washington State."

I guess we were still in denial. Blackjack would not be the same. It wasn't an optimal period in U.S. history to be locked into a business model dependent on carrying large amounts of cash through airport security constantly. On the thirteenth I drove out to Fargo. Roth called that night. The trip in Seattle was off. Airplanes weren't even flying yet. "And we don't know what it's going to be like with the security stuff once they are. We can't carry bankroll right now. We have to expect them to find it, and not only that—there are going to be all these questions about terrorist finance and whatnot. Cash in this environment's a problem. It sucks, Axe. The world just changed."

Other things had been changing besides. Conditions on the Strip were growing worse. Premium joints like Mirage were turning to eight-deck shoes, worth less to counters than six. Rules were deteriorating everywhere.

You found hit-seventeen on the Strip now. This seemingly moderate rule change increased the house edge about 60 percent in a shoe game.

Eight-deck and hit-seventeen games at least remained beatable. Another new development was worse. A company named ShuffleMaster, maker of automatic shuffling machines, had introduced a device known as the King continuous shuffler. These insidious black boxes had taken the place of the dealing shoes in a number of casinos in Las Vegas. Inside, they kept multiple decks shuffling on an ongoing basis. Every couple rounds, the dealer would insert the latest discards into the top of the unit; those cards could reappear as soon as the very next round. It resembled a shoe made of infinite decks. Counting was worthless against it.

The King threatened to end the game outright. At one point the Rio adopted it. They put it on every single table on their main floor. The casino was completely unplayable. Later they removed all their Kings, but soon other casinos were trying it. The typical preference was to use it on only a limited number of tables. What was happening overall, it seemed to us, was that the major casinos were sharply cutting back the number of high-value (i.e., six-deck, stand-seventeen, noncontinuous-shuffler) games on their floors. They offered some games with Kings, some games with hit-seventeen, and a mixture of eight-deck and six. We were left with fewer tables to select from, and it stood to reason that surveillance would devote more scrutiny to the few games they knew we would like. They could focus their attention more effectively. The heat had indeed gotten faster.

Aldous Kaufman in particular had been arguing for some time that call-ins in Vegas were dying. It was a strange thing to hear as my personal bankroll was swelling—I won hundreds of Gs for the team in '01, and my income was over $120,000 that year. I wanted to think it could last. Roth said it could; Matcha was ambivalent; Mateo didn't care one way or the other—he had already started to play less, turning new attention to poker. When the terrorists hit and the team went into hibernation for six weeks, everybody had time to mull.

We resumed play slowly. In October we drove to AC. None of us wanted to fly. The next trip was in Minnesota: I took Surrender, Aldous took his new BMW and brought Roth along. We got most of the money there that way. Afterward we caravanned to Vegas, running call-ins again in November, on the occasion of the opening of the Palms.

By the start of '02, we were comfortable flying—not that it did us much good. The first quarter that year was the first losing quarter since the team had begun its expansion in late '99. We lost in Chicago. We lost in AC. We won in Biloxi but lost in Las Vegas and Foxwoods. Hundreds of hours of work, thousands of miles of travel, and we had less than nothing to show for it. Variance, at times, gets painful like that.

The big news came in the summer. I heard it from Neal: Jon and Bridget had gotten engaged. "So that's it," Neal said. We were sitting in his living room. (Neal was living in Vegas year-round and had a place of his own.)

"Happily ever after, huh?"

"Maybe for them." He offered a smoke. I declined. "That's it for Jon Roth and Mossad. He's not going to play anymore. It's big, right?"

"Holy fucking shit, mac."

"I know, mac. I know."

"What does this mean?" There *was* no Mossad without Roth. "What happens?"

"The future's in our hands, boy. We can decide."

"What's Jon going to do?"

"I don't know. He was talking about trading on his own account. He's not really hurting for cash. I think he's going to try to live stably, you know. Wake up the same place every day. . . . He said he wants the team to stay intact."

"They're going to have kids?"

"People do."

"That's fucked up."

"The species must continue, mac. Remember."

I shrugged. "How's it gonna work?"

"With the team? I could see playing more, running some trips. Aldous is a question mark. Where do you stand?"

"I wasn't going to give it up quite yet."

"Bankroll's no problem. I'm sure Jon would want to invest, if we need passive money. If Aldous stays in, then we probably don't need it." He nodded toward the window. The Stratosphere was framed almost perfectly in the center. "You can run more trips if you want."

I'd become a junior-level manager. In Vegas I trained new gorillas and was also charged with overseeing the pipeline of gorillas—making sure new faces kept coming. Aside from the cell plays and a handful of solo trips, all of which were independent ventures, I'd also run a full-scale call-in bank: a $500-unit play in Tunica (it lost). With Jon gone I started doing more.

I ran another Mississippi junket. We won. Then I led a crew in AC. On the New Year's trip, everybody played. But Neal stepped back at the start of '03—he, too, was thriving with poker. He was happy to invest, happy to play from time to time, but he didn't want ongoing responsibility for keeping Mossad intact. Aldous was also playing poker, and trading some stocks on his own. He wanted to play just occasionally. Jimmy had started with poker full-time. Chuck had a straight-person job but still joined trips now and then. Players like Sammy, Buck, Trudy, Virginia, and Perry were still generally down, but they didn't want to play tons of trips and they couldn't contribute much in investments. The team *existed,* but it was fatigued.

I had the opportunity to save it or grow it. The groundwork was already laid: we had accounting forms printed, procedures drawn up, a database that tracked people's heat. It was potentially my chance to turn into a Roth. The question was whether I wanted to—and whether I was smart enough, strong enough. What *were* my longer-term goals? From early '01 until early '02, I'd been geared toward net worth. I wanted a hundred grand, and then got it. I took my mom to Italy for a vacation. Next, I thought, *two hundred* grand. With two hundred Gs you can do things. Maybe I would open a bar. I could buy a hot-air balloon and paint genitals on it, then float around Salt Lake City perturbing the Mormons.

Counting still worked. You could do it. Plus-one, minus-one, boom. To profit you maximize volume. Find a way to get down, and then do it again and again. "Repeat until rich," as Jon Roth used to say—though always in Roth's mouth the phrase had an undertone of irony; he was rich already. He'd started because counting was fun, and eventually, I think, contempt for the casinos kept his motivation high.

Contempt became a factor for me, too. There was also some greed, some inertia. There had once been a hunger for faraway things, for extraordinary images and spectacle, for danger (within constraints). Somehow it was hard to be impressed anymore. I wasn't quite sure what had changed, but even now, on the side of the bridge with the fog-riddled swamp for a background, with Trudy awaiting her answer, the heart-poundingness and the full-bodied panic I'd known in the past weren't present. I *knew* we'd be fine with the police.

The moment had an aspect of playacting to it. "We've broken no law," I announced. "Sooner or later they'll figure that out."

"You're positive?" Virginia here adopting the role of the anxious damsel, her eyes sinking into her face.

"Even in the worst case—they come up with some charge, they arrest us—even then we'll be fine. It *will* blow over; you know this. But I don't think that's going to happen."

A rap on the window. Our friends had returned. "Perry Clutch?" White Cop said. He asked Clutch to step outside. They all marched back to the trunk. After eight minutes or so, they returned asking for Trudy. Next they took Virginia, and finally myself.

White Cop patted me down, his hands reaching under my bulky leather motorcycle jacket, over my hips, down my legs. When that was done, they started with the questions. Black did most of the talking. White was the one taking notes. Their faces were dark blanks, spastic lights blazing behind them. I was asked again where we had played. They had me recount our itinerary. Black seemed truly professional, concerned to understand the situation, wanting to know what he had on his hands. I mentioned our paperwork, and they asked for it. I collected player sheets from everyone. I also handed over the tax returns I carried with me whenever I was traveling with money; I used these as proof that I declared as a professional gambler and had done so for multiple years. The cops seemed fairly well satisfied. "You can sit down," Black said.

We were waiting in the car. Fast-food debris lay crushed on the floor. There was the smell of old french fries and unshowered flesh. Black returned. Trudy rolled the window down. He had a sheet of paper in his hand.

"Mr. Clutch?"

Perry said, "Yeah?"

"You won eight dollars at Horseshoe, I see."

"That sounds about right."

"*Eight* dollars?"

"Yes, sir."

"And you call yourself a card counter, Perry?"

Belatedly it registered as humor.

Perry said, "Look at the next session down. Harrah's Shreveport."

The cop's gaze dropped to the sheet. He lifted an eyebrow. "Good work. That's more like what we'd expect." Now he glanced around at the rest of us. "We got in touch with some casinos. They definitely know who you are. The Isle does *not* want you back there again."

He said that was all. We could go.

Forty

They hadn't even bothered with a ticket. As Zinn pulled away, those lights were still throbbing behind us. From a distance it looked like a film crew working on the side of the road. Gradually the fireworks vanished. The darkness wrapped round us again, broken by the moon overhead, spectral flat clouds gleaming like mercury globs in the sky, patches of gray fog draping the cypresses' trunks. Then the bridge ended.

Zinn kept the speed down as we passed through a woods. Soon there was a new, long, grotesque-looking, purely functional steel bridge spanning a river. The Mississippi was immense in this location. Baton Rouge glowed on the far side, a thin rung of lights trailing north. I could hear Neal's voice: *Well, mac, another gambling town.*

We took some wisp of a ramp and were on a street close to the river. Buildings looked mostly abandoned. Everything was moist, though we hadn't seen rain. The first casino we tried was the Rouge. It was a riverboat and a toilet. Zinn stopped near the entrance. Trudy said, "I'll go and look." She hopped out.

It only took a couple minutes. She reappeared, shaking her head. "They have one open shoe with a five-hundred-dollar max and eight players playing seven spots."

"Could we ask them all to leave?" Perry joked.

"We should try that."

Zinn said, "Moving right along."

The only other option was the Argosy, where I'd had extreme heat on this shift from last year. I'd bought in for twenty—they'd liked that—but then I disappointed by recovering it all. The act had been ridiculous, comical: I told the shift boss the money wasn't mine, it was actually the property of "some gentlemen over in New Orleans" to whom I'd been charged with transporting it, but I'd seen the casino and had to stop in. "Now," I said, "I *have* to win it back. Otherwise . . ." I drew a line across my throat with my finger. The shift boss responded with a grave little nod. I almost couldn't believe he could believe it. He was very unhappy to learn he'd been fooled.

"There's the door," Buck said. He'd pulled in to a service lot adjacent to the boat, a place where you weren't meant to park. Trudy sprang out to go scout the conditions. "Back in a minute," she said.

I was staring out the window. I saw the man without really caring at first. He hadn't registered yet as a cop. He was moving from his cruiser toward us. Suddenly he shouted and his gun was in his hands. He was aiming for the door Buck had mentioned.

Freeze? Did he say "Freeze"? Do they really say "Freeze"? Now this guy looks very familiar. . . .

Trudy, at the door, had her hands in the air. The cop, Black Cop, was still shouting. She turned around to face him, as instructed. "Move toward the car. Put both hands down on the hood." She complied. Through the windshield she looked at us, terrified. Buck said, "Oh. Oh, no."

"Driver. Turn off your engine." He shifted his aim to Buck's head. Zinn tried to swivel the key, but the car kept purring. *"Driver, do it now,"* the cop said.

Buck swore in a whisper, still trying with the key. Perry said, "You have it in park?"

"Oh. Fuck . . ." He shifted, killed it, raised both his hands. Perry, Virginia, and I did the same. I had my palms flat against the ceiling.

"Step out of the car. Exit with your hands up. Follow my instructions exactly." When Buck was outside, the cop had him turn, arms still in the air, and walk slowly backward. "Move toward my voice. Closer. Now *stop*. Get down on your knees. Keep your arms up." The officer was pure dominance, rushing toward Buck with that gun poised, seizing and cuffing his wrists.

Now he was aiming at me, telling me to step out. Arms up, I took backward steps toward his voice. A shot of terror skittered through my veins, leaving behind a heaving chest but also a feeling of clarity, like the smooth water trailing a wave. I'd rehearsed for this scene, dreamed about playing it for years. Each time goons chased us out of some dump, I imagined I was John fucking Dillinger: the baddest, most wanted, most feared. That was a ludicrous fantasy for a law-abiding blackjack professional in the age of al Qaeda—my dreams were September 10 dreams. We weren't bad motherfuckers at all: not in the scheme of things. "Down on your knees," the cop said. Yes, *sir*. He made the cuffs tighter than warranted.

Perry and then Virginia were summoned, the latter in tears, asking, "Why? Why are they doing this?" Trudy was last. All of us were lined up and kneeling. The asphalt was rough on your bones. Cruisers with lights in the hues of the American flag were pouring from the street and surrounding us.

Black stood before us. "You-all aren't under arrest at this time." I found that an odd point of view. "We're holding you for questioning. Be patient." He left.

White Cop came moments later. We'd identified him as the dumb one by now. He said at once, "You're under arrest. Y'all have the right to remain silent." He continued with Miranda, pacing with a bastardly swagger. Then he was gone, too. Are we fucking arrested or not? Dillinger never put up with this shit.

I'd like to say it got even worse. I'd like to say wilder things happened. I made a sudden break for it, was shot in the knee but managed to dive into the river. For an hour I swam, until I saw lights bearing down and heard the chopping of a chopper. Grabbing the rope, I held on for dear life as he hefted me up: Neal Matcha, saying, *"Muh!* Nice getaway, mac. Let's clear the fuck out of this state."

"Where are we going?"

"Jon bought a mansion in Cuba."

"Hot damn!"

"Here's a money belt. Let's make a tourniquet."

In fact they installed us in separate cruisers borrowed from Baton Rouge PD, and then the troopers and the local cops hung around shooting the shit. The legroom was bad in the backseat. The cuffs dug into your spine. But other than that, with the relaxed attitude of the policemen out there, it was hard to believe we were fucked. The one worrisome sign was the scanner I saw in the front of the car: it had a text description of our vehicle, complete with the plates, and the advisory *"Wanted for fraud."*

Time passed. Black opened my door. He knelt down, wanting to talk. "Are you going to help me?"

Did I hear that right? "You want *me* to help *you?"*

"We're trying to understand this situation."

"I think I need a lawyer from now on."

"You-all are a part of a group?"

I said, "Sure."

"Tell me how the counting stuff works."

I explained how the plus-one, minus-one went, emphasizing that it was only really thoughts going by in our heads: no devices, no cheating.

"So it's *not* illegal?"

My God, kid. When you as a cop are asking that question of a person you've just locked up, please know you've done something wrong. I said, "No."

He thanked me, then got on the phone. Ten minutes later they went around letting us out. Black Cop uncuffed me. "Go stand over there."

Buck was leaning on a brick wall, taking out a pack of smokes. He offered me one, and I had to accept. That's how the scene's supposed to go. It may be worth noting they forced us to wait, saying we had to pose for some photographs, then could be released. I could mention the photographer's not being a cop. In fact, she was casino security. Buck Zinn probably said to the police, "Are you requiring us to pose for pictures this private company wants to take of us, as a condition of our release?" I could mention that Black wouldn't answer that question, but White said, "Yes. Yes, we are." It might be worth recounting our outrage, understanding, as we very quickly did, that it was probably the Argosy, having been phoned by the police back when we were on the side of that bridge and they were calling area casinos to learn who we were, that ended up calling them back (after we'd been let go), alleging some imagined act of "fraud," prompting our ludicrous semi-arrest and eventual release without charge. I could claim we were trembling with anger, that we vowed to get revenge, all of us blinded by rage: some of these things might be true. But mainly we just felt exhausted. It was hard to be impressed anymore.

Forty-one

Fullerton Public Library, Commonwealth Avenue, Fullerton, "the OC," California . . . The first thing I picked up was Elie Wiesel's *Night*. I flipped through some chapters. I remember thinking, I can do this.

It was 2004. A week and a half earlier, I'd spent my first New Year's outside of Las Vegas since blackjack began. The Papster and I had a beer in a neighborhood bar right at midnight. He asked what the future held for his son, the professional gambler.

"Thinking of writing a book."

"What kind of a book?" my dad asked.

"Not really sure. Something *true*."

"That's pretty vague."

He was right. I set aside some time to study the matter, and there I was soon at that carrel, perusing a Holocaust memoir. I also took a look at *Naked Lunch*. The two books got me fired up. I'd always meant to be a writer. I'd figured that's what a man did. The only impediments I was aware of were lack of talent, absence of experience, stunted vocabulary, short attention span—in fact, almost a form of pre-middle-age senility that caused my mind to jump from concept to concept and percept to percept without synthesis, retention, or awareness. Probably take a couple days of practice,

I decided, before I commence with my version of *Night*. I'll be a writer by the end of the month.

With that dream as a guide, I started announcing to teammates my intention to play fewer trips. "What's your plan?" Trudy asked. "Play some poker?"

"Not for me. I suck at Texas hold 'em, you'll recall. I'd just really like to slow down. . . ."

"Is it because you made so little money last year?"

My 2003 income was barely $35K, down from 88 the previous year. I said, "No. Blackjack conditions are decent. I think it's a fine time to play. There are more tribal games now than ever. I just want to try to sit quietly. Think."

"That's pretty vague," Trudy said.

I spent some time in California with my parents, and I went to the library five days a week. I also played a number of trips. But I'd started getting ready for a different way of life. Surely there'd been enough craziness, now. I had to calm down. I had to make sure I got married. (Elke and I had split up back in 2002.) A man should be a writer, and a man should have a wife—or a husband, if that's what he wants.

Still, in the Fullerton Library, where I walked from my mom's house each day, I saw certain omens that troubled me. Among the regulars were homeless and crazies. There was a man who had an opus of his own: nearly every afternoon he was scribbling long notes in a neat, tiny print on the insides of candy wrappers scattered all over the table. A life in the library didn't guarantee you were sane or in any way stable. Some people went in there and never came out.

Forty-two

Basically it sold like *that:* the Book. It was magic. Especially since there wasn't any book. What there was was a proposal I had written. The writing in the proposal was, I believed, very poor. But I had a story, and I had a sort of platform to promote myself with.

The platform had led to an agent. This is all "inside baseball," I guess. I'd been performing in New York, doing live monologues with this group called The Moth, and from there I'd ended up on NPR a few times—discussing developments in the gambling industry for the *Marketplace* program, under the pseudonym "Lee Aaron Blair."

We sold it in March of '05. It was done. I was a writer. Hadn't *written,* but I had a contract, and for now that was almost as good. "How much did you get?" Chuck Small asked one night over beer, when I was telling him and Jon about the news.

"Three hundred Gs. Minus the agent's cut," I said.

"*Not bad!* Who's the publisher?"

"It's an imprint at Penguin."

"The Axe blew up Penguin for three hundred Gs!"

"What happens now?" Jon said.

"Now? I write."

"Do you know how to do that?"

"Um." The truth was, I had spent the past month playing poker online. I didn't know how to write a book at all. I had never even written a story I'd liked, despite trying off and on through the years. I didn't play poker well either, but it efficiently helped kill the time, of which there was tons, every day. All you had to do was wake up and log on. There was no need to get out of bed.

I'd dabbled in online hold 'em, playing here and there throughout 2004 (I broke even that year, which, after you factor in the house's rake, is sort of like winning). Aldous kept saying how good the games were. Ever since then-amateur Chris Moneymaker won an entry into the 2003 World Series of Poker through a $39 Internet tournament, proceeding to capture the $2.5 million first prize, Internet poker had boomed. The money was ample and loose, Aldous said. He made beating the games sound easy.

"The key," he'd explained, "is playing so tight you can't even believe it. Fold, fold, fold, fold, fold. I'm in there with aces, kings, queens, jacks, and I'm not too happy about the jacks. Also ace-king and ace-queen. That's *it*. Everything else I just muck."

His methods sounded fairly scientific. He would play as many as four tables, up to thirty-six opponents at once. Rather than study their individual styles by watching what they did with their hands, as one might in a live game, he had software running in the background sucking up data on what everybody did. On the rare occasions he actually got involved in a hand, he could instantly check stats on whomever he was playing against. He could know quantitatively how often they called, how often they raised. This would help with his further decisions. But, Aldous said, his hands were so good to begin with that he rarely folded once he'd played past the initial two cards. "If you see me on the flop"—the flop is the second of the four rounds of betting in hold 'em; it's followed by the turn, then the river— "you're probably going to see me on the end."

Inspired by this, but ignoring most of his technical points, I'd begun "multi-tabling" (playing simultaneous games). I would click back and forth between windows, in a torpid kind of frenzy, enjoying myself. I tried to play tight but didn't always succeed. That was fine; it was only a hobby.

Somehow, in April—the same month my book contract came in the mail—I managed to get stuck two Gs for the month. I registered this as a problem. The solution was clear: Restricting myself to one table, I started folding most hands just the way Aldous said. I finished that month in the black.

I thought it was the end of it. In May, Neal, myself, and a couple others ran a blackjack bank in Las Vegas. It felt something like a reunion. I hadn't seen Neal in almost six months, since a play we had done last November. In Vegas it was hard to get down; we ended with a trivial loss. When the bank break was over, we played pot-limit hold 'em in Neal's apartment. I was drinking, not taking it seriously, though the pots sometimes got pretty big.

On one occasion I had called with queen-deuce. It's hard to say what I was thinking. (Queen-deuce is far, far, far off the short list of playable hands someone like Aldous would restrict himself to.) The flop came queen-high. I made a small bet; Neal raised. He probably had a hand like ace-queen. This meant I was in serious trouble. Foolishly, I called, and when the turn brought a deuce, I made a pot-size bet into Neal. He looked at that deuce and then looked into my eyes. "No, mac," he said. "No. No." He almost laughed as he folded his hand. What got to me wasn't that he'd read me so well, it was that my old mentor was scolding me. I was embarrassed, and I wished I could explain that to me, regardless of the stakes, poker was only a game. It was what we used to call "silly betting"—the same thing as craps or roulette. It just wasn't that big a deal.

Forty-three

Three weeks later I went to Chase. Things had changed. The vault keeper Bev, who used to spend her working days downstairs waiting to let you in through the locked glass door, had been dismissed. There was nobody down there. I was alone in a basement. Through the wall I saw the vault. Its circular door, hanging open, looked about the size of the cross section of a giant sequoia I'd once seen in a museum. Something about it was worrisome. It's an eye. It's an eye? It's a big eye, and it's watching. Mounted on the ceiling in the hall where I stood was an actual eye—er, camera—black, shiny, staring me down with no blink. They can see what I'm thinking, I told myself. I want to throw my body through the glass.

Someone from Customer Service upstairs brought me back down and, with her keys jangling on a bracelet-size ring, got my box out and presented it.

"Thanks." I shut the closet door behind me, trembling. The odors were sweat, grimy cash, dust from the carpet, and something resembling burned metal. I took ten Gs from the box. *Money!* Forgot I was rich.

With a strap in my pocket, I climbed up the stairs. I waited on line for a teller. The familiarity of all this was part of what got to my head. I used to come with money all the time. For a while there in 2000 (before Jon gave me the lecture about financial institutions not being toys), I was doing this thing with the cash—"round-tripping your bankroll," Jon called it—where I deposited my money after each trip, let it chill a few days earning interest, then withdrew it again for the next trip: eighteen Gs, twenty, twenty-five, back and forth, in and out, like the whole fucking thing was a game. Once, in Park Slope, I ended up at a Chase I hadn't been to before. I'd been in the neighborhood shopping for wigs and was set to depart for AC from the Port Authority in just a couple hours, but I got behind schedule—there was no time to go to my regular branch, where the shenanigans with bankroll were familiar. So I strolled through the door of this branch I didn't know, filled out the slip for withdrawal of eighteen Gs, and tucked it in the slot for the teller. That was yet another time a teller freaked out. She summoned her boss. The guy started out by protesting—"We don't keep cash like that handy," blah, blah—and then, in the end, he relented. I said, "Thanks. Make it fast. I got a bus to catch, man." That almost undid the whole thing, when I mentioned the bus. I should've said I had a limo waiting.

"Afternoon," the teller said presently. "How's your day?"

"I lost all my money," I said.

"I'm *sorry*." Wonderful, an actor, I thought. You and I ought to go on a date, pal. He had no way of knowing I had actually drained five Gs and depleted my checking account playing poker on the Internet moronically. I'd proceeded with such abandon—and I suddenly had so much clout on the PartyPoker site, which had granted instant approval of Electronic Funds Transfers (EFTs) so I wouldn't have to wait for my "reloads" to clear before getting back into action—that a number of transfers had bounced. I was in hock to a Web site based in Gibraltar.

"Don't worry," I said. "I have more." I slipped ten Gs in the slot.

"Let's not go and lose all of this," he advised. The smile I read as flirtatious.

Forty-four

PARTYPOKER TRANSACTION HISTORY—JUNE 2005

DATE AND TIME	DEPOSITS TO POKER ACCOUNT	WITHDRAWALS
06/01/05 11:53 A.M.		$965
06/01/05 02:09 P.M.	$2,000	
06/01/05 02:14 P.M.	$250	
06/01/05 02:25 P.M.	$250	
06/01/05 04:10 P.M.	$250	
06/01/05 04:24 P.M.	$250	
06/01/05 04:53 P.M.	$250	
06/02/05 11:48 A.M.	$250	
06/02/05 01:55 P.M.	$250	
06/03/05 09:06 A.M.	$250	
06/03/05 09:50 A.M.	$250	
06/03/05 05:23 P.M.	$250	
06/04/05 02:54 P.M.	$250	
06/04/05 03:17 P.M.	$250	
06/04/05 03:28 P.M.	$250	
06/05/05 11:17 P.M.	$50	
06/07/05 10:34 A.M.	$50	

06/07/05 03:18 P.M.		$2,192
06/09/05 04:19 P.M.	$1,000	
06/09/05 06:34 P.M.		$59
06/18/05 11:31 P.M.*	$1,000	
06/19/05 02:53 A.M.	$1,500	
06/21/05 05:10 A.M.		$5,081
06/22/05 03:23 P.M.	$500	
06/22/05 05:32 P.M.		$729
06/23/05 03:15 A.M.	$500	
06/23/05 04:19 A.M.		$593
06/24/05 11:38 A.M.	$500	
06/24/05 05:19 P.M.	$1,500	
06/24/05 06:19 P.M.	$1,000	
06/24/05 08:38 P.M.		$1,588
06/25/05 09:53 A.M.	$1,500	
06/25/05 04:57 P.M.	$80	
06/25/05 05:08 P.M.	$1,000	
06/26/05 07:22 A.M.		$3,720
06/26/05 11:06 P.M.	$500	
06/27/05 12:00 A.M.	$1,000	
06/27/05 01:15 A.M.		$1,989
06/27/05 10:02 A.M.	$500	
06/27/05 02:45 P.M.	$1,500	
06/27/05 04:06 P.M.	$1,500	
06/27/05 06:03 P.M.	$700	
06/28/05 10:22 A.M.		$1,761
06/29/05 12:56 P.M.	$1,700	
06/30/05 12:01 P.M.	$1,000	
06/30/05 05:02 P.M.	$1,500	
06/30/05 07:01 P.M.	$250	
06/30/05 08:13 P.M.		$833

TOTAL DEPOSITS: $25,580
TOTAL WITHDRAWALS: $19,510
NET RESULT (LOSS): ($6,070)

*From June 11 to June 18, I was vacationing on an island with no electricity. To clear my head.

Forty-five

The obsessiveness of it. The impulse clearer than the light in the room when I opened my eyes with a start. It felt like a new kind of instinct.

I would stagger from the sheets, exhale, look around for water, catch sight of the Dell on my desk, reach for it, boot. I would sit in the chair with my face in my hands. It was already too late. Water, coffee, Honey Bunches of Oats, nonfat yogurt could wait. After reinstalling the software (it would always have been deleted the night before, when my session had ended—account zeroed out—and I'd made the habitual vow), depositing fresh funds, selecting a shorthanded game that would guarantee speedy results, guarantee a windfall of variance in one direction or, usually, the other, after I'd entered my groove, as it were, the physical hunger and ache from the lack of caffeine and the withering longing for water would bolster the anxiety I'd woken with, making the game, the Fucking Sick Thing I was doing, even more essential or urgent. It presented itself as a salve, as a form of relief.

In July I was in California. My uncle had been diagnosed with cancer. In the Starbucks at La Guardia, I'd detected a Wi-Fi signal, reinstalled the software—only half an hour till my flight—and devoted ten minutes to hold 'em. I barely made the plane to Colorado. In Denver I met my mom, and we drove to my uncle's in Kansas. Next I flew west to Orange County. I had to get out of New York. Things were going badly with me there. No book was being written; minute by minute the hours, then days, and apparently now whole months were being lost, in addition to the money I was burning through.

The problem by this point was clear. I accepted it as such—as a *problem*. For problems one seeks a solution. Luckily there seemed to be an answer built naturally into the structure of the summer. A very large check should be coming: the first third of the 85 percent of the three hundred Gs that was due to me ought to show up any day. When the check came, I wouldn't fuck around anymore. That would be the fulcrum. I would pull out of poker cold turkey and turn into an Eggers, a Wiesel, like *that*.

This wasn't the first exit strategy I'd developed, I should probably admit. In June, when my friends Clark and Mira brought me and a few others to a *private fucking island* in Penobscot Bay up in Maine for the traditional weeklong retreat Mira took there every year (the island had been in her family for four generations), I figured, what with the lack of electricity in the summerhouse we'd be staying in and with the splendor of nature (spruce, moose, deer, seals, fish hawks, bioluminescent aquatic bacteria glittering near the pier), and especially in light of the history of extraordinary artists getting their work done in that very house (Mira had a well-known painter for a grandfather and well-known photographer for a great-uncle), that everything would change while I was there. A week without the Internet should do it. A week on a magical island: *the cure*.

It failed. *I* failed. I felt sick in the car driving up. I was terrified about the boat and ran around announcing that I would probably get seasick and people should expect to see vomit. I was more or less making that up—I didn't have a history of trouble on boats—but somehow lately, whether I was playing poker or thinking about it or trying to avoid playing it or not thinking of it at all, I was constantly, endlessly anxious. Everything was frightening. Everything threatened me, worried me: cars, trains, boats, the subway, the sidewalks, and most of all people. I could barely hold conversations. I'd developed a stammer I didn't used to have. My thoughts raced at high speed at all times. It was hard to pay attention, impossible to try to explain myself.

I spent the first days on the island scanning the footpaths for snakes, checking under toilet seats for black widows, wondering if I was going crazy. Then I began to get calm. Exercise helped most of all: hiking through the woods, going for swims, or playing tennis. As we headed back down to New York, I was sure I was "clean," I was healed. I went home, I got ready for bed. I checked my e-mail. I was thinking of poker just dimly. I typed the letter *P* into my browser, and the PartyPoker URL filled itself in automatically. I downloaded the software, mainly out of curiosity, or so I told myself: I wanted to see how it looked to me now that it was part of my past. What was the screen like? Why had it held such attraction? Resolving not to play, I instantly made a deposit and got back into action that night.

A few weeks later, I picked up a book, *Born to Lose: Memoirs of a Compulsive Gambler,* by Bill Lee, and I read it in one night. The author's addiction (to blackjack, no less: he preferred it over other table games in part because it was fast, new hands coming all the time) had lasted for years, with incidents recurring even after he'd gone into Gamblers Anonymous. His problems spanned over four decades. I was fully aware already that the rare hard-core degenerate gambling addicts must constitute a crucial part of the industry's revenue stream: I had seen these people in action firsthand. I'd read stories in the news and in books. They were a minority of customers, yes, but a minority willing to mortgage their houses, to embezzle from the companies they worked for—ordinary middle-class people with losses running into seven figures. One of these VIPs was surely worth hundreds or thousands of typical Vegas vacationers. For a long time, I'd thought of them as freaks, very sick and very alien, probably deserving the fates they all met. But Bill Lee was clearly a human, and not only that, a human trying over and over to rescue himself. The Behavior, the Fucking Sick Thing, was powerful, evidently.

After reading his book, I took immediate action, clicking the "Responsible Gaming" link on the PartyPoker site. There was an option for a "cooling-off period." You could select to cool off for either twenty-four hours or seven days. This was pretty funny, even in the heat of the moment—seven *years* might make a difference, but a week was a joke; I knew it already, and PartyPoker had to know it, too—and, laughing morosely, I clicked "seven days," read the disclaimer, checked the appropriate box, and was presented with an error message. I tried it again, got the error again. When it happened three times, I gave up. It might well have been a real error, completely natural and unintentional, but I found it impressive regardless. The *gall* of these bastards, I thought. . . .

You could request longer exclusions via e-mail. I did this, asked for six months. They responded within six hours. I was cut off from the sauce. But there were other sites you could choose from. I was playing hold 'em on Ultimate Bet the same day I started "cooling off."

In California I was waiting for the check. They were going to FedEx it to my mom's house. While I waited, I continued playing poker. My mom was off at work. I got a surprise e-mail from Ultimate announcing that my "excellent history" had resulted in an increase in how much they'd let me deposit over any given period: via Neteller up to $5,000 a day, to a max of $10,000 a week or $20,000 in a month; via credit card or the Firepay or Citadel payment services, up to $1,000 a day, $3,000 a week, and $6,000 a month. All told, I had the go-ahead to lose over three hundred Gs per annum.

Luckily, I had an out. So I kept telling myself. Cold turkey, baby, you'll do it. Let's put the Axe back in the woodshed. As soon as that money is here, I'll be entering a new reality.

The hand was pocket eights. It was early afternoon. I had raised, because I'm an idiot. *Fold, motherfuckers,* I prayed, but a particular dude who'd been giving me trouble smooth-called from late position. Damn. And that was when the doorbell chose to ring.

One rises, of course. One simply gets up, ditches his game of ten-twenty, goes to the door, and signs for his *eighty-five Gs.* I hesitated for a second, but then I was up, I was sprinting down the hall and up the small set of stairs, throwing the screen door open and saying various rushed, loud things to the man wearing purple and black: "Give it here!"

I approximated my signature on his pad, thrust the device back to him, and grabbed at the envelope. Then I was tearing to the back of the house. When it was your turn in a game, a clock ticked, you had limited time—had to act within about thirty seconds or they might fold you out automatically.

Got it! I clicked, bet again—it was the turn—the dude raised, and I called. I check-called the river, and I lost the hand. But now I didn't know what to do. The rule was, the money comes and everything is different. Arrival of the check will be the turning point. The check, however, came *mid-hand*. It wasn't a possibility I had considered. If the check comes mid-hand, may I complete the hand? Or had I violated the rule already by doing so? If I'd already failed, there was no reason not to play on. I played on.

I played until late afternoon. Then I had to drive to my dad's house to meet him for dinner. Expecting the usual traffic, with some difficulty I forced myself to quit playing poker and get on the road earlier than I would have at another time of day. I had the check in my pocket: $85,000, right here. Staggering, sick—it was beyond comprehension. First income I'd had all year. Even accounting for taxes, my net worth had jacked up again beyond a hundred Gs. I was sitting very pretty in the scheme of things.

But I was confused, too, troubled, too, with various pains and anxieties. Had I quit playing poker or not? Would I be all right now? Hadn't I really been fine all along? Wasn't it just in my head?

The traffic was mild. Incredible! I'd already come to the 605 South and was barely ten minutes from my dad's. I had thirty-five minutes to spare. Why—what is this billboard? Hawaiian Gardens Casino? Next exit? Okay. I followed the sign down the ramp.

When I saw the casino, I laughed yet again: You ill fucking lad! It was a temporary structure, a sort of reinforced tent of white fabric, exactly like any number of newly opened tribal casinos (Sandia near Albuquerque;

Dancing Eagle, elsewhere in New Mexico; Soboba out in Hemet, California) I'd damaged, harmed, attacked, blown up, *behaved sensibly in,* for God's sake. . . . Entering, I smelled familiar smells, the almost used-bookstore-ish reek of men who'd neglected their bathing; I saw the poker tables all busy at this peculiar hour when people with actual jobs ought still to be in their offices or in their cars heading home; I saw the bent backs of the players, their postures of boredom or weariness, eyes all bulging and yellow, some of them smiling ironically, others making wicked jokes in hushed tones to the player beside them while nodding toward somebody else; and I remembered the question I'd had, and that we'd all had back in the day: What is the appeal? Vegas, we get. Neon and glitz, we can fathom. But these sordid joints are a whole other thing. It's *gambling*—no frills. You come here to lose. There isn't any way you can delude yourself.

I played six hands, ten-twenty again. I won $30. Then I had to leave for my dad's. Maybe, I thought, that was it. How far can I possibly go with this shit?

Forty-six

Nighttime, Williamsburg, north Brooklyn, no lights on in the apartment. The computer screen was the one source of light. I was on the futon, gambling compulsively, passing the time, in a subdued kind of mental pain I didn't actually mind in the slightest. I heard the front door. The sound was like a bag of potato chips being ripped open. This would be Paul, my roommate. I thought about darting from the living room.

"Hey, *hey!*" he cried out. It was, I remembered, a Friday. I'd almost been expecting to see Paul come in. I'd expected he'd catch me like this.

The lights went on in the kitchen. My heart was beating rapidly. Somehow I was unusually aware of the fact that a heart was just tissue, that it could tear, or be ripped like cellophane. He stumbled into the living room, flicking the light. He had on a big, drunk, happy smile. He said "Hey" again.

"Hey," I responded.

"Listen. Judy and I, so Judy and I, me and Judy—huh? Right?" He was slapping the back of one hand against the palm of the other. Paul was the puppeteer friend whom I knew from California. We'd met in the fifth grade, hated each other, then became best friends in the sixth. Since the end of last year, we'd been roommates. But Paul was gone most of the time. He'd been traveling at first with the national tour of *Little Shop of Horrors,* and recently he'd started a new gig puppeteering for a children's TV show. The show taped out in the Hamptons, so during the week he was out there. The production put the puppeteers up in some house. Midweek I was free to just gamble all day; I normally stopped on the weekends.

Today I'd said fuck it, and now here he was, sweat on his face, sprawled on the sofa across from me, talking about Judy, and vodka, and locking themselves in a bathroom in some East Village bar to make out. I listened but kept playing my hands.

The game was thirty-sixty. Pots could get large. If you raised pre-flop, you'd spent $60. If there was only a bet and a call on the flop you were in $90. If you bet at the turn and got raised and elected to call, the stakes having doubled, you were suddenly in for $210. Calling a bet on the river would make it $270, and that whole series of moves would play out in less than one minute. You might see eighty or a hundred hands an hour.

I was looking at queens, a fine hand, and I'd raised, and someone had reraised pre-flop and I'd reraised again. Then the flop came with an ace. He checked me, I bet, he raised, and suddenly Paul was right there looking down at my screen. "I'm sorry!" he said. "I didn't know you were playing poker. . . ." For all he knew, it was just an ordinary hobby of mine. "I would have quit gabbing. Let you concentrate."

"It doesn't really take a lot of thought." I was looking at the queens, at the ace. My delicate heart kept pounding. Both Paul and I were sweating now.

"How long have you been at it?"

"Don't know."

"Like, all day?"

I hated to fold those queens, but I managed to do it. "A number of hours," I said.

"You winning?"

"Not at the moment."

"Overall?"

"I'm stuck at this game."

"How much are you losing?"

I continued to play as we spoke. I said I was losing a trivial sum that had the potential of becoming nontrivial.

"Do you have a gambling problem?"

"Yes."

"Josh—what are you doing?"

In a dry, almost affectless voice, I said, "This is a problem. I have been wasting some time. What I've lost is some time. I found a shrink yesterday and made an appointment. I'm seeing him next week. We'll take care of this." I got an ace-jack, and I raised.

"What about Gamblers Anonymous?"

"No."

"No? What? No? Just—*no?*"

"Gamblers Anonymous has an eight-percent success rate for members in their first year. Ninety-two percent don't quit gambling. It fails way more than it works." The flop came with no jack and no ace. I bet. I got called. "It's also a cult, it also depends on belief in supernatural intervention, which means it's a *stupid* cult, and beyond that it's just not a place somebody with my particular history is going to fit in or be helpful."

I bet at the river. I knew if he called, I would lose, and he did. Paul said, "Why do you think that?"

"Can we please talk tomorrow?" I glanced at the screen. "Look at this. This is ridiculous."

Forty-seven

I was in the waiting room, staring at a page in a novel, not really reading words. The footsteps I recognized instantly: Skippy. He moves like a dog—the guy *bounds*.

"Ready?" he said.

I got up. Skippy wore a tentative smile. He had a freshman-year-of-college-type amorphous goatee that had troubled me for almost two months. He led us down the hall.

I kept my eyes on his shoes: Kenneth Coles. That would be the footwear of the underclass. I had owned a pair once. Poorly made. They're designed to look good, but they're not good. The stitchwork on the soles isn't real. I was trying to keep focused on *him*. This moment of following Skippy down the long hall when I hadn't yet given my report but knew that I must, and that Skippy would have to absorb it: this was often the very worst part.

He held the door open for me. You could see the broken vessels in his nose. He was myopic and wore no cologne, but he did have a wedding ring on. The room, meanwhile . . . it wasn't exactly a VIP suite. It was a utility closet in a rear corner of the clinic. No window. I sat on a fake-leather love seat. Skippy used a folding metal chair. There were steel shelves loaded with office supplies, plus a broom, dustpan, bucket. This is where I'd come to fix my brain.

Skippy crossed his legs in the feminine style, left thigh above right knee, and held a yellow legal pad in his hands.

He adjusted his specs.

He said, "Well?"

He had five o'clock shadow at noon. He was younger than I was and less stylish, I felt. *Married*. These women take anyone. I can't believe this douchebag is ahead of me in life.

I spit it right out. "So I played. . . ." A dismal tranquillity smothered the room. Skippy's cheeks turned a shade of gray. He was holding that pad, writing nothing. "I'd been thinking about it . . . off and on, all evening long in the city. I was having drinks with an old friend. We said good-bye, and suddenly I thought, I'm going to do it! Like that. And instantly I was *so happy*, or maybe 'relieved' is the word. I got home. I went up the stairs. Paul was in the Hamptons. Everything felt so easy just then."

He said nothing, just blinked his eyes, wiped his upper lip, straightened his back, and kept looking at me. Something was different this time. The initial few sessions had been easy, in a twisted sense at least: I was the penitent wild man who'd pushed things too far—my humbled condition a rebuttal to the whole dream I used to represent, the bright, hard dream that people like Skippy had never had the courage to live. The dream was no good, and I'd proved it. This must have come as a relief. Skippy was right to have wed, was right to pursue a career. Normalcy was best. Following convention was the nuts. He was *right* to wear Kenneth Cole shoes. He was right and, moreover, was *good:* I went totally clean from the moment I first started seeing him. As if I were cured. I finally stopped gambling cold turkey.

Honestly, it had annoyed me. His apparent success was unearned, his techniques too crude, too simplistic. I might have been his first-ever case, he was so young a shrink (he was technically an "extern," an apprentice). I'd intended to see someone else, the famous main dude who was head of this clinic, until I found out what he charged. For $350 an hour, you got the big guns; for $75 you got Skippy. Week after week I came in and he asked first thing, "Did you play?" and I said no and he got this glow on his face. He looked about as thrilled and amazed by his sudden new powers as I must have looked at the end of my first blackjack trips, flying home to New York with the money.

It had been a fluke. Skippy had just gotten lucky. The first time I answered him yes, yes, I played, my voice was so even, so controlled, the affect in it so buried—it sounded so much like it normally did—that he was shocked. He thought he hadn't heard me right. Then when he asked what I'd lost and I answered him, "Five," and he said, "Five hundred?" and heard me say, "No. Five thousand," his head must have started to spin. You could see him thinking, I thought I was *good* at this. His little reign was finished. It made me feel strong. The power was back where it should be.

Presently he lifted the legal pad. He seemed to fan his chest with it. "We've talked about Gamblers Anonymous."

"I'm not going to go there."

"I'm going to ask you to reconsider that."

"No."

He took several little breaths. It was almost hyperventilation. He looked up at the wall behind my head, then at his lap, then at me. "I've been reviewing your case with my supervisor. There are potential liability issues. If you're not going to Gamblers Anonymous, this has to be our last session."

"I understand," I said. "So that's that?"

He nodded minutely. His face looked hardened and mournful.

Forty-eight

W hat I remember is the bills. Twelve or fourteen envelopes were
stacked on the edge of my desk. I'd desisted from paying when
requested even though I wasn't broke yet at this time. But my finances were
ugly. I couldn't bear to look anymore. The spreadsheet I used as a checkbook
was like a haunted document to me. The overall poker result had gone up
and down and up and down and mainly down; my loss climbed to sixteen Gs
by September 11 of 2005. I still *was* trying to write, and I did leave the house
and would venture to Manhattan to one library or another—sometimes all
the way to Columbia, where my alumni card would get me in. But the library
had changed since I'd graduated in '96. Back then, with laptops newly
affordable, it remained unclear whether the sound caused by typing constituted too much of a distraction, whether laptops in the reading rooms violated library etiquette. That question had long been resolved. They'd
modified all the desks, installing power sockets everywhere. They also had
Wi-Fi in there. Now half the kids were staring at MySpace, pretending to
study. I would diligently sit in the Philosophy Reading Room—it had been
a favorite study space ten years before—and I would try to be the writer I
had dreamed in those days I might grow up to become. All it took was one
failed sentence for the doubt to roar up; panic would throb in my chest, and

I would click onto the Wi-Fi, and then I would fuck myself further. The day would be lost.

After one such day, when I'd gambled till midnight and then had the hourlong ride back home to the lonely apartment (it was midweek, Paul in the Hamptons), I entered my room, saw the twelve or fourteen envelopes piled up there, and thought, Fuck it. I'm suspending all activity until I get fixed. I'm paying no bills, I'm not writing, not answering calls. I'm not going to see anyone. I was down twenty Gs at this point, and that number had gotten to my head. It was simply too much; I couldn't abide it. I am a gambler, I said to myself, and the way a gambler solves a gambling problem is to gamble. Probably I should try to do it better, though.

I went to see Aldous. He lived in New Jersey. He came in his Beemer to pick me up where the bus had dropped me off. "It's all about no-limit now," Aldous said.

"That's what you'll show me?"

"Oh, yeah. Used to be the problem with no-limit was, skill mattered too much. The bad players just got broke, and it happened really fast. If you were a pro, the issue with that was you had to find games. That's what Doyle Brunson writes about in *Super System*. The guy used to live on the road. He'd go to a town, find a game, break the suckers totally, then have to go somewhere else where they had money. From a poker room's perspective, it was a problem as well. It was the poker rooms that instituted limits. With limit poker the games tend to last, since the suckers will lose more slowly. You cap how fast they get broke. But right now, with these no-limit games online, where the buy-ins are smaller, it's a different thing. Really a good thing. That's where all the fucking money is. Everybody's watching no-limit on TV, thinking they're the next Chris Moneymaker. But they still play bad, and there are *lots* of them. I'll show you what we do."

He pulled up to the handsome two-story house he was paying for through a combination of online poker and stock trading. I was aware it was possible I myself was providing income to Aldous, to Neal, to Jimmy—I could have been playing them online without ever knowing. His girlfriend, Jessica, came to say hi. She was twenty-three, lovely as hell, and had a caustic sense of humor I admired. "What are you up to?" I asked her.

"You know, hanging out with this guy. I'm making my living with poker now."

"Oh."

"You still writing that book?"

"Yeah, I'm trying."

Aldous brought me into his study. He logged on to a site I'd never seen before, and, taking notes, I watched him play for hours. "All you're trying to do is get all-in with the nuts," he instructed. "Or with something really strong." The beauty, the way he explained it, was that you had the chance with no-limit to calibrate your bets to the size of your edge on a particular hand, more or less the way we used to do with blackjack. The key was to wait for big hands. "Then fucking bet. *Muh,* like you and Neal used to say—remember that?"

"Send it?"

"Just fucking bet."

♦

I was routinized, diligent. Sunday evening Paul would say good-bye. He would be off to the Hamptons, leaving me alone until Friday. I always waited ten minutes in case he forgot something and had to come back. Paul mustn't know what I was up to. I'd neglected to inform him I'd been let go by my shrink on the grounds that I was too crazy, much less that I'd abandoned writing totally, abandoned everything, was devoted to winning my money back.

Then, grabbing the ironing board from where it hung in the kitchen, I would set it up in the living room to use as a desk. The Wi-Fi was best in the living room. (Paul and I were stealing from our neighbors.) I would balance my computer on the board, plug it in, grab a glass of water, turn on the TV and the DVD player, sit myself down, and begin. Sometimes I rented a movie—paying with a credit card the way I was paying for all things now, billing all of life to The Future. Usually I watched one of Paul's discs. He had the complete collection of the British television series *The Prisoner*—the one with the opening sequence where the star Patrick McGoohan cries in desperation, "I am not a number—I am a free man!" amid laughter from one of his captors. The first hours would be fun, in a strange way, solitary and tedious, hopeful, restless. From the air shaft, the sound of pans clattering and children crying and telephones ringing and soccer goals getting announced by a Spanish-speaking play-by-play guy on TV would echo into the apartment. I would clasp my hands, waiting.

Eventually it was Wednesday, it was Thursday. The apartment was wrecked. I was strung out and perplexed. Usually I had been losing, seated on the bad IKEA chair with the multiply coffee-stained, once-white, non-soft cushion and the straight wooden back, bent over the keys with eyes locked on the screen, mesmerized at everything, genuinely freaked and enchanted, shocked at the way life had changed. It really was a different world I had found. It was obliterating and edgy. Some of the time, I enjoyed it, I saw a certain glamour in the desperation of it. Other times I felt that I was crazy. This is a strange thing to actually feel, as opposed to just pretend to feel, hyperbolically claim that you feel. People are always saying they're feeling crazy or that they've just done crazy shit, but to have (as I did, from time to time) an oblique awareness that your mind is no longer reliable, that your own innermost will is either without purchase—effete, powerless, neutered—or simply not actually yours, that it's alien or unaccountable, a will that may well be perfectly at liberty, *free,* but inaccessible or unknowable, not yours and yet nobody else's: this fucks you up. Maybe it was an addiction—there's a degree of conflict in the medical community about what ought to count as addiction and what shouldn't count. I didn't fucking care either way what you called it. I was actually jealous of cokeheads, heroin addicts, alcoholics, people who used too much Splenda. Their problems seemed simple to me. You put the thing into your brain, introduced the drug, and *that did it.* I had nothing like that to point to. The thing in my brain was my brain. The pain didn't come from outside me. It felt like a routinized craziness, and I was completely devoted to it. I thought I could master this thing, and at the same time I knew that I couldn't, knew that it was crazy and that I was fucked.

Friday afternoon it was crunch time. I would cut myself off around four. The apartment had gone wholly to shit. Refuse from improvised meals would be strewn all over the floor. I would close the laptop, the ironing board. I would gather up the trash: paper towels, empty cereal boxes, paper wrappers from Paul's Tofutti Cuties, every one of which I would have consumed and would have to replace. I would sweep and do dishes, set my computer up at my desk, and then sit there staring at Andrew Sullivan's blog or reading op-eds in the *Times* and pretending to write. I kept hitting keys to make sound so that the moment Paul came through the door, he would hear it and know all was well.

Forty-nine

I was playing on Pacific Poker, a different site. I thought my luck might change, and it did. Not right away, though.

I would bang in for $500 and bang in for $500 and bang in for $500, each time at the $600-max no-limit game with the $3 and $6 blinds. What was different about the site was that you couldn't multi-table. You had to play one game at a time. This helped with the focus. I was thinking only a little bit more, was only a little more cautious, but soon it began to add up. Having started with my latest $500 deposit, I grew my account to three Gs, then eventually to five. Suddenly I knew what I was doing.

Aldous had been right. You shipped your money in with the nuts or with a strong hand. He'd also suggested a good deal of casual betting, something close to bluffing—raising a standard amount pre-flop on a wide range of hands, including some poor hands, and then consistently betting the same amount at the flop regardless of whether it hit you or not. You wanted opponents to think you were loose, you were a bluffer. But the trick was that anytime you bet really big, it definitely wouldn't be a bluff—you would know this, and they wouldn't know it. By then they would be used to calling you, and would call, and you would fuck them.

For a few weeks, I'd been making too many casual bets; I'd been reckless about it. Then I slowed down. I made just enough of these bets to create the impression I wanted, and beyond that I was tight. My balance grew from five Gs to ten.

Through November and December, I was playing a winning game, all of it for relatively low stakes—the $600 buy-in was the biggest no-limit game Pacific Poker offered. My balance was steadily growing. Most days I would win, and I was used to winning. I was expecting to win: all had changed. It was a grind now, and certainly boring—hand after hand, I would fold. But I was on a mission. I'd targeted twenty Gs, and when I got to twenty Gs, I shifted the target to thirty. I reached this just before Christmas.

I was in the black for Texas hold 'em, in the black online. I had won. The story could come to an end. Only I didn't see it that way. Now that I had the thing beaten, clearly there was a great deal more money to be taken off the Internet; I figured I should go ahead and take it. I could work part-time on my book and spend the rest of the time working at poker—I would probably have a six-figure income this way. It would be just like the old days, except more convenient. I wouldn't have to go on the road. For a professional gambler, Internet poker had created an opportunity that had never once existed in the past: You could earn a good, upper-middle-class income working any hours that you wanted, including normal hours, and you didn't have to live in Las Vegas or live on the highway. You could do the stunt from anywhere.

Christmas night I was at my dad's house. I was in the guest room down-stairs. On a whim I'd logged on to Pacific, and, not having the time or the solitude to play as I normally would, I went into a limit game instead of no-limit. It was a big game, 100-200. When you have thirty Gs in your account, you think you have little to worry about. The stakes of this game, although high, weren't impressive to me. I stretched out on the bed on my stomach and started to play. The room's door was open.

I got stuck pretty fast—a few Gs. That was more than I ever lost in a day of the no-limit game. I kept playing, kept losing. My dad and my step-mom were sitting in the living room where I could see them, and vice versa.

My stepmother said at one point, "Look at him, he's just so focused." It dawned on me she thought I was writing. That's what everyone assumed I was doing all day.

By the time I had lost ten Gs—around two in the morning—all the old feelings from the days of losing constantly were back; I felt shaken, reverting toward craziness. Christmas, you fucker. So pitiful. You just erased a full month of work. First thing in 2006, you'll have to earn that money right back again, kid.

Fifty

I was moving down Broadway in a state of diminished intelligence, look-ing one way and another. I could have been a homeless. I imagine the ghosts of Indians wandering, lost in Manhattan, in loincloths, paint on their cheeks, stunned the way I am, crippled in their hearts by the height of what towers remain. Asking where the forests have gone to and concerned about game and survival, awed by these vehicles rumbling, awed by the light from the sky . . .

"Game" is a word I should note.

Notepad I should have.

I have to live life differently.

Heh.

Don't we all?

I need two phalluses next time around. I also want a *really good friend*.

A person should have a Ferrari.

Scratch that.

A person should have *the wisdom you get* from Ferrari ownership.

I was still carrying the glove. It was a heavy workman's glove found under a mailbox some number of blocks uptown. I must have spent three minutes on my knees wondering if I should take it—it looked like a pretty nice glove.

At the corner of Twenty-fifth, I saw a hotel to the right. I was clutching the glove, backpack weighing on my shoulder, standing on the sidewalk outside a Comfort Inn. It had been a residential building sometime in the past. Pale stone and redbrick. You could tell from the outside it would have to have one of those impoverished elevators inside, small as a phone booth and no sturdier.

I dropped the glove on the steps going in. I'd almost brought it with me to the front desk—my brain wasn't well. The priority was not to go home.

The guy responded quickly to the bell. "Yes?"

"You have rooms?"

He said, "Yes."

"What's the rate?"

It was $229. I stood thinking, touching the counter with one hand and looking down. Then I said, "Thank you. Good night."

"Good luck, sir."

I stepped on the glove going out. I walked back to Broadway, continued downtown. A Comfort Inn is a Comfort Inn is a dump whether they charge $230 or $60. A cab home would cost $18, net of tip; people go home at the end of their days. I know all the basic procedures. Brush your teeth and floss. Mumble to your spouse and grab hold of that flab at her side, something to clutch through the night.

It was the quiet stretch below Twenty-third and above Union Square, where no business was open, no person was seen. I stopped at the display window of a particular high-end store and was staring at stemware. It was all crystal, with facets cut in. I like things like that. I happen to own a pillow with silk case that I paid $90 for, in '02. The exact word for its color is "nacarat," red tinged with orange; it's a cognate of "nacre," meaning mother-of-pearl: the pillow has a nacreous sheen. I was a big fan of it when I bought it—I was a big fan of myself *while I was doing the buying,* aware of the decadence of (a) having a throw pillow at all and (b) having a throw pillow that fucking expensive, as well as of the deeper decadence of not truly thinking, in my heart, the purchase was all that extravagant. The most decadent decadence is unreflexive, unaware, opaque to itself.

In the middle of the next street, I challenged a cab, and he slowed; he was nailing the horn. I did not flip him the bird. I proceeded to cross the street at a pace so reduced you almost couldn't tell I was moving. His engine roared as soon as he could pass me.

Muscles all over my body were sore. My feet hurt—I'd been walking three miles, almost. I was hungry, and I wanted alcohol. I liked not knowing quite where I would sleep. It reminded me of being on the road in the old days, a long time ago, in a galaxy way the fuck out there.

Fifty-one

U nion Square was less dead, but still dead. The Barnes & Noble looked gloomy. The new books displayed in the window were like an affront. Screw them.

Approaching the corner of Park Avenue, I was staring at the W across the street. This is a decent hotel. The building is old and granite and limestone, ingeniously renovated, massive neon glowing from the roof in a color not far from nacarat, gorgeous giant windows by the sidewalk, so the geeks can peer in and the meatheads inside can show off their three-figure blue jeans, three-figure T-shirts, or four-figure jackets, and how much they spend on their drinks. I always found that kind of vanity highly provocative and enraging.

As I entered the lobby, I practically slipped. They take good care of their floors. The handsome wooden banister at the left side of the curved stair shone as if it were metal. The woman at the desk smiled graciously.

I asked if they had vacancies.

"Yes. . . ."

"What's the best rate at this hour?"

"Best I can do is three-eighty," she said.

"What time is checkout?"

"Eleven."

"I would have the room for—what, seven hours . . . ? I'm a member of the Auto Club."

"The triple-A rate is the same. Hold on a moment." She was keying something in, looking pained. "I can give you three-forty."

I was holding my silver CitiCard, pausing, with no other idea than the thought that I *mustn't go home*. Paul would be there, and I couldn't look at Paul.

I couldn't have Paul look at me. I'd spent the day playing poker at Columbia, losing three Gs. . . . Had to try to put it all behind me. "Could I get a late checkout?"

"Of course."

♦

Next morning, in the $340 room, I wasn't hungover alcoholically with thorough physical sickness, nausea, and head pain. This hangover was different. It was all in the brain and the chest.

I tried showering. But that couldn't help. My face's reflection looked sickly. My skin *couldn't become clean*. My skull throbbed, and my thoughts were all scrambled. I was feeling the restlessness still.

On the train home, all I could think as I sucked bad coffee heavily sugared was that I needed to shower my *mind,* rinse or scrub or exfoliate in there somehow. Hose it down, if I could.

There's no way.

In any case. In any case.

I'm a strong bitch.

My might has been proved by now.

You could ask the Aladdin about it.

In the building I climbed the three flights. Someone had been smoking on the stairwell again. I got to the green metal door of the dump Paul and I called a home.

As soon as I stepped inside, the throb and the anxiety quickened. It was like a bass drum getting frantic. Fruit flies bobbed in the kitchen. I bade them good day.

I got out my laptop from the backpack and went stumbling into my room. I collapsed at my desk. I had paid $600 for the desk. I'd gotten a number of furnishings in '02 when I moved into Manhattan for a year. The days of wine and poses, long ago.

What is this—2005?

It's '06, kemo sabe. Get a grip. Bush is the president. War in Iraq. The terror alert is at orange. Things hunky-dory in general.

Katrina—remember? The toilets in Biloxi were destroyed. The Grand lay smashed on the coast. The Isle of Capri *disappeared*. No one ever saw the thing again. It was like a fulfillment: God's vengeance upon the casinos. A beautiful sight!

Yeah, I remember that day. I'd been playing poker compulsively on the Internet, feeling rather spavined, and losing. They had all those warnings on the news, predictions of where it would strike. The ominousness was terrific. I was stretched out on the futon and played through the night, hoping for something tremendous.

The laptop had finished booting up. I rose from my chair, and I paced. Dust motes were swarming the air. My bed was disheveled, of course. I sat on the mattress.

I yawned. I had to live life differently. You must, boy, you must. These thoughts just hung in my head: must, *must*. They were in there, all right. I moved to the desk, reinstalled the software, began another day in the life.

Fifty-two

Grace opened the door and said, "Wow." She beckoned, I entered. The room had a view of the lake. Obviously, it was romantic.

I know it doesn't sound like I should've had a girlfriend, but I had one. She'd known me before I'd gone nuts. We'd had a little fling, it had ended, and one day last fall I had taken her to dinner and afterward, grabbed her by the waist and implored her to please be my woman. There was a chain-link fence behind her, and I was crushing her against it so it rattled. That did the trick. But she really didn't know who I was anymore.

I'd struggled to keep it like that, and in consequence I stayed away from her a lot, spent nights by myself. I was utterly lost with the poker. I was dead. I'd given up the no-limit game even though it had worked. I was now playing limit for very high stakes, the 100-200 games and often shorthanded so they played fast and big. The thirty Gs I'd won had disappeared. I was back in the hole again, big time.

We stood at the window, not touching. Then Grace sat on the couch. I sat down beside her. I put my face over hers, and we kissed. Taking hold of her shoulders, I tried to push her light body down so we could stretch out together and cuddle, but something went wrong. "Ow," she said.

It was a wedding—that's why we were here. The entire wedding party stayed in cabins by a lake upstate. The first night, a Friday, after dinner and drinking, Grace and I lay in our bed. She'd fallen asleep. I was thinking about the shorthanded 100-200 game at Pacific. I must have stayed awake half the night. I was visualizing hands, seeing myself dominant at the table, testing out a brave new style, more aggressive than ever. I thought I saw a way to beat the game.

During the ceremony and afterward at the reception, while people were dancing and doing merry people-things together, joking and laughing and hugging and crying, feeling their people emotions, I was visualizing hands. I had the table in my mind at all times.

We rode a van back to the city with eight other people. It was a rental, and we had to drop it off in Manhattan. When we hopped out, I told Grace, "I think I'm going home."

"All right," she said. She was used to this.

Paul had gone to Southern California, so I was completely alone. I set myself up on the living-room futon and burst into action once more. I had a couple Gs in the account and in the course of the next twenty-four hours I built it up to twenty grand. It wasn't a straight shot—there were serious ups and downs, including a rough spell where I gave back eight Gs in twenty minutes—but overall my strategy was working. I was betting almost constantly. I was trying to come off as a madman and cow my opponents. The winning was good—was essential, in fact: I was desperate for the money. My overall loss as of yesterday had been forty-five Gs. The six-figure net worth from last summer was toast. Yesterday I'd had barely twenty Gs left to my name (I wasn't working otherwise, and expenses kept coming), but now I'd doubled my worth in a day. I slept a few hours Tuesday night and was up before dawn, rolling again, and one of the players who might have been a pro (I saw him on the site all the time) started really coming back at my aggressive play, constantly reraising and building giant pots well into four figures. I'd given back ten Gs by noon, and I had a sense of where things were heading. My head and my body both throbbed—waves of savage energy kept pouring through me. It felt as if I were caught

up in a giant traumatic experience like a hurricane or an earthquake, something much bigger than myself, a force of nature, almost. I knew in a rational nook of my brain that I was fucked, I was doomed, it wasn't good, I was
making it worse every minute, but this part of me had no authority. My
body and heart were locked down, and they couldn't be pulled away. I kept
pressing the buttons, shipping out hopeless bets, praying for that bastard to
fold. When my stack was short—down to the last $800—intellectually I
knew without doubt I had to leave the table. I had to play lower stakes and
build a bankroll again, or I would push all-in in a panic and probably be
done. Then it happened. My adversary reraised pre-flop and was betting
anew on the flop, where I'd gotten a straight draw. I tried to bet out on the
turn, my draw having missed, but he raised me. Why can't you fold? I was
all-in, and the last card appeared, and that was that, the account was at zero.
Minus twenty Gs for the day.

There was a quiet moment. It was evening, and the shaft outside the
window was gray. I felt very bad. My brain seemed out of control. It was
spinning, sharp pains rearing up in the center of it, agonizing sounds rip-
ping through; fragments of voices were muttering, my own voice among
them, but just as fragmentary and incomprehensible, spitting out a series of
syllables as if hoping simply by luck it could utter something meaningful.
More than ever I felt that I was occupied by a strange power and could not
be relied on. This wasn't *my* mind—or it was mine, but really nuts now,
not as a joke anymore: it was lost.

Googling Gamblers Anonymous and finding an immediate meeting took
only a couple minutes. I dashed around looking for wallet, keys, socks that
didn't reek, and soon I was flying down the stairs and outside to the fresh
air of May. The neighborhood was busy at this hour. At an intersection cars
bore down heedless of stop signs and white-painted stripes. Bicyclists were
coming in the wrong direction. Pedestrians ahead in separate packs had
distributed their bodies in a manner that made them collectively impossible
to pass. Stray cats were pacing with expressions both of power and of fear.

There were planes overhead, engines sighing like balloons leaking air. I had to wait for the light at Grand Avenue.

On the other side of the street, as I rushed up Union toward the subway, it felt like I was running in a dream. My strides were long and hard, but the progress was barely perceptible. As if I had stopped and stared for minutes and taken mental notes, like a man who's just fallen in love and put his woman in a cab and intends to remember the setting the rest of his life, I was holding the images, everything was vibrant and significant: the piece of graffiti someone had written in marker on a mailing label stuck to the front of a plastic rack dispensing free newspapers, its message saying "Your [*sic*] only fooling yourself"; the site of long-abandoned construction consisting of a two-story rusted steel frame, some of the beams lashed crazily with lengths of rope to the building next door, as if that's what were holding them up; the Empire State Building just visible over the BQE, looking taller than normal, statelier and more aged and more enduring than ever, her spire iconic and bringing to mind other pictures that I'd seen of her, in postcards and books and in movies, so it seemed she herself even now a couple miles away were a symbol of some absent structure; and then the subway platform, which was timeless. For a fraction of a second, it felt like I'd stood here waiting for this very train the whole time I'd lived in New York.

On the train it was worse. My mind had a constant thrumming undertone, like an engine being pushed toward the limit. I couldn't look at anyone, because everyone frightened me. There was nothing to look at or hold. I'd brought no book, and I wouldn't have been able to read if I had. My gaze darted dizzyingly from one pair of feet to the next. When we left the Bedford station and descended below the East River, gathering speed, I felt that disaster was coming, that the train would jump its tracks or that the river with its full mass would crush down upon us.

Reaching the street at Sixth Avenue, I went west a half block to the YMCA. The lobby was well lit, with shiny floor and a lone guard reading a tabloid at a big desk. "Gamblers Anonymous?" I asked.

He pointed to a door near my left. Its window was covered from the inside. Later I would learn that the piece of construction paper over it was taped up anew at the start of each meeting. "Do I knock?"

"You can just go on in."

I opened the door. It was as if I had shown up late to a class I'd never gone to before. A dozen people sat in low plastic chairs with yellow backs around a rectangular table. A man stood alone at the desk's far end, directly across from me, speaking. When he saw me, he nodded. "Sit down."

He continued his speech. He was discussing a sex addiction that had evidently followed his gambling addiction. Eyes kept drifting over to check me out. I was trying to stay focused on him. The thrumming in my head was softer but still plaguing me, and I needed to settle it somehow. I wanted to talk myself, wanted to say *the thing*—the classic formulation beginning with "My name is Josh"—wanted it out there and done with. That would be my anchor. That would be a thing I could touch, a thing I could hold: I would lash myself to it.

The people were mostly male, and one woman. Most were a good decade older than I was. A couple wore suits, a couple more—including the gaunt man presiding at the front, who looked like a Steve Buscemi haunted by terrible memories—wore the hodgepodge of khakis and button-down shirts and plain ties that qualified as business casual.

"What's your name?" he asked presently. Everyone turned to face me. I told them my name. "Why are you here, Josh?"

"Poker on the Internet."

"When was the last time you played?"

"Just now. I tapped out again just before I came here. I lost twenty thousand dollars in the past day." There were a couple nods in response to this. An elderly man with narrow eyes and a mustache was staring with special attention. It occurred to me he might be envious, might miss the sort of feelings I'd had throughout the day.

The leader asked, "How long has this been a problem for you?"

"It's been almost full-time for a year." I didn't know what I should say about blackjack. But then he asked, "Only a year? Often it would take a little longer of a history to build up to your level of intensity."

"It's a strange thing. But I used to play blackjack for a living. I supported myself counting cards for five years. That was something different."

This was met with absolute silence. Then he said, "Right. George, you want to take him through the questions?"

"Okay." George was a taller, equally thin man with heavy-metal hair down to his neck. Opening a yellow stapled-together booklet of fewer than forty pages, he cleared his throat, looked at me, then began reading from a list. "'Did you ever lose time from work or school due to gambling?'"

"Yes."

"'Has gambling ever made your home life unhappy?'"

"Yes."

"'Did gambling affect your reputation?'"

"Yes."

"'Have you ever felt remorse after gambling?'"

"Yes."

"'Did you ever gamble to get money with which to pay debts or otherwise solve financial difficulties?'"

"Yes."

"'Did gambling cause a decrease in your ambition or efficiency?'"

"Yes."

"'After losing did you feel you must return as soon as possible and win back your losses?'"

"Yes."

"'After a win did you have a strong urge to return and win more?'"

"Yes."

"'Did you often gamble until your last dollar was gone?'"

"Yes."

"'Did you ever borrow to finance your gambling?'"

"No."

"'Have you ever sold anything to finance gambling?'"

"No."

"'Were you reluctant to use "gambling money" for normal expenditures?'"

"No."

"'Did gambling make you careless of the welfare of yourself or your family?'"

"It did."

"'Did you ever gamble longer than you had planned?'"

"Yes."

"'Have you ever gambled to escape worry, trouble, boredom or loneliness?'"

"Yes."

"'Have you ever committed, or considered committing, an illegal act to finance gambling?'"

"I'm not sure about that one."

"'Did gambling cause you to have difficulty in sleeping?'"

"Yes."

"'Do arguments, disappointments or frustrations create within you an urge to gamble?'"

"Yes."

"'Did you ever have an urge to celebrate any good fortune by a few hours of gambling?'"

"Yes."

"'Have you ever considered self-destruction or suicide as a result of your gambling?'"

"Yes." Suicidal fantasies were the latest addition to my menagerie of mental shenanigans. That pretty much came with the territory, I'd figured, and it hadn't bothered me a whole lot. More bothersome at the moment was the fact that I was answering *these fucking questions* in earnest—the same twenty questions could be found in brochures at casino cashiers in toilets around the country, and in the old days we had a running routine of reading them aloud to one another, answering yes to most, and just thinking it was so damn funny. The behavior of a professional, positive-expectation gambler with a real edge in the game he has mastered in many ways is identical to that of a sucker or a maniac. Psychologically they're not even that far apart: the need for the tingle in your heart and the sense of touching some vital, significant force you can't find anywhere else is the same in both cases, I can testify. Your life feels extraordinary while you're in action, regardless of which mode you're in. It's only a small aspect of the overall situation that distinguishes one from the other.

George had finished the questions. The man in the front of the room said, "Most compulsive gamblers answer yes to at least seven of those questions. You had sixteen. Do you think you're a compulsive gambler, Josh?"

Big time, I thought. And then I got to say what I'd been meaning to.

Fifty-three

After the meeting, a man I hadn't talked to before, Jesse, introduced himself, offered a cigarette (we were outside on Fourteenth Street), then asked for my phone number. "Your first days going into recovery will be hard. I'm going to call you. Whatever you do, don't gamble." I promised I wouldn't; he promised again he would call. Then I called Grace, and I went to her place and explained where I'd been, and she held me. She was proud of me for going to the meeting, she said. About the poker, she wasn't surprised. She acted like she'd known it all along. We watched an episode of *Family Guy* on her laptop, and she went to sleep.

In the morning Grace left for her job. I waited for her brother (and roommate) to leave the apartment, then showered, went out for a coffee and an egg sandwich, came back, tried to get going with my book about what a great gambler I was. It was due in November, just seven months off. The writing was not coming easily.

The next several days were fitful, difficult, confused, but I didn't play poker again. I stayed at Grace's place. Saturday morning I went back to my apartment, where Paul remained absent. The agenda for the day was a special one: Grace's birthday was Tuesday, and I'd decided I was getting her a guinea pig. She'd had one in childhood and loved it. I even made a note in my calendar: "Pig."

It was natural to check e-mail and then fuck around on the Web. This is what most people do when left alone for a few minutes, and it was certainly what I did. After going from the *New York Times* to Andrew Sullivan to Gawker to Tony Pierce's blog, then Googling the woman I'd lost my virginity to in sophomore year of college, then examining some photographs from the surface of Mars, looking up the word "plebiscite" in Wikipedia, spending a few minutes trying to find a large, clear JPEG of a Monet painting of cliffs by a beach that I'd seen several times at the Met, I was thinking about pigs again and how I needed to identify quality pet shops in Manhattan. I typed in *p,* for "pet," and Pacific Poker came up. That's very funny, I thought.

I beamed in $500. I went ahead and played for a while, and by noontime I had a four-figure bankroll and resurgent ambition. But then at higher stakes some money got lost back, and before I knew it I was down to the low-limit games, playing one-two, trying to build my $500 back. It was three in the afternoon when I switched to micro-limit. I was betting in 50-cent increments. I realized I was verging on being out of control once again. I wondered about pet stores, how late they were open. I was supposed to spend tonight and all day tomorrow with Grace—tomorrow evening there were cocktails with friends in honor of her birthday, and that's when I wanted to give her the pig.

By 5:00 P.M. it seemed plausible I could be fucked. I intended to stop gambling. I intended to rise from my seat. As a hand came to an end, my one thought would be, *Do it, get up, we are done here, now we will leave.* I am leaving, I would think, and with no other thought in my head, no other identifiable intention, with my will as pure and as articulate and manifest as it had ever been, I would see the new cards appear at the bottom of the window—between rounds in online poker, there's no pause for the dealer to shuffle; cards simply appear, like that—and, the hand having been dealt,

I would play it, thinking all the while I was done, must get up, had to leave.

At seven I lost my last dollar. Thank God! It was too late for Manhattan, but I did find a pet store in my neighborhood, which is not a great neighborhood. Williamsburg near the East River and north of Grand Avenue is a place of wealth, privilege, lounging in cafés all day pretending to write screenplays while actually just Googling old lovers and reading gossip on the Internet—you wouldn't believe the way these hipster bastards waste their time—but farther inland where I was, south of Grand, it's different, it's gritty, with project housing everywhere, people who dress like they're poor for reasons not strictly aesthetic, lots of stray cats and obesity.

The little store was jammed with smells of shit, dander, urine, caged animals in shoddy health. A man asked to help me. He was built like André the Giant but had plucked eyebrows and very red lips. "Guinea pig?" I asked.

"We have one left." He sort of sang the words.

I followed him to a terrarium in the rear, but I saw no guinea pig in it. There were eight fat bunnies with yellowish, stained-looking fur. They were dog-piled on top of one another. André said, "He might be underneath. . . ."

Lifting the lid off, he dug through the bunnies, finally producing a creature the size of a twenty-four-ounce beer bottle, colored like a calico cat and almost totally inert. "You want to hold her?"

"No, thank you. That's a guinea pig, right?"

He said, "Yes."

"How much do they cost?"

She was $25, he told me. I had no choice but to take her. Adding a terrarium, bedding, and food to the equation brought the total to over $100. I paid with a credit card—plastic was becoming a survival strategy now that it seemed unlikely I would be submitting a manuscript anytime soon; the theoretical extra payments attached to the book's publication were no more tangible than Social Security to me. By charging my whole life and then paying only the monthly minimums on the cards, the cash I had remaining might last a couple years (unless I lost it all on the Internet). I'd also stopped insuring my health, which helped, too.

Stumbling up the street bearing the glass terrarium, I was accosted by a nine-year-old boy who'd slipped away from his mother. His eyes peeped through the glass, and his gait was synced to mine. I didn't slow down for the kid. "What is that?" he asked with fascination.

"Guinea pig," I said.

"Is it alive?"

"If it isn't, I just got fucked up the ass."

He was gone. The mother had grabbed his shoulder and yanked the boy away from me. I remained in a daze from the gambling, and I hadn't showered yet. I got home with the pig, bathed, called a car service, then phoned Grace's neighbor Vladimir, a college friend of mine, and arranged to ditch the terrarium in his and his wife Emily's apartment for the night.

I surprised Grace with it the next day, and she was delighted. Compulsive gamblers still have good tricks up their sleeves now and then. It lived till the following weekend and then, without warning, was dead.

Fifty-four

At my second meeting, the following Wednesday, Jesse approached me before the proceedings began. "I'm sorry I didn't call you," he said. "I'll definitely call you this week. You all right?"

"Yeah. I think."

He patted my shoulder. The Steve Buscemi lookalike brought us to order. He said the leader of this week's meeting would be George. Each week one of the members would select a meeting theme and give the first speech before we went around the table, all of us saying a few words on that theme. George had selected "anger." Before he spoke, we read aloud in unison from the same booklet George had read the questions from last week.

The production quality wasn't great in this booklet. The cover said "Gamblers Anonymous" in a sans-serif font, all in caps. Below this they'd printed the serenity prayer. Inside, there was another little prayer, in poem form, with an inconsistent meter, mentioning "soul" and "God." I found the religiosity off-putting and irrelevant. The writing throughout the book was childlike, distressingly simple—almost too glib to take seriously. The grammar was slack and erroneous. Yet *this* was our text, *this* was our testament: from these same uninspired pages, some of the people in the room here with me had been reading for over a decade.

We also read the twelve steps together. One-third of these involved a Higher Power. To an atheist it was gibberish. Gamblers Anonymous implied on their Web site that atheists would fit right in, but it didn't look that way from close range. Here and there the text invoked the God "of our understanding," perhaps allowing wiggle room for people in my camp, but taken as a whole the steps referred distinctly to a unitary deity possessed of a will and determining the fate of human lives. There was nothing I could ask of such a God.

George spoke. He hadn't placed a bet in four years. (Every speech began with the formula "My name is X, and I'm a compulsive gambler. It's been Y days/years since I placed my last bet.") After that we each had our turn. There was one person here I hadn't seen the week prior, a handsome, middle-aged black man in a fine suit who introduced himself as a regular at a different meeting elsewhere in the city. He'd stopped by to check on old friends, he explained. He hadn't placed a bet in nine years.

My turn came. I said I hadn't bet in four days. I'd been nervous to confess that I'd gambled since the previous meeting, but no one seemed surprised. In an effort to sum up my gambling history and the relationship I'd experienced between card counting, poker, and anger, I might have lingered on blackjack too much. I realized I was possibly the only person who'd ever shown up in this place with a positive lifetime gambling result. I feared it might be in bad form to discuss, or even allude to.

At the end of the meeting, just as we'd done last week, we all held hands and we lowered our heads and we prayed or we pretended. The man to my right was an old guy with rough skin like rusted iron. He hadn't placed a bet in three months. He'd been trying to quit gambling off and on for twenty years, he'd said earlier during his speech. His tone betrayed very little hope. He was at least in his seventies, and he claimed to have six figures in gambling-related debt. He would never pay it off in this lifetime.

I hated to be touching this person, feeling his jittery fingers twitching and the coldness of his skin. I hated to think he and I were caught in a common predicament, or had anything in common at all. I hated his insipid groveling voice, his poor storytelling talents, his refusal to stick to the theme. I hated that he pitied himself. I hated the room and the small chairs in it, I hated the doughnuts they bought. I hated the undeniable poignancy of the moment the plate went around—these broke motherfuckers producing their wallets and parting with single dollar bills or even just quarters with obvious discomfort and fatigue. I hated the whole game plan, and especially the repetition: identifying yourself foremostly, at least once a week (though really, I think, you were supposed to do it in your prayers every day), as broken, as an addict, as diseased, as incapable of correcting your life on your own, and repeating this self-defeating mantra on and on for four years or nine years or forever.

I found a new thing to hate once the meeting was over and the unfamiliar man in the fine suit stepped hastily toward me and said in tones of tough love bordering on brutality, "The stuff about the card counting? Winning? Supporting yourself? Professional gambler? You can just forget about it now. *This* is reality." He stared down for a minute, apparently disgusted with my speech. I don't think he'd believed it. I wasn't sure I believed it myself anymore.

Fifty-five

I went to a third meeting and a fourth. The third time Jesse apologized again for not calling, again saying he would. He never called. The fourth time he didn't even mention it. I was in a sense being rejected by the lowest, most devastated individuals I had ever encountered.

That rejection was mutual. I didn't know what to make of them any more than they knew what to make of me. A kid younger than I was, who also had Internet poker issues and claimed to have lost seven figures online, made a long and impassioned speech about the game's being fundamentally unbeatable, which isn't correct. It's just that people like us can't beat it. There wasn't any point in correcting him.

I came to suspect that the existence of professional gamblers had been expunged from the Gamblers Anonymous worldview. The booklet had a section discussing the "dream world" of the compulsive gambler, and the way it described that alternate universe of luxury and wonder and intensified experience reminded me exactly of the world I used to inhabit. The dream world was real; it could truly be reached, it could truly be reached via gambling. These people had had the right instinct. *They'd all been correct.* A richer life was actually achievable. It might not be sustainable, but it could be lived, and the living could be very good. It appeared to me that the ongoing sanity of the Gamblers Anonymous members required denying that such a world ever could exist. To know that it was out there, and know that you had lost access to it forever by virtue of having approached the wrong way, would be more than most people could bear.

Fifty-six

Between meeting two and meeting three, I again played poker. After that I stopped, for a time. I understood if I continued playing in the same manner, I would be damned to that room, damned to spending time with those people, holding their infected hands, acknowledging my sickness every week or every day, praying to impossible gods to take over my brain and direct me. The thought was so revolting it made me stay straight. I was resolved to find my own way back to health; I didn't want to be in those meetings. For two weeks I was clean.

Then, in June, I played on a total of three separate days the whole month, winning $2,200. In July I played on two separate days and lost $2,400. In August I played on three days and lost $1,300. My pace was slowing down overall.

In September I played only one day, the twenty-ninth, and lost $500. I might have quit after that—I can't say. The trend suggested progress. Then, on the thirtieth, both houses of Congress approved an Internet gambling amendment to an unrelated bill concerned with port security. Known as the Unlawful Internet Gambling Enforcement Act of 2006—the UIGEA— the bill gave the federal government new power to impede an activity that had always been technically illegal. The Web sites had managed to operate with effective impunity because they were based in other countries, but the new law changed the situation, both by clarifying the U.S. position and by going after banks doing business in the States. Banks could be criminally liable for allowing fund transfers between domestic accounts and online gambling Web sites. This eliminated one way of funding accounts. Moreover, the bill's language prompted all Internet gambling enterprises listed on the major stock exchanges (PartyPoker, for example, whose parent company was listed on the London exchange) to stop doing business with American players.

It also prompted me to quit for good. I believed poker was gone. I believed my action wasn't welcome anymore on the Web sites. I didn't understand, at the time, that plenty of sites that were privately held—with no boards of directors, shareholders, British law-enforcement agencies to answer to—had continued to accept U.S. bets. The game remained accessible, but I didn't know. About six weeks later, I read on the Internet that American gamblers continued to play. The temptation endured—I could log on whenever I wanted. By that point, however, I'd gotten in touch with my editor and with my agent and explained that my story had changed. "There's a twist," I informed them. These conversations were cumbersome. Nobody had wanted any twist. I told them all about what I'd been through with poker. "It's all right, though," I said. "It ends happily."

It *had* to end happily. I was feeling strongly about that. Happy endings may be bullshit, but they're needed. Suspending disbelief, I went back to pretending that poker was dead on the Internet. I pretended I was clean, and then I was.

Fifty-seven

I was also distracted, which helped. I had work to do. I was a writer, albeit the nonwriting kind. I had no manuscript, my story had gotten on top of me—shattered my brains and then eaten itself. Everything was screwy. The whole book was due six weeks after the date of the gambling law's passage.

The publisher would grant more time, provided I turn in *something* to show them some progress. That was something more than what I had. I still didn't know how to write. I'd never really written a thing. The proposal had been artless but marketable—in other words, corrupt to the core. Instead of an author, I was a whore. The worst kind: a whore with delusions. I should have written a book before selling one. An author, I'd thought, ought to struggle—no one should pay him on spec. He's supposed to have to borrow to be able to eat. My models were Henry Miller, the Marquis de Sade, Giacomo Casanova, Gary Gilmore, Jack Henry Abbott, Neal Cassady, and Peter Abelard. Cassady and Gilmore in particular, since *they barely wrote. . . .*

I cranked out eighty pages by mid-November. They were good enough to score the extension. That is to say, they sucked but were serviceable.

In truth, I couldn't write, in part because I didn't know how to live. My character was *me*, but who was I? Some kind of nut, evidently.

My cash was running low; I was living off credit cards fully. The fact that even McDonald's had begun taking plastic wasn't lost on me. I owed money on a quiver of MasterCards, as well as to American Express, to Discover, to the Internal Revenue Service, to the accountant who'd prepared the unpaid tax returns from '05. Then, during an episode of especially poor judgment, I got heat exhaustion playing basketball on the asphalt a little past noon in August of 2007. I started getting bills from a hospital.

I couldn't afford to work because I needed time to write. I couldn't write because I was broke. It was difficult to think straight. In eight months, or seven months, the cash I was using to pay the growing monthly minimums on all those cards would run out. . . . A book about *what a great gambler I am?* The whole fucking thing was a joke.

Hemingway, scolding: "All you have to do is write one true sentence." This I believed absolutely. If I could write a single true sentence, I would know I could do a whole book. Everything would fall into place, I was sure. But I had never written such a sentence.

It would have to do with Vegas, this sentence. . . . Here was the dilemma. Vegas had once looked like heaven to me. It was *glorious,* it was . . . something. I used to have very keen feelings about it. They were no longer accessible. I'd murdered the boy who had once been in love with the valley, way back; how could I speak in his voice now?

Many things happened in a hurry. . . . Grace dumped my ass; I felt this was appropriate under the circumstances. . . . Then there were long walks with Paul. Our relationship was deep and peculiar. He offered me money; I took it. He paid off twenty grand's worth of credit cards, simply to save me the interest. . . . This seemed delicious, at first, even if it was irrational, overly generous, *baseless.* The only hope of paying him back was to finish the book. I still wasn't able to start it. Every couple days when he asked how the writing was going, I cringed. "Coming along, coming along . . ." I would sputter. Oh, God! Living with a creditor is dolorous. Debt was building anyhow, *again*. I wasn't gambling—honest. I was just trying to get laid. I was trying to lead some sort of life. A person needs clothes, he needs blue jeans, cut a certain way and hence costly. My liquidity was nearing its end.

We were walking one night in the dark. This might have been close to the river. I have a memory or two, and they're mixed up. . . . In one, or maybe both of them, Paul is asking stuff about the book and I'm hedging. He sees that I'm hedging, *he knows,* he can tell there's no progress, and he touches my shoulder, absolute forgiveness in his eyes, a kind of limitless compassion (is it love?) that I don't even know what to do with. "It doesn't matter to me if you do it," he says. "It doesn't matter. The money is irrelevant—forget that. I don't need to get paid back." I can't even speak when he says this. "If you do finish, though"—and he's smiling—"it'll be something. I doubt any professional gambling book ever gotten written like *this*." I say he can say that again, and we laugh.

Then, perhaps another night, I'm either with Paul or alone. I'm thinking of throwing a party. It's my fifteenth anniversary of living in New York, and I want the occasion remembered. The problem is, I'm broke. The party is going to cost money. I'll need at least a G's worth of booze to do it the way I've been wanting. We'll need music—I'm thinking a harpist. Hired ladies drifting around in no clothes giving back rubs to guests . . . The sort of party a *gambler* would throw. Should I do this, I'm thinking, or not? Is this the right use for the last of one's cash? Is the decadence over for me? Have I left the high living in Vegas?

Maybe I was asking Paul about it. I remember approaching the East River, coming to the little beach at the end of Metropolitan Avenue. The water was black, and it glistened. It thrashed against the rocks on the shoreline. To the west was Manhattan, and, rising from the south end of it, twin beams of light reached into the sky. It was September. It was around the anniversary of the attacks. They looked like the Luxor in duplicate. Vegas had followed me home.

♦

I threw the party. Then I was broke. I was strolling Park Avenue in the afternoon one day. I noticed a sign in a window: CASH LOANS FOR GOLD. I was wearing my grandfather's watch.

"It's plated," the man said. He stood behind bulletproof glass examining the back of the timepiece.

"Look," I said, "the thing is solid gold."

"Let me see." He took it away for a minute. Then he came back saying, "You're right. I can offer you six hundred dollars."

"That's a five-thousand-dollar watch." It was a Bulgari. I'd priced it a long time ago, just because I was curious.

"They're worth closer to seven grand, actually, now. But if I have to sell it as a pawn, I'm telling you I get six hundred. Rolex is the only thing they want." He slipped it back under the window.

I held the watch, thinking for a minute. "Thank you. Maybe later on."

"Hope you find what you need."

I said, "Right." What I needed, of course, was a cash advance on a credit card. I used this to pay off the mins on a number of cards, and I had $150 left over. Officially, I thought, I'm fucking up.

Fifty-eight

I'm omitting the darkest parts of this story, as they have no narrative content. They followed the poker; poker was done, and remained so. It had gone the way of counting cards. I didn't want it back anymore, but living without it was hard. I had lost a figure so large in such an irrational manner (just north of fifty dimes by the time I was finished) that I could seldom bear to think of it directly, seldom bear to hold the number in my mind or to say it aloud to myself. Sometimes I would remember it suddenly the second I opened my eyes in the morning. I would be staggered and frightened: it was like waking up in a state of immediate danger—in the wrong dimension, wrong house, in a dungeon, in some fairyland haunted by ghouls where you realize that anything is possible, that no one is there to protect you and your own defenses are worthless.

Even without benefit of therapy, I could see the symbolic aspect to what I had done, could see how I had undermined myself and nullified the cornerstone of my biography. The platform I'd built was demolished. The crossroader, the highwayman, the canny thug I'd tried to represent was exposed as a sucker and a fool. To the extent I used to doubt I deserved my strange blessings, I'd proved those doubts to be right. What I hadn't deserved, I wouldn't retain. It was fair.

Life continued. You had to go on, but the terms had been altered. The source of enchantment was gone. I felt like I was stranded half the time. The one blessing was exercise—running—and it was worth a lot to me every now and then. Often I was wrecked. I couldn't believe in myself. I hadn't even had the dignity to turn into a genuine psychopath. I was in a graceless position but had failed to go so far into debt that an exit wasn't conceivable. Even as an addict, I had hedged. You could make the argument that the book that would spare me financially if it ever were to really get written would be richer because of these traumas. I hadn't crossed the final line, robbed a bank or shot myself in the head like a Michigan policeman once did in the same high-limit room in Detroit where I discovered my talents for placing large bets. I'd pulled back from the line.

I might never have gotten quite near it. It's possible I'd never seen what Sergeant Solomon Bell managed to glimpse between the moment when the dealer made her hand and the moment he lifted his weapon, placed it to his temple, shouted one word, the word "no"—he was stuck between $15,000 and $20,000 on the day—and fired it into his brain. Or I might have simply lacked the handgun.

I might have lacked balls. Whatever the case, it was finished. The appeal of madness had ebbed. The longing for strange sights had slipped away without ever once getting sated. It was by nature insatiable—this might have been part of the lesson. But merely because there's a lesson and the lesson is true and you've learned it doesn't mean you'll know how to go on. The truth could turn out to be terrible. The truth could be too hard to live with. The truth could be *dull*, uninspiring. The truth could be the last thing you need. There's no way to know till you've found it.

◆

Neither fish nor foul nor good Jewish kid, I did what I must: got a job. That was a small miracle, under the circumstances. I had to put blackjack on the résumé: "I'm a famous professional gambler, but I'm broke. Is that cool? I haven't had a job in nine years." Luckily for me, they were desperate.

I worked an early shift at a public-relations firm (five in the morning till ten), then got on the train, spent a full hour getting home, napped for twenty minutes, then showered. If I was lucky, I could get in six hours of writing before I turned to beer and melatonin, gobbled some food, and passed out. It was a grind and went on that way for a year.

March of 2009—I guess that was only six months ago. Once again I didn't have a manuscript. There was one draft, it was bad, and it had to be junked. The grind would continue indefinitely. After this grind was finished, another would come. The prospect of continuing on and continuing on I found almost as staggering sometimes as the thought of all the money I had vaporized. There weren't any miracles left—there were no other worlds, only the present gray mess of New York with its exasperated people crammed onto underground trains with remorse in their hearts, filled with self-loathing and infinite doubt. This was life. This was reality.

I looked for new outlets. I drank. I managed to find a new woman. I pledged her all I had, which wasn't much. She moved to Seattle with some other dude. I considered this a phase, remaining faithful.

For no good reason I'd developed the practice of sitting very still in one place like a statue of Buddha, but this was as useless as anything. I had friends who would sit in this way, and they made enormous claims about its potency. It could give you a new lease on life, change how you saw things, and so on. All it did for me was kill some time.

I no longer hoped for any miracles, but even so I wanted some relief. I would find it wherever I could. Every couple days I would sit on my butt in my room, trying to calm my brain (you were supposed to calm your brain), focus on breathing, relax. Finally I went to take a meditation class. The instructor woman looked at me and said, "Sit up straight." That was the thrust of the lesson.

She was right, it turned out: a straight spine made all the difference. Everything fell into place. It happened right there on the cushion with the redheaded teacher staring down at me, nodding her head. My muscles relaxed and my lungs opened up. I found it easier to quiet my thoughts. My mind really had gotten calmer. The body and the brain were connected somehow.

A revelation, almost. It was something. It was odd. It wasn't too much, in the beginning. I got an indirect glimpse of a new state of mind. Then, at the same Buddhist outfit where I'd taken the class, I went to what they called "public sitting." This ran from five-thirty to seven, five evenings a week, and you didn't have to pay any money. I went for the last half an hour one night, and as soon as I entered the room in which six total strangers with hands on their knees and their eyes barely open sat cross-legged and silent, I felt some kind of a "power," some sort of a "force," maybe an "energy" or a "spell," a mysterious whatsit characterized more by what it lacked than what it had. It was a room with almost no stimulation—the quietest in all of Manhattan, perhaps. I joined the proceedings, sat down, arranged my legs and feet, concentrated on my breathing, and had just begun to hush my thoughts when a man in the front of the room whacked a brass bowl with a stick. Meditation was over.

I found myself back the next day, and right at five-thirty this time. I sat for the full ninety minutes. The experience progressively deepened. I got to the point more than once where I had no words in my brain. At first this would last a few seconds, then it would last a full breath—in and out—and then several breaths would go by. It would dawn on me later that I'd never gone so long at any prior moment in my life with no verbal thoughts whatsoever. It felt distinctly weird. It was an altered state of consciousness and no doubt about it. The present moment seemed to rush over me like the air when you're in a convertible. There was something breathtaking about this, and before long, as my gaze remained fixed on the floorboards, everything in sight seemed to tremble or twitch. Perceptually, it felt like marijuana, except that my mind didn't drift. I was fixed on the grains of the wood of the floor—a particular whorl had grabbed me. If I blinked, I didn't notice. At one point I started to drool. I must not have been swallowing. It was longer and longer since I'd last had a word or a sound or some recollected image or thought in my brain, and the calmer my mind became, the more reduced and purified it got, the more seedlike and tiny, the bigger the things in the room seemed to grow. The floor appeared almost to bulge. The back of the person in front of me might have belonged to a giant. Her shoulders were swollen and round. Everything was fraught and close to bursting. The bowl again was whacked, and for a second no one moved. Soon I was back at the closet retrieving my boots, having spoken to nobody. I was feeling pretty weird. I opted for the stairs, even though an elevator was right there waiting. The six stories felt like a thousand.

I got to the bottom, with the altered state continuing and shifting in a way that made me nervous. It was like an acid trip at some kind of difficult juncture. It threatened to take a bad turn. Gradually I shuffled toward the door. The first thing I saw stepping out was the whole of the street—I was taking it all in at once. I couldn't focus on particular things. I almost had to look toward the ground. It was cold, and the traffic was light on Twenty-second Street, thicker ahead on Sixth Avenue. A truck was moving slowly down the street. His headlights were dim, like oysters under half a foot of ocean. He had a snub face and looked menacing. Pedestrians adjusted their paths to get around me. I was barely moving forward at all. Just ahead, the cars were like a mob. Reflected on windshields were vistas of infinite motion, too complex to ever apprehend. The sky was close to dark, and yet the asphalt seemed almost to glow with the softest gray warmth, like an antique television just turning on. Between rows of cars, battered and vanishing gray-white lanes stretched like contrails lit by the moon. A manhole cover shone like a penny. The sun must have set, but the city was sparkling. It was bright and it was bright and it was so strange, I thought, so improbable. . . .

HOW TO COUNT CARDS IF YOU MUST

Casinos like card counting. The existence of counting, the books about it, the stories about it, all help to perpetuate blackjack's reputation as a fair and even a beatable game, attracting more business for them. Aspiring card counters are an especially valuable source of revenue. They're often willing to lose more money than the average gambler because they're able to justify losses as part of a rational undertaking. Perversely, the more familiar a student gets with the mathematics of gambling, the more comfortable she'll be losing money. She'll understand that short-term results are a poor indication of the fundamental value of her play, which, she will have learned, is obscured by statistical swings. Meanwhile, in reality, most aspiring and amateur counters are no threat to casinos at all. It's easy to get to the point where you believe you have an edge but don't and are comfortable with losses that should bother you. It's easy to mess yourself up with this stuff.

Easy. The basics aren't even that difficult. It's easy to begin learning, make some clear progress, and think you know more than you do. I'm going to spell out the basics presently amid a lot of caveats.

Step 1: Learn Basic Strategy

Basic strategy is the collection of mathematically optimal moves for every hand you can be dealt. It's still a losing strategy unless you're also counting, but it keeps the house edge to a minimum. Depending on the rules in effect (rules at blackjack vary in significant ways from one game to the next), a player using perfect basic strategy faces approximately a 0.5 percent house edge: in the long run, he'll lose 50 cents for every $100 bet.

In blackjack you select from the following playing options:

1. *Insurance*. Insurance is a separate wager placed after your original bet. You may take insurance only if the dealer shows an ace; insurance bets are limited to one-half the amount of your starting bet. The insurance bet wins if the dealer has a ten-valued card in the hole and loses in all other cases. This is a terrible bet (unless the count is very high). In basic you never insure.

2. *Surrender*. Surrendering means backing out of a hand without playing it at all, in exchange for a 50 percent refund of your original bet. This option, unavailable in most casinos, is especially favorable to counters.

3. *Split*. You can split a hand if your original two cards are the same (a pair of threes, for example; the suits don't have to match), and you can usually (but not always) resplit if you're dealt the same card another time. To split you place a new bet equal to your original bet. The dealer will divide your cards into two separate hands, add a new second card to each of these hands, and you'll play the new hands independently.

4. *Double down*. When you double, you agree to take one and only one additional card, and you double your original wager. Doubling for less than your original wager is generally permitted, but you should never do this.

5. *Hit or stand*. Hitting means taking more cards. Standing is ending the play of your hand.

Basic strategy is printed below. The key is beneath the chart. The figures along the top row (2, 3, 4, 5, 6, 7, 8, 9, T, A) represent the dealer's upcard. ("T" means any ten-valued card—a ten or any face card.) The leftmost column represents your hand. To find the play for a given situation, look for the box in the chart where the dealer's upcard intersects with your hand. Before learning to count, you should memorize basic completely. You'll want to be able to play with no effort, keeping as much of your mind as possible free for the task of counting. Drawing up index cards is helpful. You can also find a free, Internet-based basic-strategy training module at Blackjackinfo.com.

YOUR HAND	DEALER'S UPCARD									
	2	3	4	5	6	7	8	9	T	A
4 to 8	H	H	H	H	H	H	H	H	H	H
9	H	D	D	D	D	H	H	H	H	H
10	D	D	D	D	D	D	D	D	H	H
11	D	D	D	D	D	D	D	D	D	H
12	H	H	S	S	S	H	H	H	H	H
13	S	S	S	S	S	H	H	H	H	H
14	S	S	S	S	S	H	H	H	H	H
15	S	S	S	S	S	H	H	H	U/H	H
16	S	S	S	S	S	H	H	U/H	U/H	U/H
17	S	S	S	S	S	S	S	S	S	S

SOFT HANDS										
A, 2	H	H	H	D	D	H	H	H	H	H
A, 3	H	H	H	D	D	H	H	H	H	H
A, 4	H	H	D	D	D	H	H	H	H	H
A, 5	H	H	D	D	D	H	H	H	H	H
A, 6	H	D	D	D	D	H	H	H	H	H
A, 7	S	D/S	D/S	D/S	D/S	S	S	H	H	H
A, 8	S	S	S	S	S	S	S	S	S	S
A, 9	S	S	S	S	S	S	S	S	S	S

SPLITS	DEALER'S UPCARD									
	2	3	4	5	6	7	8	9	T	A
2, 2	P	P	P	P	P	P	H	H	H	H
3, 3	P	P	P	P	P	P	H	H	H	H
4, 4	H	H	H	P	P	H	H	H	H	H
5, 5	D	D	D	D	D	D	D	D	H	H
6, 6	P	P	P	P	P	H	H	H	H	H
7, 7	P	P	P	P	P	P	H	H	H	H
8, 8	P	P	P	P	P	P	P	P	P	P
9, 9	P	P	P	P	P	S	P	P	S	S
T, T	S	S	S	S	S	S	S	S	S	S
A, A	P	P	P	P	P	P	P	P	P	P

Source: Wizardofodds.com

KEY

U/H	Surrender if possible, otherwise hit
P	Split
D	Double if possible, otherwise hit
D/S	Double if possible, otherwise stand
H	Hit
S	Stand

Note: Rules at blackjack vary. Certain sets of rules require adjustments to basic strategy. Do not use this chart in games where you are not allowed to double after split. (Double-after-split is allowed in most games.) If you're unsure of the rules, ask the dealer before sitting down.

Also note: In games with exceptionally poor rules, your disadvantage will be much worse than the 0.5 percent mentioned above. One of the worst (and least honest) games available in Las Vegas today is a variant in which the hand of blackjack pays six-to-five, instead of three-to-two as it should. The difference is meant to seem trivial; in reality it's not. The house edge is approximately tripled. This game is often dealt from one deck, in an effort to confuse gamblers into thinking they've found an honest, old-fashioned, 1960s-style single-deck game. Please don't be hustled by this.

Step 2: Keep the Running Count

The running count is a single tally—one number—you keep in your head while you play. This tally is a measure of the value of the deck. It represents the relative concentration of certain player-favorable cards among whatever remains to be dealt. Those cards are the ten-valued cards (the tens and the face cards), plus aces. You want a deck rich in such cards.

There are actually a number of valid counting systems to choose from, all with the same function of identifying favorable decks. Mossad, MIT, and many professional players use High-Low because it has a nice balance of simplicity and power. This count was first introduced by engineer Harvey Dubner in 1963 (and popularized when Ed Thorp published it in the second edition of *Beat the Dealer*). It assigns values known as "count tags" to the three types of cards it distinguishes: player-favorable, house-favorable, and neutral. These are the assignments:

CARDS	TYPE	TAG
2, 3, 4, 5, 6	House-favorable	Plus-one
7, 8, 9	Neutral	Zero
T, J, Q, K, A	Player-favorable	Minus-one

During play, a card counter adds up the tags of each card dealt. He has to play perfect basic strategy on his own hand at the same time. He'll see his cards two separate ways: If he's dealt, say, a ten and a five, he'll see the hand as fifteen for basic-strategy purposes, but also as zero (for his running count: $-1 + 1 = 0$). You can do this only if basic is effortless for you.

Counting should be close to effortless, too, before you ever try it live. You can practice at home by holding a deck in your hands and flipping through the cards. Remove one or two cards first, then count through as fast as you can. A complete deck should count to zero; you can check yourself at the end by adding the cards you left out to the running count in your head. As you improve, start timing yourself. A good benchmark is consistent, perfect counting in twenty seconds or less.

Step 3: Calculate the True Count

High, positive running counts are what you're looking for. The value of the count (and the size of your edge) will depend on the number of cards left to play. In order to know your edge, then, you have to adjust your running count to reflect where you are in the shoe. The adjusted count, known as the "true count," is equal to the running count divided by the number of decks remaining.

You estimate remaining decks visually. Casinos inadvertently facilitate this by leaving the discards in full view during a game. Discards are stored in a tray at the dealer's right side. With two decks stacked in the tray, if you're playing with a six-deck shoe, you'll know you have four decks remaining. (If in doubt, you can ask the dealer how many decks are in use.) Accuracy with your estimates requires practice at home.

Once you have an estimate, divide.

Step 4: Playing Deviations

The true count is used for two things: deciding how much to bet and deviating from basic strategy. Deviations increase your edge. They help you make better plays to take advantage of the altered composition of the deck in high counts.

Different counters use different sets of deviations; there are plenty to learn—over a hundred if you really want to geek out—but most add little value to your play. I've listed my recommendations below. The "index number" is the true count at which the play becomes correct. You should make the deviation whenever the true count is equal to or higher than the number. The numbers here were computed by Stanford Wong and published in his book *Professional Blackjack*, a thorough and essential reference for any serious High-Low player.

PLAY	INDEX NUMBER
Take insurance	3
Stand 16 versus T (when surrender is not available)	Any positive running count (the index is 0)
Stand 16 versus 9 (when surrender is not available)	5
Stand 15 versus T (when surrender is not available)	4
Stand 12 versus 2	3
Stand 12 versus 3	2
Double 11 versus A	1
Double 10 (or 5, 5) versus A	4
Double 10 (or 5, 5) versus T	4
Double 9 versus 2	1
Double 9 versus 7	3
Surrender 15 versus A	2
Surrender 15 versus 9	2
Surrender 14 versus T	3

Step 5: Betting Decisions

The greater your edge, as measured by the true count, the more you should bet. Some counters use simplified guidelines, such as betting the true count in black chips (betting two black chips at true two, four at true four, etc.). Generally, you'll win at a faster rate by playing two hands in positive counts. The increments in which you bet (known as "betting units"; the unit was a black chip in the example just now) will depend on your overall bankroll, as well as on your appetite for risk.

A formula I would recommend is dividing your bankroll by 660 and using the result for your two-hand unit. A $33,000 bankroll would allow you to bet in increments of $50 on each of two spots. This formula is known as "half-Kelly" because it represents betting half as much as would be indicated by the risk-management system known as the Kelly criterion. Most pros use Kelly when computing their units; few actually bet the exact amount Kelly would call for, because the swings under "full Kelly" betting are very dramatic. Mossad played half-Kelly; the MIT players I originally trained with used only one-third of the Kelly amount. Betting more than permitted by Kelly is increasingly perilous the further you push it; if you overbet your bankroll enough, you will definitely lose all your money in the long run, even if your counting is flawless in other regards. Note that rigorous Kelly betting requires you to increase or decrease your unit as your bankroll grows or shrinks.

Note also that you really want to bet only when you have an advantage. Your units apply only when there's a favorable count. At all other times, you want to bet less than your unit.

When do you have an advantage? Whenever the true count is high enough to overcome the initial house edge. Stanford Wong notes that each extra point in your true count improves your situation by (approximately) half a percent. On a typical game, where the house starts out with a 0.5 percent edge, a true of plus-one means you're even: the house edge is balanced by the count, but you don't yet have an advantage. Once the true reaches two, you become the favorite and can start betting your two-hand unit. A recommended approach—common to both teams I've mentioned—is betting "true-minus-one": subtracting one from your true count and betting the result, in units, on each of two spots. With a $50 unit, a true two would call for two hands of $50, a true four would call for two hands of $150, and so on.

Step 6: Repeat Until Rich

How much less than your unit can you get away with betting when you *don't* have an edge?

It's really up to you to figure out. The optimal bet would be zero; you can achieve this using Stanford Wong's technique of "back-counting" (or "Wonging") in which a counter stands behind shoes watching the cards and doesn't even sit down at a table until she has at least a true two. This isn't much fun, but then again a card counter doesn't go into a casino to have fun.

You have to spread your bets. The minimum spread you need depends on what game you're playing. Single- and double-deck games require much less of a spread, but they have other problems, including the fact that it's easy for a boss to study your play for a minute or two and identify you as a counter. In a six- or an eight-deck game, I would want a minimum bet about half the size of my unit: $25 in the example we've been using. This, too, will be conspicuous. There aren't a lot of great ways to generate reliable EV without risking some attention from the house. If your ultimate goal is not to get barred, consider craps or roulette instead of counting cards. Counters get barred. They get barred and then return and get re-barred. Repeat until rich. Best of luck.

ACKNOWLEDGMENTS

This book had emotional problems, was suicidal, and might have destroyed itself. Susan Elia MacNeal prevented that from happening. She was a sort of literary miracle worker who rescued this thing and taught it how to learn and how to speak despite its own blindness and deafness. Daniel Greenberg, my agent, kept it alive at a time when the prognosis was extremely grim. In lesser hands than his, it would have perished. Eamon Dolan edited with a mixture of ruthlessness, compassion, and insight, for which I remain grateful. I also want to thank Scott Moyers for his initial counsel and for-bearance, Jim Levine and Monika Verma at Levine Greenberg, and Nicole Hughes at Penguin Press.

This book owes its inception to Catherine Burns and Lea Thau of *The Moth*. Its gestation is due to the efforts of Joshua Wolf Shenk, Ilya Bernstein, and Reina Hardy. For their reading and intelligence and encouragement, I want to thank Sarah Porter, Todd Polenberg, Noel MacNeal, Jay Michaelson, Emily Klein, Tom Sugiura, Sally and Daniel McKleinfeld, Maggie Cino, Joshua Polenberg, Judy Prays, Robert Ooghe, Nellie Kurtzman, Martin Dockery, Lydia Ooghe, Ali Lemer, Siveya Ethersmith, Susanna Myers, and Bridget Dyer.

My teammates and friends from the blackjack world were beyond gracious in allowing me to share these experiences in print. They were also the best teachers I have ever had in life. Particular thanks to Maria, Goose, Extract, Mrs. Extract, Wizard, Alex, Peter, the Arse, Yo-yo, Goldy, the Big Bopper, Vin, Queen Ro, Robert Jayne, Jefe, the Dog, Jon, J. Ro, Xaco Duxbury, Murphy, Robin, Jupe, Todd, Zodiac, Jane, Julie, Hurricane, Slime, Gordo, and Wild Bill.

Thank you, Paul. Thank you, Mom, Dad, Sylvia, Penny, Robby, and Bruce. Thank you, Laura and Steve. Thank you, Ilse. Thank you, Leslie. Thank you, Guy Tower. Thank you, Mike Daisey. My thanks to the late Ellen Miller.

Throughout my blackjack career and in preparing these pages I drew on the research and writings of Ed Thorp, Arnold Snyder, Stanford Wong, Don Schlesinger, James Grosjean, and Ken Uston. The appendix (*How To Count Cards If You Must*) uses data provided by Michael Shackleford of Wizardofodds.com.

Finally, this book would not have been possible without the generous support of the American casino industry. Thank you for the action and good times.

ABOUT THE AUTHOR

Josh Axelrad played blackjack professionally for five years and poker unprofessionally for one. A graduate of Columbia College, he languished briefly in investment banking before he turned to cards. His personal win as a card counter, at $700,000, has left him 86'd from the finest casinos in Vegas and around the United States. His subsequent losses at poker (exceeding $50,000) have cost him credit privileges at the Internet's most reputable poker rooms. A commentator on the casino industry for National Public Radio's *Marketplace* program, Josh also performs at Stories at the Moth in New York City and has been featured on the award-winning Moth Podcast. For more information visit axelrad.net.